S0-EJW-123

Crimes of Power &
States of Impunity

UTSA DT LIBRARY RENEWALS 458-2440
DATE DUE

GAYLORD			PRINTED IN U.S.A.

CRITICAL ISSUES IN CRIME AND SOCIETY
Raymond J. Michalowski, Series Editor

Critical Issues in Crime and Society is oriented toward critical analysis of contemporary problems in crime and justice. The series is open to a broad range of topics including specific types of crime, wrongful behavior by economically or politically powerful actors, controversies over justice system practices, and issues related to the intersection of identity, crime, and justice. It is committed to offering thoughtful works that will be accessible to scholars and professional criminologists, general readers, and students.

Tammy L. Anderson, ed., *Neither Villain Nor Victim: Empowerment and Agency among Women Substance Abusers*

Mary Bosworth and Jeanne Flavin, eds., *Race, Gender, and Punishment: From Colonialism to the War on Terror*

Loretta Capeheart and Dragan Milovanovic, *Social Justice: Theories, Issues, and Movements* Patricia E. Erickson and Steven K. Erickson, *Crime, Punishment, and Mental Illness: Law and the Behaviroal Science in Conflict*

Luis A. Fernandez, *Policing Dissent: Social Control and the Anti-Globalization Movement*

Michael J. Lynch, *Big Prisons, Big Dreams: Crime and the Failure of America's Penal System*

Raymond J. Michalowski and Ronald C. Kramer, eds., *State-Corporate Crime: Wrongdoing at the Intersection of Business and Government*

Susan L. Miller, *Victims as Offenders: The Paradox of Women's Violence in Relationships*

Susan F. Sharp, *Hidden Victims: The Effects of the Death Penalty on Families of the Accused*

Robert H. Tillman and Michael L. Indergaard, *Pump and Dump: The Rancid Rules of the New Economy*

Mariana Valverde, *Law and Order: Images, Meanings, Myths*

Michael Welch, *Scapegoats of September 11th: Hate Crimes and State Crimes in the War on Terror*

Crimes of Power & States of Impunity

THE U.S. RESPONSE TO TERROR

MICHAEL WELCH

RUTGERS UNIVERSITY PRESS
New Brunswick, New Jersey, and London

Library
University of Texas
at San Antonio

LIBRARY OF CONGRESS CATALOGING-IN-PUBLICATION DATA

Welch, Michael, Ph. D.
   Crimes of power & states of impunity : the U.S. response to terror / Michael
Welch.
      p. cm.—(Critical issues in crime and society)
   Includes bibliographical references and index.
   ISBN 978-0-8135-4434-2 (hardcover : alk. paper)
   ISBN 978-0-8135-4435-9 (pbk. : alk. paper)
   1. Terrorism–Government policy–United States. 2. National security–United
States. 3. Intelligence service–United States. 4. Subversive activities–United States.
I. Title. II. Title: Crimes of power and states of impunity.
   HV6432.W43 2009
   363.325'1560973–dc22

                                                                2008016718

A British Cataloging-in-Publication record for this book is available
from the British Library.

Copyright © 2009 by Michael Welch

All rights reserved

No part of this book may be reproduced or utilized in any form or by any means,
electronic or mechanical, or by any information storage and retrieval system, without
written permission from the publisher. Please contact Rutgers University Press, 100
Joyce Kilmer Avenue, Piscataway, NJ 08854-8099. The only exception to this
prohibition is "fair use" as defined by U.S. copyright law.

Visit our Web site: http://rutgerspress.rutgers.edu

Manufactured in the United States of America

To Stan Cohen—a Powerful Influence

Contents

PREFACE AND ACKNOWLEDGMENTS

SEVERAL YEARS INTO A post–9/11 world, conflict, domination, and wars persist but what is new is that many of those human rights abuses are carried out in the name of preserving national security. The war on terror—the United State's prevailing response to the attacks on the World Trade Center and the Pentagon—has gained considerable momentum. In many ways, it appears that we are witnessing a new configuration of power. Certainly, that unchecked authority situated at the core of the executive branch of the U.S. government has produced a long list of policies and practices that run roughshod over the rule of law. Those crimes of power as this work describes are particularly troubling since they occur within a zone of immunity that protects government officials from grave breaches of domestic and international law. Continuing from my previous writings on the subject, most notably *Scapegoats of September 11th: Hate Crimes and State Crimes in the War on Terror* (Rutgers University Press, 2006), this project examines in detail the underlying political, economic, and cultural forces shaping both power and impunity. I depart from the domestic concerns addressed in *Scapegoats of September 11th*, however, by focusing primarily upon manifestations of U.S. power that inflict harm on people beyond its borders.

The transnational element of this undertaking benefits from my residence outside the United States. Living in London during the research phase of the project enabled me to view the U.S.—and the U.K.—government with a sharper perspective. Particularly since 9/11, government officials in both nations have adopted controversial measures in confronting political violence, even though the British experience is informed by a lengthy campaign against the Irish Republican Army. As a sociologist, I attempt to decipher the world around us, and even in the face of tragic events it is important to maintain a cool analytical stance. On September 11th, I was living less than two miles from what would come to be called Ground Zero. Being at such close range let me see the devastating impact of political violence while keeping a critical eye on how the U.S. government reacted, especially as it abandoned its commitment to the rule of law (e.g., the unlawful enemy combatant designation, abuse and of torture of terror suspects).

Correspondingly, in 2005, I was residing in London during the July 7 bombings; in fact, that morning an e-mail was circulated by Nikolas Rose at the London School of Economics informing us that the farewell retirement event for Stan Cohen was canceled as a result of the disruption. For days, weeks, and months after the attacks, Londoners—hearing my North American accent—would offer their personal insights. Without dismissing the tragedies, many local people seem to shrug off the threat of "new" terrorism (i.e., Islamic radicals), citing years of enduring the "old" version of political violence (i.e., the IRA). Still, I was alarmed by some other comments. On the evening of the July 7 explosions, I was walking across the Waterloo Bridge (as the Underground was shut down). As I approached the half-way point, a police officer instructed me and fellow pedestrians to retreat because there was concern over an unidentified package resting on the footpath. Overhearing my accent as I spoke briefly to the police, a well-dressed man looked at me sternly and griped, "Your country has the proper answer to terrorists, you lock'em up and throw away the key"—an obvious reference to the U.S. detention center at Guantánamo Bay.

My trans-Atlantic comparisons, to be sure, go beyond informal encounters with Londoners. This study is designed to offer an in-depth examination of the United States' response to terror from an international standpoint while drawing on important theoretical influences. The critique of power unpacked in the pages to follow trail in the footsteps of Michel Foucault, David Garland, and Stanley Cohen—to whom this book is dedicated. In addition, the project benefits from recent work by Giorgio Agamben, Richard V. Ericson, Conor Gearty, Derek Gregory, and Jonathan Simon. This work is essentially the end-product of a sabbatical that I was awarded at Rutgers University in tandem with a visiting fellowship at the Centre for the Study of Human Rights at the London School of Economics. Individual expressions of appreciation are extended to my colleagues at Rutgers: Arnold Hyndman, Holly Smith, Ed Rhodes, Allan Horwitz, Ellen Idler, Lennox Hinds, Al Roberts, Pat Carr, Paul Hirschfield, Lisa Miller, and Anne Piehl. Likewise, I appreciate the tireless work of Betty McCoy and Sarah Laboy-Almodovar.

At the Centre for the Study of Human Rights at the LSE, I am indebted to the following persons who made my stay particularly rewarding: Conor Gearty, Stan Cohen, Francesca Klug, Margot Salomon, Claire Moon, Nick Guilhot, Joy Whyte, Zoe Gillard, Harriet Gallagher, Helen Wildbore, and Ahmad Qandeel. Also I appreciate the company of other visiting fellows, namely, Linda Rabben, Dorothy Q. Thomas, Leslie Vinjamuri, and Matthew Zagor. Of course, Tim Newburn, the director of the Mannheim Centre for Criminology at the LSE, and David Downes provided much inspiration and support. This project also was improved considerably by way of invitations to speak at many universities in continental Europe and the United Kingdom over the course of 2006–2008. For those opportunities, I wish to thank Dario Melossi (University of Bologna, Italy), Maartje van der Woude (Leiden University, the Netherlands), Chris Birkbeck (University of Salford), Ben Bowling (King's College, London), Stephen Parrott (Birkbeck University, London), Leonardo J. Raznovich (Canterbury Christ Church University, Kent), Justin Foxworthy (University of London, Institute of Commonwealth Studies), Maximo Sozzo (Universidad nacional del Litoral, Argentina), Lynn Chancer (Hunter College of the City University of New York), Bernard Harcourt (University of Chicago), and Scott Bonn (Drew University, New Jersey).

Elsewhere in London, I am enormously grateful to Kevin Coyne at the International Students House, which provided extraordinary accommodations.

Likewise in Paris—my summertime home—thanks to Elisabeth Ban and Nick Stevens for making available a terrific flat. Cheers to my many friends who keep my trans-Atlantic life interesting, in particular Melissa Abernathy, Lynn Hofher, Stephen Nathan, and Liza Schuster. I am especially grateful to my long-distance companion, Melissa Macuare, who sends to me steady streams of wonderful e-mails, Chevere!

Finally, numerous people were involved in preparing this work for publication: Warm thanks to the staff at Rutgers University Press: Marlie Wasserman (director), Adi Hovav (editor), Beth Kressel (associate editor), Marilyn Campbell (prepress director), Alicia Nadkarni (production editor), and Joe Parson (copy editor). Also I appreciate the feedback and input from Raymond J. Michalowski (editor of the Critical Issues in Crime and Society series at the Press), David Kauzlarich, and Jeffrey Ian Ross.

Michael Welch
Paris, France

PART ONE

 Presenting History

CHAPTER 1

A Post–9/11 World

WHAT HAS HAPPENED DURING the past seven years in response to the attacks on September 11 that killed nearly 3,000 victims? Here is a capsule:

- President Bush moves to suspend existing criminal law so as to process terror suspects—termed unlawful enemy combatants—by way of military tribunals rather than by criminal courts.
- A detention center in Guantánamo Bay, Cuba is opened, housing more than 400 terror suspects while others are shuttled to secret prisons run by the CIA. A select few detainees will undergo military tribunals, but most will not, and none will receive what could be characterized under international law as a fair trial.
- Considered a dormant problem in the United States, torture and abuse of terror suspects reemerges as policy and practice. Even more boldly, White House legal advisors go to great lengths to rewrite prohibitions on torture whereby those who order and carry out such acts are immunized from prosecution, even in cases where there exists credible evidence of war crimes.
- Key players in the Bush administration concoct a disinformation campaign linking Al-Qaeda to Saddam Hussein who is accused of possessing weapons of mass destruction (WMDs) and biological and chemical agents that threaten U.S. national security, prompting the war in Iraq.
- Under the rules of international law, the invasion of Iraq is deemed illegal.
- When inspectors fail to find WMDs, the overriding rationale for the occupation of Iraq shifts to the war on terror.
- As of June 2008, nearly 4,100 American military personnel have died since the start of the Iraq war in 2003. Civilian deaths in Iraq are more difficult to ascertain, but estimates suggest that more than 3,000 Iraqis die each month—roughly the total number of deaths in the September 11 attacks.

Of course, that's just a short list. As this book demonstrates in detail, there are other key developments in America's response to terror, many of which constitute state crimes committed on behalf of the U.S. government. Such crimes of power are particularly distinct from ordinary street-level offenses and even other political, corporate, and organizational violations because they are perpetuated in large part to various forms of immunity from prosecution and penalties. It is because of those states of impunity that crimes of power appear to have few bounds.

With those concerns in mind, this project sets out to study state crime in America's war on terror with particular focus on the nature of power. Indeed, the new configuration of power drafted since September 11 has given rise to serious breaches of international law and abuses of human rights, including the invasion of Iraq, the unlawful enemy combatant designation, and extraordinary renditions, as well as the mistreatment and torture of detainees. In deciphering those crimes, the approach transcends the straightforward legal—albeit important—arguments, reaching for a broader sociological interpretation for what can be viewed a post–9/11 world. Since the tragic events of September 11, the U.S. government, often with little or no resistance from its citizens, has trampled the rule of law. So that we may appreciate the meaning of those recent developments, it is fitting that we turn to a brief overview of an emerging field of scholarship that unveils elite crime.

ELITE CRIME, POLITICAL ECONOMY & HUMAN RIGHTS

During the past few decades, a growing number of criminologists have been committed to throwing light on illegal and unethical actions carried out by state, corporate, and organizational elites.[1] Despite the significance of such critical scholarship, the field of criminology has generally neglected those forms of sophisticated criminality: for instance, a recent review of the leading criminology journals found that a mere 3 percent of published articles involved studies on state, economic, or political violations (Michalowski and Kramer 2006a).[2] Nonetheless, crimes by the powerful have immense reach and consequence, as the following passage suggests:

> GREAT POWER AND GREAT CRIME ARE INSEPARABLE. It is only those with great political and economic power who can, with the stroke of a pen, the utterance of an order, or even a knowing nod of the head send thousands to their deaths or consign millions to lives of unrelenting want and misery. When economic and political powers pursue common interests, the potential for harm is magnified further. (Michalowski and Kramer 2006b, 1)

Tracing the sources of elite crime ultimately brings us to the political economy. There we find a system whereby political and economic players synthesize their mutual interests, often with a shared vision of a desired social—global—order (Hardt and Negri 2000, 2003). Consider, for example, the exchange between elected leaders and defense contractors: an entity that has come to be known as the military-industrial complex (Mills 1956). Together those political and economic elites determine the path of foreign affairs and military intervention, including the 2003 invasion of Iraq (Hartung 2004). The war in Iraq serves as a timely subject for criminologists concerned with elite criminality in the form of state crime as well as the more nuanced state-corporate crime.

Hardt and Negri observe that war has become the "organizing principle of society" and "what appears as civil peace . . . only puts an end to one form of war and opens the way for another" (2004, 12). Although the cycle of mass violence offers opportunities for war profiteers, there remain concerns over other paradoxes of contemporary military aggression. Ruggiero (2007) recognizes that modern war is actually demodernizing insofar as the military targets are bombed back to the Stone Age: destroying cities along with their infrastructures, electrical grids, sanitation devices, and related public health services. Similarly, food distribution and medical care is disrupted, contributing to hunger and disease; hence, bomb now, die later. Concurrently, war is remodernizing by way of enormous reconstruction contracts awarded by the state to its private partners; moreover, the political economy is revamped so as to accommodate external investment (Klein 2007). "In this way, logical continuity is established between the space of war and the space of peace, between war actors and civilian groups, while inimical countries, now annihilated offer maximum predatory potential to industrial conglomerates" (Ruggiero 2007, 212; see Ruggiero and Welch 2009).

To offset the conceits of nation-building in the aftermath of war, it is crucial to acknowledge that war is criminogenic: that is, it becomes a central source of crime beyond those committed by state and corporate actors. In *Criminality and Economic Conditions* (1916), Dutch criminologist Willem Bonger put forth a roster of social problems stemming from war: families are separated, children orphaned, and basic social services cease to function properly. Rising unemployment, idleness, and desperation breed street crime, robbery, and looting. In the vacuum of war-torn regions, black markets emerge not only out of a sense of survival but also propelled further by greed and exploitation. The underground economy also invites violence as a means of protecting commercial turf in pursuit of revenue. Those illicit activities occur when local criminal justice systems are at their weakest; therefore, people acting out of the criminogenics of war often go unpunished (Bonger 1936; Jamieson 1998). More to the point of this project, war also is criminogenic in ways that contribute to various war crimes: namely, torture and the mistreatment of prisoners (e.g., Abu Ghraib). Likewise, many of those perpetrators have yet to be brought to justice, especially the government officials who ordered such brutality (Hersh 2004; Sands 2006).

It is with those concerns in mind that we seek to broaden our understanding of state crime. Whereas much of the dialogue on the subject implies strong support for human rights, it is useful to go a step further. Borrowing from Green and Ward, who insist that criminology should not be neutral between human rights violators and their victims, this study adopts their definition of state crime as "state organisational deviance involving the violation of human rights" (2004, 2; 2000). As we shall explore closely, state crimes embodied in the war on terror invite us to consider the conceptual and concrete aspects of the state, organizational deviance, and human rights abuses.[3] Bridging those matters, we acknowledge the interplay between the political and economic elements of the social order, particularly because they also provide a foundation for elite crime committed within an array of antiterrorism maneuvers. In reference to more global notions of domination, Green and Ward argue that the war on terror has "become the key strategic device through with the United States is enforcing its hegemony through a series of military incursions in some to the world's most unstable regions" (2004, 191; 2005).

A study of state crime, of course, would prove incomplete without taking into account strategies for curbing such harm. According to Ross, "Controlling state crime can be accomplished through sound theoretical conceptualization that both identifies the criminal actions committed by the state as well as the mechanisms that sustain those actions and devises methods to control these illegalities and hence to minimize the abuse of coercive power" (2000a, 10). Ross also attends to criminogenic situations, organizations, and networks as sources of state crime, most notably the military-industrial complex and national security agencies, which draw on political and economic vectors in pursuit of power. Rather than retreating into nebulous conspiracy theories, Ross emphasizes the importance of identifying key political and economic players who are instrumental in formulating and carrying out policies and practices. Controlling state crime is often easier said than done, as many incidents since September 11 demonstrate. Echoing the call by human rights groups, Ross insists that state and corporate elites ought to be subjected to greater democratic controls, governmental checks and balances, and oversight by civil society, the media, and nongovernmental organizations. Scholarship aimed at elite crime—particularly from the perspective of human rights—tends to be at once critical and interdisciplinary: drawing on conceptual influences from sociology, social psychology, economics, law, history, political philosophy, human geography, cultural studies, ethics, and so on. Although empirical evidence is crucial to substantiate accusations of wrongdoing, it is also important to attend to theoretical constructs located at the macro- (historical, economic), meso- (organizational), and micro- (interactional) levels (Kauzlarich and Matthews 2006; Kramer and Michalowski 2006). By refining our understanding of elite crime in its various permutations (e.g., state crime, corporate crime, state-corporate) we might improve further the capacity to minimize such atrocities while holding violators accountable.

As noted in the preface, this work builds on a previous study of state crime contained in *Scapegoats of September 11th* (Welch 2006a). Since 9/11 there have been continued acts of wrongdoing against U.S. citizens. Consider, for example, recent revelations of the illegal surveillance program: compounded by the government's eagerness to grant immunity to telephone and Internet providers from consumer lawsuits citing violations of privacy (*New York Times* 2008; Risen 2006; Weiner 2007). Shifting attention beyond U.S. borders, the project explores the war on terror as it expands globally, leaving a long trail of deaths, injuries, and various harms to people elsewhere. The analysis delves deep into the historical, economic, and political forces that shape current responses to political violence. Setting the conceptual groundwork, we take a probing look at power especially as it contributes to state crime in a post–9/11 world.

POWER AND THE ARCHAEOLOGY OF STATE CRIME

Much of the analysis within this work draws on the insights of philosopher Michel Foucault, who continues to leave a deep imprint on the work of many contemporary sociologists as well as a growing number of criminologists. To optimize our appreciation of Foucault, it is fitting that we address his general method, since it offers significant lessons for criminological scholarship. Blending fragments of philosophy, history, and sociology, Foucault puts forth a unique brand of phenomenology: a study of consciousness and the ways individuals experience the social world around them. In stepping toward his subject matter whether it be prisons, discourse, or sexuality, Foucault introduces " 'propositions,' 'game openings' where those who may be interested are invited to join in; they are not meant as dogmatic assertions that have to be taken or left en bloc" (1991a, 74). Those reading Foucault in search of a unified social theory will be disappointed, because there isn't one. Nevertheless, his projects have "a serial continuity with each other. They all concern the modern organization of theoretical and practical knowledges and their relation to certain practices and forms of social organization. But the problems that Foucault's analyses address are each different. They do not sum up nor do they exemplify a single methodological principle" (Cousins and Hussain 1984, 1). That limitation largely explains why Foucault's followers tend draw on extractions rather than the totality of his work; still, his influence serves to improve particular understandings of social relations within certain contexts (Hardt and Negri 2000; Stenson 1993).

Although Foucault continues to have a unique impact on sociology—what is generally called Foucauldian—the use of his concepts present a challenge, because they tend to be rather fluid, making them difficult to nail down.

Consider, for instance, Foucault's notion of power, which has provoked considerable scholarly debate (see Burchell, Gordon, and Miller 1991). Cousins and Hussain contend, "Foucault is alleged to have sired a general theory of power which is an alternative to the conventional theories of power. We shall argue that while Foucault's treatment of power relations is distinctive and novel, this does not constitute a general theory" (1984, 4). For some sociologists, however, that apparent lack of precision seems to invite further interest in the way Foucault approaches power. Particularly with respect to how power unfolds in the prison and other social control projects, Cohen recognizes that orthodox Marxist theorists find weaknesses in Foucault's conception of power as a "thing" not reducible to the workings of labor and capital; however, he considers that to be a strength, adding, "to write about punishment and classification without Foucault, is like talking about the unconscious without Freud" (1985, 10; 1979). For Foucault, power refers to "the various forms of domination and subordination and the asymmetrical balance of forces which operate whenever social relations exist," and in that sense, power "operates 'through' individuals rather than 'against' them" (Garland 1990, 138; Foucault 1980, 98). As Garland points out, "Many sociologists will have little trouble accepting the Foucauldian claim that power is dispersed throughout society as well as being concentrated in the state, and that power operates through networks of action that traverse the legal-constitutional divisions that supposedly separate the state from civil society" (1997a, 205). Foucault rejects the view of a holistic conception of society, leaning more in the direction of open-ended pluralism, containing an array of overlapping social relations and institutions, described by Max Weber (see Hirst and Woolley 1982; Mann 1986). Despite its basic contribution to sociology, Foucault's conceptualization of power benefits from some additional reworking, as Garland has done.

> Power is not a thing in itself, despite Foucault's tendency to use the term 'power' as if it were a proper noun. Power instead is a relational concept. It is the name we give to the capacity to realize a desired goal in a particular situation, and in human cultures the goals which may be valued and sought after are many and varied. If we wish to abstract our analysis away from real situations, it is possible to discuss technologies of power without reference to values. . . . But once we move on from there to analyze the actual operation of forms of power in society, then a crucial question will always be: what values does this power serve? (1990, 169; see Dreyfus and Rabinow 1983)

A recasting of power figures prominently in this work on state crime since it sets out to ground Foucauldian analysis within a post–9/11 society where key political actors and strategists (i.e., the Bush administration) possess and exercise power in ways that serve what they contend to be the state's values (e.g., freedom) and interests (e.g., economic prosperity). Again, Garland faults Foucault for rejecting the notion that power is a thing that is "held" by someone, insisting that ultimately we need to know "who are the people in positions of power and how they came to be there"(1990, 170). Garland goes on to characterize Foucault's conception of power as apolitical, an empty structure, devoid of influential decision makers. Breaking away from that bare technological scaffolding, Garland's revision of Foucauldian power provides better a groundwork for comprehending state crime, especially those actions carried out in the name of national security (extraordinary renditions, the abuse and torture of terrorist suspects, etc.; see Welch 2007a).

Adding both range and depth to his work, Foucault turns to Friedrich Nietzsche (1996 [1887]), whose genealogical method skeptically explores all phenomena for their signs, symbols, and meaning of power (see Garland 1990). For Nietzsche, taking a genealogical approach goes beyond merely identifying origins narrowly conceived as single punctual events; rather, it is an in-depth examination of the emergence of complex interaction within an array of diverse and competing forces. Foucault and Nietzsche attend closely to historical developments, but in doing so each takes a critical stance by liberating the present from previous claims, offering fresh—at times harsh— interpretations of modern society. Nietzsche in particular questions the process by which historical narratives are constructed and to which ends and in the service of which interests. Moreover, he contests not only the accepted historical truths but also the very notion of truth itself. To that end, Nietzsche points to the dynamic role of power in shaping culture insofar as it produces meanings that are never fixed but instead are subject to being redefined in an ongoing struggle over values. Nietzsche also "rejects the progressive notion of history as a necessary, rule-governed development which finds its fulfillment either in the present or in some deferred future" (Smith 1996, xiii). Perhaps even more bluntly, according to his translator Douglas Smith, Nietzsche views all civilization as a product of "economically sanctioned violence" that perpetuates a "history of cruelty" instead one marked by progressive equality (1996, xiii).

Throughout much of his writing, Foucault frequently visits Nietzsche and then moves toward a different interpretation of the subject—for instance, the history of ideas. Nietzsche's genealogical approach nevertheless remains in the backdrop of Foucault's analysis as he questions the widely accepted chronology of the social order, further digging for truth buried deep beneath layers of knowledge. Foucault (1972 [1969]) embarks on archaeology of knowledge, excavating history so as to reassemble a better understanding of the present. Borrowing from what French historian of science Georges Canguilhem called "sanctioned history," Foucault sees a general conceptualization of history as one in which "the past is read through the teleological grid of the present, and in which the present functions as the standard of reason (Cousins and Hussain 1984, 4). Much like Nietzsche before him, Foucault rejects any such use of the category of progress in his analyses.

Especially when taking into consideration a world shaped by domination, conflict, and war—as well as state crime—it is crucial to remain skeptical of the government's version of events because very often history is written by the winners. In that vein, Howard Zinn (2003) reminds us of the importance of adopting a critical approach to history because it provides a foundation for fact checking whatever the government claims to be true. It precisely when commonly accepted and "self-evident" notions of history are confronted that we see the significance of archaeology of knowledge, paving the way for a revised history of the present. Such close analysis indeed drives this unique study of state crime, raising questions about history in the making, especially in a post–9/11 world. With a steady eye on political and economic forces, notably in the form of imperial adventures, this projects sets out to reveal the inner workings of the war on terror, thereby challenging widely circulated rationales and motives for pursuing certain strategies in the name of national security. Along the way, critical notions of power embedded in various social institutions and their practices remain at the forefront of discussion, thereby demonstrating how such potent entities contribute to not only state crime but also thick walls of impunity guarding perpetrators from prosecution. To be clear, the state per se does not commit crimes; instead actors—economic, political, military—who perform on behalf of the state, its values, and its interests do so.

Contrary to mainstream criminologists who dismiss Foucault as being too abstract, too philosophical, and too historical, one must bear in mind that his work is actually quite grounded, even while it looks deep into the sources and expressions of power. During a rather frank interview about his writings, Foucault noted, "The only important problem is what happens on the ground" (1991a, 83). What's more, for activists who find his work simply not practical for intervention, Foucault vehemently insists that critique—which is ultimately what he produces—should "be an instrument for those who fight, those who resist, and refuse what is" (1991a, 84; see 1996; Hardt and Negri 2000).

IN THE PAGES TO FOLLOW

To sort out and examine critically the various crimes of power and their states of impunity, this book offers a series of detailed chapters aimed at different facets of America's war on terror. Admittedly, the problems at hand are complex and have their own unique histories and genealogies. Nevertheless, archaeology of state crime is within reach. The overarching goal of the work is to explore the increasingly controversial features of antiterrorism strategies in order to not only establish their unethical and in many cases unlawful nature but also provide an explanation of how such abuses of power frequently go unchecked. The first theme of this project, a history of the present, continues in the second chapter, where I examine the ways in which power has become reconfigured in the wake of September 11. To be sure, such sociolegal transformations have attracted considerable scholarly attention (Agamben 2005; Butler 2004; Ericson 2007). Chief among recent changes that enhance power—especially in the form of the executive—is the suspension of law, producing tactics and interventions deemed illegal under international law (i.e., the unlawful enemy combatant designation, torture, and the invasion of Iraq). The chapter attends to recent analyses on sovereignty, governmentality, counter-law, and states of exception in an effort to elaborate on state impunity because it is regarded as an important phenomenon warranting greater consideration. Because of an absence of accountability that would otherwise hold specific government actors responsible, key counter-terrorism strategies perpetuate serious state crimes. The discussion situates those transgressions within a conceptual context that deepens our understanding of power in post–9/11 world while inviting further critique on the war on terror as it undermines the rule of law and widely recognized human rights protections.

Adding more precision to how the Bush team moved forward with its reconfigured power, the next three chapters follows the theme of prime targeting. Chapter 3 investigates in detail the emergence of the unlawful enemy combatant designation. To issue a more nuanced interpretation of executive power, the analysis focuses on shifts in military maneuvering that grant the president—operating as commander-in-chief—even greater latitude in administering the war on terror. By doing so, another layer of impunity is imposed that immunizes from wrongdoing the executive and others working under the tent of the presidency. The chapter also benefits from Foucauldian thought, in particular notes on the nature of penal power in the classical age that gradual gives way to counter-law, the undoing of criminal law (Ericson 2007). The phenomenon of counter-law demonstrates how criminal law is undermined, producing less due process rather than more safeguards against arbitrary prosecution. The Military Commissions Act (MCA) of 2006, for example, embodies a new form of militarized power aimed at unlawful enemy combatants, serving to redistribute of the economy of penal power within an increasingly centralized political hierarchy.

Of course, those persons designated unlawful enemy combatants are not merely detained but are placed in a highly specialized penal institution located beyond the shores of the United States, situated inside a military installation at Guantánamo Bay, Cuba. That institution has without question become one of the most notorious prisons in a post–9/11 world, raising sharp questions about its legality under international law as well as reports of harsh conditions of confinement, coercive interrogations, torture, and indefinite detention. Whereas there is a fast-growing literature addressing each of those issues, there are few penological excursions into the distinctive nature of Guantánamo Bay and its internal workings. Chapter 4 attempts to offer a coherent theoretical interpretation of Guantánamo Bay as a unique—Foucauldian—supermax prison. While it is true that Foucault has undergone considerable critique for his writings on imprisonment, there remains much potential for improving our understanding of the prison and specifically the role Guantánamo Bay in the war on terror. The analysis sets out to decipher the significance of penal discourse, technologies, and resistance as they unfold at Guantánamo Bay; by doing so, critical insights into emerging forms of modern power are illuminated alongside their unintended consequences.

The theme involving prime targets in the war on terror extends to matters of interrogation and torture, as presented in chapter 5. While photographs of abused and tortured prisoners at Abu Ghraib were being revealed to a global audience, the U.S. government rushed forward a campaign of denial and damage control, claiming that such sadistic cruelty was confined to a small unit of "bad apples." Those with knowledge of the history of covert actions, however, immediately recognized the tell-tale signs of CIA torture techniques dating back five decades. The chapter embarks on a genealogy of modern torture by tracing its origins from the Cold War to its current use in America's war on terror. Correspondingly, a "science" of interrogation is critiqued so as to bring into sharp relief the significance of power. The analysis takes into specific account Foucauldian concepts known as translation, governmentality, and discourse. Together, those theoretical devices explain how torture policies are transmitted through various agencies and levels of participation. Acknowledging the importance of political rationalities (i.e., the why) and governmental technologies (i.e., the how), the discussion sheds light on the process of transforming "unthinkable" interrogation methods into ones regarded as not only "thinkable" but also argued to be necessary and effective.

The next two chapters illustrate the expanding range of America's response to terror, particularly given the invasion and occupation of Iraq. Contradicting U.S. claims that the invasion was both justified and legal, it is necessary to recognize that under international law only the United Nations Security Council can authorize military action to disarm an aggressor. A primary reason for that stipulation is to ensure that disarmament is the real objective rather than a pursuit of other political or economic interests (Beyani 2003). From that standpoint, the invasion of Iraq is not only a blatant breach of the rule of law but further constitutes a war of aggression that the Nuremberg Charter describes as supreme international crime: the most reprehensible and destabilizing of all state crimes (Kramer and Michalowski 2005; Kramer, Michalowski, and Rothe 2005). Chapter 6 goes beyond issues of legality to examine in greater detail the colonial dimensions of the occupation. In light of the degree of economic realignment in Iraq, there is mounting criticism that the United States is in violation of international humanitarian law (IHL, or law of armed conflict) on the grounds that the Fourth Geneva Convention (1949) bans occupying powers from restructuring the economy in their own vision (see Gregory 2004; Whyte 2007). Similarly, chapter 7 examines collateral damage, a military euphemism for civilians killed or maimed while being caught in the crossfire or hit by an errant missile veering off course. As will be discussed, the failure of an occupying power to provide security and protect civilians also violates international humanitarian law. Certainly, the rationale behind the United States' claims that it is not an occupying power in Iraq is to skirt the country's obligations under international law that holds foreign military and political officials accountable for failed security measures. Much like the other crimes of power compounded by states of impunity examined in this study, there is little recourse for victims of collateral damage. Whereas some families have been granted relatively small sums of cash for errors in the use of lethal force, most of those who have lost loved ones are rarely acknowledged by the U.S. military (Keen 2006; Shiner 2007).

The final part of the analysis surveys lasting legacies of the U.S. response to terror just as crimes of power and states of impunity become firmly rooted in America's political and popular cultures. Following in the steps of Jonathan Simon (2007), whose treatise on governing through crime has had an immediate impact on criminology, chapter 8 explores further how the state has adopted antiterrorism rhetoric and strategies to legitimate its claim to rule. Mirroring the campaign against crime, the war on terror expands government and delivers a more powerful—and authoritarian—executive, superseding a passive legislature and defensive judiciary. The emergent autocratic politics do not occur in a vacuum but, rather, draw enormously from a growing populism in American culture. In the end, however, governing through terror does not actually mean delivering greater security and safety; instead, it is the way in which the state expresses its power in general and in particular its ambition to manage the population within its territory. It is regrettable that, while pandering to populism, governors of terror refuse to recognize the underlying sources of political violence.

The concluding chapter fixes squarely on the second twin pillar of America's response to terror: the states of impunity. As another lasting legacy, the dense wall of immunity keeps at bay any attempt to bring to justice violators of domestic or international law. To be certain, some low-level military personnel have been punished for their participation in the mistreatment of detainees at Abu Ghraib, as just one example. Nevertheless, the authors and architects of such abuse—and torture—remain outside the zone of prosecution, leaving them immune from accountability. Contributing to the states of impunity is a wider public culture that either endorses current strategies (e.g., torturing terror suspects, launching large-scale military strikes upon other countries) or reluctantly turns a blind eye to the "lesser evils" inherent to the war on terror (Dershowitz 2002; Ignatieff 2004). Whichever the case, there prevails a strong sense of denial that such extreme measures to fighting terror are simply not effective and even make matters worse, leaving behind an ugly trail of human rights casualties. In order to stitch together the various levels of denial contributing to states of impunity, chapter 9 extracts key observations from Cohen's (2001) treatise on how governments and their citizens insulate themselves against a full realization of serious human rights violations. For Cohen, denial refers to "the maintenance of social worlds in which an undesirable situation (event, condition, phenomenon) is unrecognized, ignored or made to seem normal" (2001, 52). As the following pages show, America's trampling of human rights in a post–9/11 world is rife with denial.

The book closes on an activist note: calling for action against human rights abuses in the war on terror. Although the war in Iraq is simply too obvious to ignore, other antiterrorism measures are easily overlooked because they unfold secretly, such as extraordinary renditions and the mistreatment and torture of detainees. The project intends to bring to the forefront of conversation important ethical issues surrounding those crimes of power. Moreover, in an effort to dismantle states of impunity it echoes Cohen, who reminds us that the human rights movement is not only aimed at confronting government but also aspires to promote a general awareness: "We must make it difficult for people to say that they 'don't know' " (2001, 11).

CHAPTER 2

A New Configuration of Power

IN RESPONSE TO THE attacks on September 11, the U.S. government has embarked on a campaign that significantly redrafts the legal landscape, prompting political commentators to take notice. In an editorial titled "Mr. Cheney's Imperial Presidency," the *New York Times* chronicles chief developments over the past few years:

> George W. Bush has quipped several times during his political career that it would be so much easier to govern in a dictatorship. Apparently, he never told his vice president that this was a joke. Virtually from the time he chose himself to be Mr. Bush's running mate in 2000, Dick Cheney has spearheaded an extraordinary expansion of the powers of the presidency—from writing energy policy behind close doors with oil executives to abrogating longstanding treaties and using the 9/11 attacks as a pretext to invade Iraq, scrap the Geneva Conventions and spy on American citizens. (December 23, 2005, A26)

The "Bush/Cheney regime" indeed makes good fodder for political conversation embedded in America's 9/11 culture (Croft 2006). Many scholars and human rights organizations, however, are not amused by the recent suspension of law and question the claim that such sweeping shifts in governance are justified by a national "emergency" brought on by terrorism.

INTRODUCTION

With certain tactics in the war on terror, such as designation of unlawful enemy combatant, torture, and the war in Iraq, being characterized as lawless, intellectuals have delved into the nature of power to determine which specific sociolegal transformations have occurred and what they mean in a post–9/11 world. Judith Butler, a leading voice in the dialogue on power, sovereignty, and governmentality, looks critically at what she calls the "new war prison" (i.e., Guantánamo Bay). Wondering about the legal innovations that serve as its basis, she asks, "What does it say about the contemporary formation and extension of state power?" (2004, 51). Similar to the views of Richard V. Ericson (2007) and

Giorgio Agamben (2005), Butler explores not only the suspension of law in the wake of September 11 but also the precise entity of power that fills its void. While reviewing various interpretations of those shifts in power, this chapter sets out to elaborate on one of its key dimensions—namely, impunity. In light of a new exercise of state sovereignty, it is distressing for human rights advocates to learn that decisions over who is detained (perhaps indefinitely), tortured, or even executed take place in the absence of clear accountability (Human Rights Watch 2007, 2006a). That particular form of impunity fuels scholarly debate over power, sovereignty, and governmentality. Moreover, in large part because of its detachment from mechanisms of social control aimed at holding perpetrators responsible for their transgressions, such immunity is a major source for state crimes. The position established here is that the unlawful enemy combatant designation, torture, and the war of Iraq qualify as serious state crimes (Kramer and Michalowski 2005; Welch 2006a). Those lawless tactics in the war on terror, as studied in this work, are intimately linked to a newly configured form of power that has taken hold since 9/11.

The discussion begins with an overview of Ericson's (2007) discovery of counter-law, or laws against law, as situated in risk society theory. Ericson's concerns over the suspension of law parallel those of Agamben (2005), who issues a probing look at states of exception and how those ruptures in democratic power are not merely passing moments but also have become a working paradigm of government. In search of added insight into that sociolegal phenomenon, Ericson further explores Butler's (2004) theoretical framework on power. The conceptual destination of this project lies in the realm of impunity since alongside a new configuration of power comes unique forms of immunization. In the wake of 9/11, the U.S. government has introduced greater administrative measures in dealing with terror suspects that shield against prosecutions for war crimes the architects of those policies as well as those who carry out its tactics. The notion of impunity is significant because it not only strands those in custody from access to meaningful legal remedies but also insulates state and executive power from accountability and the rule of law, enhancing the likelihood that such abuses will persist in an endless war on terror. To be clear, it is the nature of immunity embodied in the campaign war on terror that contributes to the erosion democratic institutions, thereby deepening our insight into counter-law within the state of exception. To illustrate those transformations, the focus concentrates on the unlawful enemy combatant designation, torture, and the invasion of Iraq. Joining Young (2003) and Mythen and Walklate (2006), the analysis seeks to connect criminology to sociology, with special consideration given to power as it produces state crime and human rights abuses. It concludes with observations on contemporary war and its victims as trapped in the colonial present, a concept that refers to grids of time and space where domination and violence are framed as justified (Gregory 2004).

Criminology has made significant inroads into the risk society literature with insightful studies on crime, risk, and uncertainty (Amoore and De Goede 2005; Levi and Wall 2004; Mythen and Walklate 2006). Recent work by Richard V. Ericson (2007) is of particular interest because it illuminates the linkages between recent legal transformations and a neoliberal political culture preoccupied with uncertainty. According to Ericson, as uncertainty intensifies, a precautionary logic leads to extreme—and frantic—security measures intended to ward off imagined sources of harm (see Taylor 2004). In the realm of national security, terrorism is the politics of uncertainty because, as a form of political violence, it plays on randomness to press entire populations into mindsets of fear and anxiety. Terrorism also exposes an inherent feature of modern societies—that is, their potential ungovernability whereby those with little power can undo formidable institutions (see Deflem 2004, 2008).

In response such threats, state actors move toward intensified security measures by putting into motion distinct legal maneuvers. Such changes include not only an expansion and revision of criminal law but also new civil and administrative tactics; paradoxically, those transformations erode key aspects of due process intended to safeguard suspects' rights under traditional criminal proceedings. Whereas Ashworth (2000, 2003, 2004) points to political opportunism as a driving force behind such changes, Ericson further contextualizes those developments within the risk society framework. In addition, Ericson's analysis is informed by Foucault, who recognized that asymmetries of power were widened by suspensions of law, a phenomenon he called counter-law (1977, 30; 1991).[1] Blending risk society theory with Foucauldian thought, Ericson characterizes counter-law as the enactment of new laws (and civil and administrative devices) "to erode or eliminate traditional principles, standards, and procedures of criminal law that get in the way of preempting imagined sources of harm" (2007, 24). To be clear, Ericson's use of the term *counter-law* should not be separated from his theoretical considerations on risk. Counter-law is not simply a power shift that passes new legislation to replace existing ones; it is a sociolegal transformation within the state as it strives to harness risk. Whereas many crimes, including terrorism, fall into the purview of criminal law, counter-law provides a concept that allows us to see risk as a driving force that justifies reassigning those offenses (and even mere threats or suspicions of such harm) into the sphere of civil and administrative proceedings where there is less uncertainty in trying to manage the putative problem (see Crawford 2003, 2006; Ericson and Haggerty 1997; Stenson 2003). As Ericson writes,

> The legal transformation through counter-law is not only a response to scientific uncertainty about risk, but also the law itself as a source of

uncertainty. For example, when it sustains high standards of due process, evidence, proof and culpability, criminal law creates a great deal of uncertainty in the capacity of the criminal justice system to prevent, discover, build a case against, and successfully prosecute criminal behavior. In the precautionary urge for greater certainty in crime control, these standards of criminal law are weakened [and] the lower standards of civil and administrative law are substituted. (2007, 25–26; see also O'Malley 2004)

Counter-law serves as a transparent tactic by political authorities to gain the upper hand in the politics of authority. That is particularly significant in the wake of a catastrophic event such as September 11 that reveals key weaknesses in the government's ability to protect national security. Consequently, counter-law becomes a dominant political strategy representing the boldest statement of authoritative certainty by the state, even when its authority and certainty may be at its weakest.

Ericson (2007) situates counter-law within a neoliberal search for security, a dubious quest given that uncertainty is a basic condition of human knowledge (see Welch 2006b). Although advocates of counter-law claim that to have achieved an advantage in managing society as it faces risks embedded in late modernity, such strategies undermine democratic institutions and provide a dangerous foundation for human rights abuses. In its war on terror, the U.S. government has adopted several counter-law tactics that restricts the rights of its own citizens (e.g., the USA Patriot Act). Still as we shall elaborate on in this work, there are other tactics that target persons outside of America's borders. The unlawful enemy combatant designation, the opening of Guantánamo Bay, and revised definitions of torture are all counter-terrorism measures that operate beyond law as conventionally conceived in international terms. Turning critical attention to those matters, Ericson discusses the importance of counter-law as it is emerges in a state of exception, an idea developed by Agamben (2005). The state of exception stems from a catastrophic event that the state depicts as an emergency, thereby justifying a suspension of normal legal principles and procedures. As the national (or even international) emergency expands so do uncertainty and putative threat; as one might expect, a state of exception has profound sociolegal effects. For Agamben, it seems that "the legal order must be broken to save the social order" (2005, 26). Ericson and Agamben share the view that counter-law and the state of exception are not momentary suspensions of the legal order but have become the new normal, serving as the dominant paradigm of government. Those developments offer important implications to state crimes as they occur within a zone of immunity. Nevertheless, before making the leap into matters of state crime, it is useful to sort through some conceptual considerations as they pertain to sovereignty and a new configuration of power, especially in light of recent writings by Judith Butler (2004).

In light of the rapid pace at which changes in the legal order have occurred since September 11, scholars have asked probing questions about the contemporary formation and extension of state power. Butler (2004) joins the forum by giving serious thought as to how Foucault's (1991b) conceptions of sovereignty and governmentality can be reworked, producing a clearer understanding the nature of power in a post–9/11 world. In Foucauldian terms, sovereignty provides a guarantor for the representational claims for state power (see Welch 2007a). By contrast, governmentality refers to a mode of power directed at the maintenance and control of a population by way of policies carried out by various managerial and bureaucratic agencies that gain their authority under state power. Foucault proclaims, it is governmentalization that has permitted the state to survive (1991, 52). Still, he concedes that sovereignty and governmentality actually coexist. Deciphering that particular form of coexistence became Butler's project. Speaking about the emergence of Guantánamo Bay, as a "new war prison," Butler concludes that "the current configuration of state power, in relation both to the management of populations (the hallmark of governmentality) and the exercise of sovereignty in the acts that suspend and limit the jurisdiction of law itself, are reconfigured" (2004, 53). The suspension of law can be properly interpreted as a tactic of governmentality, although it also opens an opportunity for the resurgence of sovereignty, permitting both entities to operate in tandem. That convergence then disarticulates the state into a set of administrative powers residing outside the apparatus of the state. Moreover, "the forms of sovereignty resurrected in its midst mark the persistence of forms of sovereign political power for the executive that precede the emergence of the state in its modern form" (Butler 2004, 55–56).

The new configuration of power described by Butler points to a significant sociolegal transformation in a post–9/11 world insofar as the war on terror is administered by recently created petty sovereigns who are mobilized by tactics of power they do not fully control. Nevertheless, they are granted the power to render unilateral decisions, "accountable to no law and without any legitimate authority" (2004, 56). Without question, that form of power is lawless or, in Butler's words, constitutes "a 'rogue' power par excellence" (2004, 56). As discussed below, that "rogue" power figures prominently in the process of deeming certain persons as unlawful enemy combatants. Nonetheless, it is important to emphasize that those decisions take place in the context of a "state of emergency" that has set the conditions for removing accountability from the field of operations (Brown 2005). The "emergency" ushers in rules (governmentality) that replace laws (juridical), reinstating sovereign power that distributes managerial authority as it enjoys full and unreviewable discretion. As a result, pseudo-institutions are produced for the administration of the war on terror, most notably "a law that is not a law, a court that is not a court, a process that is not a process" (Butler 2004, 62).

SOVEREIGN IMPUNITY AND STATE CRIMES

Certainly recent sociolegal developments have all the markings of a literary narrative, perhaps best captured by Franz Kafka in *The Trial* (1999), in which an ordinary man is forced to appear before a tribunal, but the government refuses to inform him of the charges he faces. In a similar fashion, the new configuration of power as described above has potential to reach beyond the sociology of law and into the realm of state crimes. Integrating ideas contained in counter-law (Ericson 2007), state of exception (Agamben 2005), and what might be called sovereign governmentality (Butler 2004), this project proposes an extended concept. As the term implies, sovereign impunity, is embedded into a newly configured form of power while accentuating its inherent lack accountability. It is that feature of power which serves as key source for state crimes in the war on terror, specifically indefinite detention and torture, as well as the war in Iraq. Sovereign impunity not only immunizes state actors and their operatives from wrongdoing but also erases all avenues for victim compensation. Together, those dimensions of sovereign impunity create the likelihood that state crimes will persist, particularly within a wider political culture that reframes such actions as necessary to protect national security. Sovereign impunity emphasizes further the dark side of the new configuration of power, an area that is of keen interest for criminologists focusing on transgressions of the state. Moreover, it also brings into relief elements of justice inseparable from human rights. Stanley Cohen (1995a) reminds us that justice does not necessarily mean exacting punishment onto guilty parties; it refers to a process of establishing accountability.

There are varied definitions of state crimes alluding to governmental crime, political crime, and state-organized crime. Nonetheless, it is generally agreed that such violations constitute "illegal, socially injurious [harmful], or unjust acts which are committed for the benefit of a state or its agencies, and not for the personal gain of some individual agent of the state" (Kauzlarich, Matthews, and Miller 2001, 175; see Chambliss 1989; Friedrichs 1998; Ross 2000a). That interpretation of state crime clearly lends itself to an array of unlawful acts and human rights atrocities in the war on terror (see Kramer, Michalowski, and Rothe 2005; Welch 2003, 2005). In this section, three instances of state crime occurring in the name of national security are examined: the designation of unlawful enemy combatants, torture, and the American (and British) invasion of Iraq. To remain mindful of recent sociolegal transformations, we consider the role played by the newly configured power in the reproduction of sovereign impunity. Certainly, what distinguishes those state crimes from the run of the mill street-level offenses (and even many political, corporate, and organizational crimes) is their total immunity, adding to speculation that such crimes have no bounds.

Unlawful Enemy Combatant Designation

The decision by President Bush to process terror suspects by way of military tribunals rather than by criminal courts is notable because it reveals how the president opted to interpret and exercise the particular powers of the office. As the record demonstrates, Bush issued a military order rather than an executive one.[2] As a result, the war on terror became militarized in ways that goes beyond popular metaphor, becoming a carefully planned strategy housed within the Department of Defense. The military order mandated the establishment of military tribunals according to rules and regulations dictated by the Pentagon's civilian general counsel, William J. Haynes II, and submitted to Secretary of Defense Donald Rumsfeld for departmental promulgation.[3] Among other aspects, the new military tribunals depart from past practices by specifically targeting non-U.S. citizens; previous tribunals never distinguished between citizens and foreign nationals (see Katyal and Tribe 2002; Welch 2008a).

By initiating a military strategy, Bush's choice of options is especially significant. "For the first time in American history, the characterization of terrorism as a criminal act to be dealt with by the civilian courts would be superseded by its characterization as an act of war" (Pious 2006, 225). To give the appearance that his military order was not unilateral, Bush claimed that Congress provided its support in the joint resolution authorizing the president "to use all necessary and appropriate force against those nations, organizations, or persons he determines planned, authorized, committed, or aided the terrorist attacks that occurred on September 11, 2001."[4] Those events set the stage for a series of crucial political and military decisions that reconfigure power in the war on terror. As we shall see, the Bush administration put into motion several unusual strategies to detain and prosecute terror suspects, tactics that continue to raise serious questions about their constitutionality and legality under international law (Jinks and Sloss 2004; Kacprowski 2004; Margulies 2004).

Precisely how the Bush administration exercises the unlawful enemy combatant designation has been subject to legal scrutiny. In 2006 the Supreme Court in *Hamdi v. Rumsfeld* (2004; see *Rasul v. Bush and United States* 2004) invalidated the system of military commissions Bush had set up for trying terrorism suspects, saying that the tribunals required Congressional authorization. The court also required that suspects be treated in accordance with a provision of the Geneva Conventions, Common Article 3, which prohibits cruel and inhumane treatment, including "outrages upon personal dignity." In response to that ruling, Congress set out to assemble a tribunal system believed to be congruent with the decision of the Supreme Court. After months of (relatively narrow) debate, Congress passed the Military Commissions Act (MCA) of 2006, a measure that Bush swiftly signed into law (Stolberg 2006a). Under the revised proceedings, the government—specifically, the executive branch and the military—enjoys numerous built-in advantages in determining whether a suspect fits the classification of unlawful enemy combatant. The MCA reconfigures and recentralizes power in the war on terror in ways that gut due process and meaningful judicial oversight; in fact, the MCA created few differences from its predecessor that Bush ordered into effect in November 1, 2001. Likewise, the new law poses serious threats to international human rights by preventing suspects from filing suit via the writ of habeas corpus to challenge the legality of their detention or to raise claims of torture and other abuses (see Swanson 2004). Human rights advocates complain that MCA tribunal system does not meet the fair trial provisions required by the Geneva Conventions and human rights law (Cole 2003; Kacprowski 2004; Paust 2005). Scholars studying conceptions of power have take a keen interest in the unlawful enemy combatant designation, particularly as it points to a newly configured form of power. Butler's remarks on the subject are instructive:

> In the current war prison, officials of governmentality wield sovereign power, understood here as a lawless and unaccountable operation of power, once legal rule is effectively suspended and military codes take its place. Once again, a lost or injured sovereign becomes reanimated through rules that allocate final decisions about life and death to the executive branch or to officials with no elected status and bound no constitutional constraints. (2004, xv)

Butler's observations on the lawless nature by which persons are designated as unlawful enemy combatant further the notion of sovereign impunity because it points to the absence of accountability. Indeed, indefinite detention, as a form of state crime, not only contradicts principles of due process contained in the rule of law but also obliterates basic ideals of justice. Agamben (1998, 2005) also weighs into the controversy, arguing that persons denied legal rights, including unlawful enemy combatants, are stripped completely of protection, rendering them vulnerable to the whims of the state, including acts of crime. Agamben enriches his analysis by invoking the concept *homo sacer* (sacred man) that has its origin in Roman law. *Homo sacer* refers to those who could not be sacrificed according to ritual because they were outside the zone of divine law, thus their lives had no value to the gods. Nevertheless, they could still be killed with impunity because they also remained out of the reach of juridical law, which meant their lives had no value to their contemporaries. The notion of *homo sacer* has profound ontological implications pertaining to unlawful enemy combatants as they intersect with sovereign impunity. In essence, those who are refused their rights are also denied a sense of belonging to any community. Moreover, the sovereign (one who decides the exception) who orders the exclusion possesses an unreviewable power and is, therefore, totally unaccountable (see Schmitt 1985; Human Rights Watch 2004, 2005, 2007; Amnesty International 2005).

Torture

The United States is not immune to charges of state crimes. For example, U.S. operatives engaged in torture in Southeast Asia during the 1960s and 1970s as well as in Latin America in the 1980s (Harbury 2005; McCoy 2006). What is new about torture's reemergence in the current campaign against terror is the attempt by government officials to justify it in legal terms. Its advocates argue that, given the state of emergency surrounding the war on terror, the United States is engaged in a fourth-generation warfare involving a nation-state against a nonstate actor (Cheney 2005; Lind et al. 1989). Such tactics have a clear policy objective: to correct the information deficit on Al-Qaeda since the U.S. government had relatively little formalized intelligence on a network of terrorists who had thrown a wrench into the American imperial project (Clarke 2004; Scheuer 2004). In attempting to meet that objective, the White House once again has entered the domain of sovereign impunity. By deliberately rewriting the prohibitions on torture, the authors and architects of American policy, along with those who order and carry out torture, would be immunized from punishment, even in cases in which there exists credible evidence of war crimes (Danner 2004; Welch 2006a).

Keeping in mind the notion of sovereign impunity, there is compelling documentation on precisely how the executive branch of the U.S. government set out to remove itself from the rule of law in planning a policy of torture. In *The Torture Papers: The Road to Abu Ghraib*, Greenberg and Dratel (2005) reveal in stark detail the Bush administration's playbook by which it would concoct a legal defense for the use of torture in the war on terror (also see Hersh 2004). The legal narrative contained in official memos exhibits three aims that would facilitate the unilateral and unfettered detention, interrogation, abuse, judgment, and punishment of prisoners: "(1) the desire to place the detainees beyond the reach of any court or law; (2) the desire to abrogate the Geneva Convention with respect to the treatment of persons seized in the context of armed hostilities; and (3) the desire to absolve those implementing the policies of any liability for war crimes under U.S. and international law" (Dratel 2005, xxi). Among the revelations amplified by *The Torture Papers* is the now infamous White House definition of torture that contradicted the standard interpretation established in the Convention against Torture, a deliberate weakening of the document the United States ratified in 1994. A memorandum by Jay S. Bybee, assistant attorney general for Alberto R. Gonzales (then White House counsel and later attorney general) altered the meaning of the longstanding Convention against Torture by arguing, "Physical pain amounting to torture must be equivalent in intensity to the pain accompanying serious injury, such as organ failure, impairment of bodily function, or even death" (Greenberg and Dratel 2005, 172–214; Danner 2004).[5]

As a paper trail of legal arguments favoring torture and as a tainted historical record fixed squarely onto the Bush presidency, *The Torture Papers* is nothing less than remarkable. Dratel notes, "Rarely, if ever, has such a guilty governmental conscience been so starkly illuminated in advance" (2005, xxi). Unquestionably, that guilty conscience is fraught such denial that it has produced a steady stream of rationalizations attempting to justify a blatantly indefensible position in support of torture (S. Cohen 2001, 2006). The Bush team resorted to a "corporatization" of government lawyering in which torture policy architects began with a specific objective and work backward without benefit of a moral compass that could brake their client's descent into unconscionable conduct (Dratel 2005; Greenberg 2005). The "corporatization" of government lawyering coupled with counter-law figures prominently into sovereign impunity insofar, as wrongdoing is the product of an organizational system, however small, and its collective decision making. As Ericson (2007) points out, there is a tendency to lay blame on a few malicious persons and scapegoat them in ways that reproduce the myths of accountability when the actual problems reside in the structure and organization of those responsible for formulating policy. *The Torture Papers* provide indisputable evidence that the abuse and torture of prisoners Abu Ghraib was the product of policy initiatives and not an isolated incident involving a bunch "bad apple" servicemen and women who disgraced themselves and the military they served (Lewis 2005).

While human rights advocates fret over the consequences of sovereign impunity, some legal scholars have added to the controversy by supporting the state's policy of torture. Dershowitz (2002) suggests that "torture warrants" be prepared in the courts to immunize government torturers from criminal prosecution (see Ignatieff 2004; Steel 2004). Other techniques of immunization are found in renditions whereby terror suspects are outsourced to a third party (e.g., Egypt, Jordan, Morocco, and Syria) as a means to skip over legal prohibitions contained the Convention against Torture. In a similar vein, the employment of privatized "interrogators" who are not bound by legal or military codes provides another avenue for impunity. Commenting on the lack of accountability, Peter Singer said, "Legally speaking [military contractors] fall into the same grey zone as the unlawful combatants detained at Guantanamo Bay" (Singer 2005, 121; Newburn 2007). It is true that the *Hamdan* ruling raised questions over the legality of the Bush administration's secret CIA detention program while "making clear that the abusive interrogation techniques used by the CIA violated the United States' obligations under international law and that CIA operatives could be held criminally liable for such abuses" (Human Rights Watch 2006a, 1). However, because the CIA exists within the sovereignty of presidential power, it remains conveniently insulated by virtue being a covert agency shrouded in secrecy and its own lack of any political will to prosecute its personnel for state crimes involving torture.

War in Iraq

The 2003 U.S. (U.K.) invasion of Iraq has drawn critical attention from a growing group of criminologists who characterize the war—along with a host of interrelated human rights abuses—as a key form of state crime. Indeed, should criminologists be committed to fully comprehending and significantly reducing violence, wars of aggression ought to be subject to critical analysis. Kramer and Michalowski insist, "Wars of aggression are, by far, the most destructive and destabilizing of all state crimes. In the words of the Nuremberg Charter, they are the 'supreme international crime' " (2005, 446). With an eye on history and the political economy, several criminologists offer a critique of American imperialism as a force that produces war, aggression, and state crime (Kramer and Michalowski 2005; Whyte 2007). As the examination of power moves forward, it is useful to recognize America's imperial history that has served as a political foundation for the war in Iraq and the launching of a militarized war on terror.[6]

Niall Ferguson (2005) presents his case that the United States has been an imperial project in the making since its early years as a republic (see Garrison 2004; Hardt and Negri 2000). Nevertheless, as Ferguson purports, Americans suffer from an infliction that he calls "imperial denial," and liberals and conservatives project different versions of the same disclaimer. Ferguson's thesis permits us to view in-depth the nature of American political rhetoric that shakes off accusations of empire while inserting carefully spun justifications for military action. Consider the words of President George W. Bush's on April 13, 2004: "We're not an imperial power. We're a liberating power" (Ferguson 2005, ix). The persistent use of the slogan "spreading freedom" to characterize the American invasion of Iraq (and Afghanistan) is not a new political invention. Along with its companion mantra "making the world safe for democracy," efforts to "spread freedom" by way of military force have been recycled from one historical period to the next: the First and Second World Wars, the Korean War, the Vietnam War, and adventures in Central America. Further deepening American denial is the belief that the United States is a reluctant interventionist and acts only out of a sense of moral duty to protect freedom. Moreover, the commercial facets of American expansionism also help float "imperial denial" insofar as it is based on the strategy of controlling without owning, a sharp departure from previous colonial regimes (Chomsky 2003; W. A. Williams 1969, 1988).[7]

While serving as defense aecretary under the first President Bush, Dick Cheney worked closely with neoconservatives Paul Wolfowitz and I. Lewis (Scooter) Libby, who produced the Defense Planning Guidance (DPG), a classified internal document that outlined the neocon agenda aimed to reshape American military—and economic—agenda. The DPG "depicted a world dominated by the United States, which would maintain its superpower status through a combination of positive guidance and overwhelming military might. The image was one of a "heavily armed City on a Hill" (Armstrong 2002, 78). The plan included strategies to prevent the reemergence of a new rival while keeping in its reserve options for the use of preemptive military strikes to ensure its supremacy (Chomsky 2003). It is interesting to note that the document was leaked to the press and President G. H. W. Bush and Secretary Cheney distanced themselves from the neocon agenda while maintaining a less odious form of imperialism known as the New World Order (Aronowitz and Gautney 2003; Soros 2004). For the time being, the DPG would be shelved until September 11, 2001, a catalyzing event that unleashed the fury of the neocon plan that could thrive under the conditions of a "state of exception" (Agamben 2005).

The attacks on the Pentagon and the World Trade Center not only jarred the nation into a state of anger and insecurity but also provided an opportunity for the neocons to fill the "blank threat" vacated by the Soviet Union, dubbed the Evil Empire by President Reagan. While Al-Qaeda and Osama Bin Laden emerged as the new evildoers responsible for 9/11, the neocons pushed forward a major disinformation campaign to connect the terrorists to Saddam Hussein and Iraq—a member a group of nations that President George W. Bush called the "axis of evil" (Clarke 2004; Suskind 2004). As the claim linking Hussein with Al-Qaeda began to lose political currency—especially given the failure to find weapons of mass destruction and biological and chemical agents—the invasion and occupation of Iraq would become synonymous with the war on terror (Scheuer 2004; Woodward 2004). Experts on state crime, however, point out that motivations and opportunity alone are not sufficient to produce organizational deviance. "Although policy planners who supported aggressive American unilateralism [i.e., neocons] as a route to global dominance enjoyed insider positions in a presidential administration willing to embrace just such a strategy, this alone is not a sufficient explanation of how the United States found itself on a pathway to committing state crime against Iraq and the Iraqi people" (Kramer and Michalowski 2005, 460).

Kramer and Michalowski (2005) go on to explain that strong social control mechanisms could have blocked the march to war. As evidence of sovereignty that resists attempts to hold accountable high level political and military officials for state crime, Kramer and Michalowski direct attention to weakened mechanisms situated at three levels: structural, organizational, and interactional. At the international level, the United Nations could not produce a sufficiently robust deterrent to keep the United States—a hegemonic power—from proceeding forward with its war plans, even in the face of worldwide negative opinion. Also Congress and the media failed to meet their obligations to confront the White House and question its justifications for going to war. At the interactional level, the Bush administration insulated itself from self-criticism by resorting to "groupthink" whereby loyalty and shared beliefs in the inherent morality of their position reign supreme (Janus 1982; Suskind 2004). The Bush team and its supporters further rationalized the state crimes in ways consistent with the classic "techniques of neutralization," a set of social psychological dynamics that facilitate, rather than inhibit, wrongdoing (Sykes and Matza 1957). Kramer and Michalowski are trenchant in their characterization of the Bush administration's justifications for war against Iraq:

> They denied responsibility (the war was Saddam's fault), denied the victims (most were terrorists), denied injury (there was only limited 'collateral damage'), condemned the condemners (protestors were unpatriotic and the French were ungrateful and cowardly) and appealed to higher loyalties (God directed Bush to liberate the Iraqi people). (2005, 463)

In addition the aforementioned actions depicted as state crimes, four specific war crimes violating international humanitarian law (IHL, or law of armed conflict) have been documented in the course of occupying Iraq. First, is the illegal transformation of the Iraqi economy, a violation that reflects key designs of a belligerent American imperial project. Under the Fourth Geneva Convention of 1949, occupying powers are banned from restructuring the economy in the vision of the conqueror. As American forces gained control over Iraq, the state-dominated economy was overhauled to fit the imperatives of a market economy committed to neoliberal free trade, supply-side tax policy, privatization, and foreign ownership (Greider 2003; Juhasz 2004; Klein 2003a). Second, is the failure of the occupying power to secure public safety and protect civilian rights in the wake of widespread looting and violence along with a host of home demolitions and arbitrary arrests leading to detentions (Amnesty International 2005). Third, indiscriminate responses to Iraqi resistance have contributed to a greater number of civilian casualties. Examples of "overkill" have been documented in such sieges as in Fallujah, where American military had resorted to an inordinate level of force and destruction (Normand 2004; Parenti 2004). Fourth, there are war crimes involving the abuse and torture of Iraqi prisoners. Most important, those crimes are not just isolated incidents of "bad apple" soldiers ventilating their frustration against perceived enemies but, rather, represent highly organized and systematic tactics; therefore, affirming the view that torture has been devised as policy by the U.S. government (Hersh 2004; Human Rights Watch 2006b; Knowlton 2005).

Although it is instructive to conceptualize the war in Iraq as a form of state crime boasting clear imperial features, there is, of course, room to refine our interpretation of that event as it figures into the critique of power and sovereign impunity. In his *The Colonial Present*, Derek Gregory borrows from a host of intellecuals, among them Foucault, Agamben, and Butler, to stitch together meanings of time and space as they factor into contemporary war. Gregory notes that even the best-run empires are violent enterprises, adding: "I believe that 'the roots of the global crisis which erupted on September 11 lie in precisely those colonial experiences and the informal quasi-imperial system that succeeded them' " (2004, 10). Still, as a human geographer, he directs attention to perceptual grids that suggest spaces where some populations are expendable, most notably civilians killed by invading powers, or what the military refers to as "collateral damage." Those victims of state crime are marked as *homo sacer* (capable of being killed but not sacrificed) confined not only in a state of exception but also space of exception. That space of exception is deliberately removed from the visual field whereby such victimization often is concealed from a Western audience that otherwise might feel sympathy or even outrage at such atrocities. Indeed, Gregory depicts the war in Iraq as a "war without witness" (2004, 53; see S. Cohen 2001). Whereas Americans mourn the deaths of its "fallen heroes" who perished in the war, civilian fatalities are officially unrecognized by the U.S. military that claims that it does not even record such statistics. As Chomsky puts it, most of these men, women, and children were killed or maimed "not by design but because it did not matter," which suggests the existence of an "even deeper level of moral depravity" (2002a, 144). It is by way of what Gilroy (2002) calls the "imperial topography," which dictates whether deaths in war are honored or ignored.

CONCLUSION

Setting out to sharpen our understanding of a newly configured power that operates within a zone of unaccountability, this chapter turns attention to key concepts resonating in a post–9/11 world, including Agamben's (1998, 2005) states of exception and *homo sacer* as well as Butler's reworking of sovereignty and governmentality. The analysis demonstrates the significance of unaccountability since it serves as a major source for state crimes in the war on terror despite claims that the United States is conducting foreign policy in accordance with the rule of law. As Agamben (2005, 87) recognizes, "The normative aspect of law can thus be obliterated and contradicted with the impunity by a governmental violence that—while ignoring international law externally and producing a permanent state of exception internally— nevertheless still claims to be applying the law." Gilroy similarly writes that the consequences of contemporary a colonial economy are exacted according to a calculus of power that differentially makes "some human bodies are more easily and appropriately humiliated, imprisoned, shackled, starved and destroyed than others" (2003, 263).

So as to not lose sight of our starting point with Ericson's notion of counter-law, it is important to revisit the conceptual backdrop of his perspective—namely, risk society theory as it pertains to late modernity. To be clear, laws against law as discussed by Ericson emerge not only amid a state of exception in the wake of a catastrophic event but also within a political culture preoccupied with harnessing uncertainty. The problem of uncertainty, according to Ericson, subsumes and replaces the problem of order; still, he goes further by situating uncertainty—rather than risk—at the center of analysis (see Beck 1992; Beck, Giddens, and Lash 1994; Giddens 1990). The undoing of law occurs when uncertainty is perceived as a viable threat because "the higher the enforced standards of due process, evidence, and culpability in law, the greater the uncertainty in the capacity of the legal system to prevent, discover, build a case against, and successfully prosecute offenders. Justice is surrounded by uncertainty, and thus viewed as a problem to be overcome" (Ericson 2007, 206). Controversies over the enemy combatant designation and the use of torture in the war on terror ought to be interpreted paradoxically:

> Ironically, when law and other democratic institutions are most threatened, the response is to devise new legal measures that further threaten these institutions. Law is transformed into an instrument of suspicion, discriminatory practices, invasion of privacy, denial of rights, and exclusion. (Ericson 2007, 209)

All things considered, it is the absence of accountability featured in the new configuration of power that is a primary concern because it is within that orbit of impunity that the state and its operatives continue to engage in crimes and human rights abuses without fear of penalties. Furthermore, the prevailing political culture that facilitates the unraveling of law is reinforced by a wider public culture that sees those sociolegal transformations as contingent on safeguarding national security in what is nowadays viewed as a "dangerous" world (Bonn 2007; Croft 2006; Welch 2006b). The convergence of those mutually reinforcing levels of culture has clearly crystallized among some military personnel who consider themselves on the front line in the war on terror. In *Guantanamo: America's War on Human Rights*, David Rose describes a scenario—however, unlikely—involving an interrogator being charged with torture, noting: "he would have two lines of defence: that it was 'necessary' to prevent a terrorist attack, or that it had been performed in self-defence" (2004, 94; see Campbell and Connolly 2006).

PART TWO

 Prime Targeting

CHAPTER 3

Unlawful Enemy Combatants

THE LEGAL BATTLES OVER how the Bush administration defines and applies the unlawful enemy combatant designation continue to unfold in the U.S. courts. In late 2004, federal judge Joyce Hens Green was still interested in scanning the limits of presidential power to detain enemy combatants and whether the White House satisfied the requirement laid out in the June (2004) U.S. Supreme Court decision to provide a justification for their detention acceptable to federal courts. In court, Green introduced a hypothetical case to Brian Boyle, a justice department lawyer: Could the president of the United States imprison "a little old lady from Switzerland" as an enemy combatant if she donated to a charity not knowing that her money was eventually used to finance the activities of Al-Qaeda terrorists? After a long pause, Boyle responded, "Possibly" (Lewis 2004, A36). Boyle then went on to explain that the enemy combatant definition "is not limited to someone who carries a weapon." Especially in light of the global reach of the enemy combatant definition, Green pressed Boyle about the temporal scope of the war on terror and the application of the powers under the enemy combatant order, "When will they end?" To which Boyle conceded, "I wish I could give you an answer" (Lewis 2004, A36).

INTRODUCTION

Deepening his exploration of power and punishment, Foucault (1977) contends that penality (or the penal order) performs functions that extend beyond mere retribution and is enveloped into a broader network of power relations that exist outside the immediate orbit of the penal regime. Indeed, punitive methods should not be accepted as mere consequences of legislation but rather as signposts for emerging social structures and shifting dynamics of power. By taking a critical look at the recent controversy over the unlawful enemy combatants in the war on terror, we are afforded an opportunity to recognize several of Foucault's insights concerning the reach of power. At its most basic level, the unlawful enemy combatant designation is a form of classification that speaks to Foucault's interest in how power gives way to the chores of social sorting: that is, assigning people into socially constructed categories (see Hacking 1986). As a point of departure from Foucault's apolitical depiction of power in *Discipline and Punish* as not belonging to any pregiven group or individuals, however, this chapter sets out to demonstrate that the war on terror is very much a product of how the Bush team has chosen to conduct its counterterrorism strategy in the wake of September 11. One could argue that another presidential administration might very well have followed a different path of prosecution and punishment; in fact, there has been (and continues to be) sharp dissent even within Bush's inner circle (Cooper and Sanger 2006).

> In the aftermath of 9/11, President Bush requested that White House Counsel Alberto Gonzales organize a working group to determine what procedures to use with al Qaeda prisoners once they were tracked down and captured. Gonzales created an interagency task force headed by Pierre-Richard Prosper, a State Department official and expert on war crimes. While some officials in the task force wanted to apply the military justice, Attorney General Ashcroft and his deputy Michael Chertoff, proposed that terrorists be tried in civilian courts. Gonzales, along with Vice President Cheney, broke the deadlock, and President Bush issued a military order based on his power as commander-in-chief. (Pious 2006, 224)

The decision by President Bush to administer the war on terror by way of military tribunals rather than by criminal courts is notable because it reveals how the president opted to use the particular powers of the office. To be clear, Bush issued a military order rather than an executive one.[1] Consequently, the war on terror became militarized in ways that goes beyond literary metaphor, becoming a carefully planned strategy situated in the Department of Defense. The military order mandated the establishment of military tribunals according to rules and regulations dictated by the Pentagon's civilian general counsel, William J. Haynes II, and submitted to Secretary of Defense Donald Rumsfeld for departmental promulgation.[2] As noted previously, the new military tribunals depart from past practices since they specifically targeted non-U.S. citizens; previous tribunals never distinguished between citizens and foreign nationals (see Katyal and Tribe 2002).

By initiating a military strategy, Bush's choice of options is especially significant. "For the first time in American history, the characterization of terrorism as a criminal act to be dealt with by the civilian courts would be superseded by its characterization as an act of war" (Pious 2006, 225). To create the appearance that his military order was not unilateral, Bush claimed that Congress provided its support in the joint resolution authorizing the president "to use all necessary and appropriate force against those nations, organizations, or persons he determines planned, authorized, committed, or aided the terrorist attacks that occurred on September 11, 2001."[3] Those events set the stage for a series of crucial political and military decisions that reconfigure the economy of the power of punishment in the war on terror. As we shall see, the Bush administration introduced several unique strategies to detain and prosecute terror suspects, tactics that continue to raise serious questions over their constitutionality and legality under international law (Jinks and Sloss 2004; Kacprowski 2004; Margulies 2004).

That form of militarized prosecution in the war on terror is given close Foucauldian consideration in this chapter. To contextualize the formulation of the enemy combatant designation in both historical and theoretical terms, the discussion opens with Foucault's notes on the nature of penal power in the classical age. In due course, the analysis takes into account penal reform in the eighteenth century, gradually giving way to counter-law. The phenomenon of counter-law is significant because it undermines criminal law, producing less due process rather than more safeguards against human error, prosecutorial corruption, or a combination of both. At the heart of the examination is militarized penal power emanating from the Military Commissions Act (MCA) of 2006. That legislation and similar militarized tactics in the detaining (indefinitely) and trying unlawful enemy combatants point to key transformations in the redistribution of penal power toward a structure that is highly centralized with the Bush political and military hierarchy.

MONARCHICAL POWER IN THE CLASSICAL AGE

As a starting point, we extend our view of the history of the present as it pertains to the construction of the unlawful enemy combatant, beginning with a glimpse at the classical age and the nature of monarchical power. Foucault refers to the classical age as the ancièn régime period in eighteenth-century France when the monarchy wielded absolutist power over people. That form of power, to be sure, was viewed in light of a divinely ordained political theology, relying on revenge and militarism to defend itself against rebellion. During that era,

> any crime signified an attack on the sovereign's will. Punishment is thus an act of vengeance, justified by the sovereign's right to make war on his or her enemies and conducted in appropriate warlike terms. In keeping with the military sources of this sovereign power, justice is a manifestation of armed violence, an exercise in terror intended to remind the populace of the unrestrained power behind the law. (Garland 1990, 140; see Foucault 1977, 47–48)

The public spectacle, most vividly expressed in brutal executions, provided an elaborate ceremony by which the monarchical power was reaffirmed (Spierenburg 1984). The entire process serves a juridico-political function, which implies that the monarchy itself was the real victim and seeks to have its full power restored. "It is a ceremony by which a momentarily injured sovereignty is reconstituted . . . Its aim is not so much to re-establish a balance as to bring into

CRIMES OF POWER & STATES OF IMPUNITY

play, as its extreme point, the dissymmetry between the subject who has dared to violate the law and the all-powerful sovereign who displays his strength" (Foucault 1977, 48–49). The excesses inherent in the open spectacle were deliberately used to express the monarchies intrinsic superiority whereby the symbolic and physical strength of the sovereign both figuratively and literally beat down upon the body of the adversary and masters it. It is clear that the ultimate target of punishment was the offender's body, an entity that is explored more graphically in the chapter on torture. Still, at this juncture of analysis it is important to stress that the "public execution did not re-establish justice; it reactivated power" (Foucault 1977, 49). Moreover, the absolute power of the sovereign gained even greater control over the people since the monarchy could exercise the authority to suspend punishment and issue pardons.

The militaristic features of punishment during the classical age also augmented the sheer dominance of the monarchical power. Returning to *Discipline and Punish*,

> The justice of the king was shown to be an armed justice. The sword that punished the guilty was also the sword that destroyed enemies. A whole military machine surrounded the scaffold: cavalry of the watch, archers, guardsmen, soldiers . . . it was also a reminder that every crime constituted as it were a rebellion against the law that that the criminal was the enemy of the prince [*crimen majestatis*]. (Foucault 1977, 50)

The monarch not only ruled over an armed law but also sat as head of justice (*fons justitae*) and head of war. Punishment, therefore, marked both a battle and a victory, bringing a solemn end to a war. Enhancing further the political theology embodied in the militaristic monarchical power, executions with all their fanfare and drama closed with glorious shouts of "God save the King." The public spectacle folded nicely into to a series of royal rituals: coronation, entry of the king into a conquered city, and the submission of rebellious subjects (Foucault 1977, 48, 53). Throughout *Discipline and Punish*, Foucault uses the term *supplice*, which, although it does not have a precise equivalent in the English language, is meant to capture the spectacular essence of public torture and executions. In a word, *supplice* characterizes the prevailing trait of the ancièn régime of penalty (see Foucault 1977, translator's note; Cousins and Hussain 1984).

FROM PENAL REFORM TO COUNTER-LAW

Discipline and Punish directs critical attention at the emergence of the prison. It should not, however, be treated as a historical work per se (Cousins and Hussain 1984; Dreyfus and Rabinow 1983; Garland 1990). Rather, Foucault exhibits a strong fascination with the ways in which the penitentiary came to replace *supplice* as the leading form of punishment (see also Ignatieff

1978; Melossi and Pavarini 1981; Rothman 1971). Whereas the prison did in fact exist under the ancièn régime, it did not take center stage in the field of penality until reformers pushed to improve the criminal justice system, its procedures, and its institutions, thereby attempting to make the courts fair and punishment more humane. Attacks on corrupt judiciaries and corporal punishment in the later part of the eighteenth century were led by such thinkers as Cesare Beccaria (1856 [1764]) and Jeremy Bentham (1970 [1789]) who influenced reformers across much of Europe. Over time, *supplice*—most notably the public spectacle—was displaced by confinement, representing a modern approach to crime inviting new theories that, for example, examined the role of environment in criminal behavior.

Still, Foucault does not lose sight of the elements of power as legal reformers redistributed the economy of penality. The judiciary under the ancièn régime was criticized for its corrupt method of appointments along with a host of external constraints on the trial process, a dysfunction stemming from what Foucault calls "surplus power" (*surpouvoir,* or superpower) referring to the personal and absolutist power of the sovereign. Because legal offices belonged to the king, he had the latitude to sell them to generate revenue, creating a system driven by market forces rather than judicial competence. Moreover, the monarchy remained an important influence over the magistrates by issuing orders by fiat; consequently assembling a penal regime riddled by loopholes and vast disparities in sentences from one court to another along with royal pardons that made the system all the more capricious. Penal reformers recognized that power was too asymmetric, leaving the accused enormously disadvantaged in their efforts to be properly and adequately defended. In Foucault's terminology, reformers positioned themselves on two fronts: challenging the "surplus power" (*surpouvior*) of the monarchy as well as the "infra-power" of the people "to indulge in little illegalities without fear of punishment" (Cousins and Hussain 1984, 178). The sovereign had indeed perpetuated both brutal forms of punishment on the one hand while absolving some people from the duty to adhere to certain laws, both of which contributed to a feeling that the entire social order lacked justice and legitimacy.

To penal reformers the answers apparently were clear, revamp the courts and institute more humane forms of punishment: thus injecting a sense of credibility into the system. By doing so, penality would become a linchpin in the functioning of a just society. That new economy of the power to punish also benefited from utilitarian notion of penal calculus from which prison sentences would be assigned according to a highly arithmetic logic: days, months, and years (Foucault 1977). Such standardized quantification throughout the court system not only added to an appearance of fairness (and deterrence) but eventually streamlined a form of prison management that could grant or deduct "time" for good behavior. The birth of the prison is not necessarily attached to a particular date in history but rather refers to a time when the practice of incarceration became "self-evident" as the prevailing mode of punishment, leaving behind the scaffold and other barbaric, uncivilized forms of monarchical vengeance (see Foucault 1991a).[4]

From that point in the evolution of penology, scholars often then turn their attention to the prison as an institution operated by newly developed technologies designed to reform convicts into docile and useful members of an increasingly industrialized society and beyond (see Lyon 2006; Mathiesen 1997). Indeed, in the next chapter we shall explore how such panoptic practices have shaped the prison regime at Guantánamo Bay. Before doing so, however, it is important to sustain an interest in the broader legal transformations that affect not only the contemporary criminal justice system but also recent developments in the war on terror. With a critical eye on the economy of the power to punish, Foucault offers some particularly insightful notes on shifting legality. Foucault anticipated the suspension of law, referring to that phenomenon as counter-law that operates "on the underside of the law, a machinery that is both immense and minute, which supports, reinforces, multiplies the asymmetry of power and undermines the limits that are traced around the law" (1977, 222). He goes on to say that law has the potential to invert and "pass outside itself" whereby counter-law "becomes the effective and institutional content of the juridical forms" (223). Counter-law, in essence, emerges as a paradox facing democratic governance.

As mentioned previously, Richard V. Ericson (2007) attends to counter-law, or laws against law, where it interfaces with neoliberal political cultures troubled by the prospects of greater risk and uncertainty in late modern society. In an effort to manage and reduce such risk, a precautionary logic leads political actors to adopt extreme security measures to protect society from crime, terrorism, and various threats to national security. Those precautions take the form of specific legal transformations that undermine traditional criminal law and due process (Ashworth 2000, 2003, 2004). Within the context of a risk society, Ericson characterizes counter-law as a type of legal maneuvering in which political authorities strive to gain an advantage in governance by chipping away at long standing safeguards intended to protect persons against unfair and unconstitutional tactics in criminal prosecution. Recent examples of counter-law cited earlier include the convergence of immigration and criminal laws and various provisions contained in the USA Patriot Act (Chang 2002; Welch 2006a). A later chapter contends with counter-law in the realm of torture, but it is fitting here to address similar observations on the unlawful enemy combatant designation, especially since it appears to resemble the classical age of monarchical power and recentralization of penality.

MILITARIZED PENAL POWER IN THE WAR ON TERROR

Foucault (1977) reminds us that reformers of the eighteenth century went to great lengths to separate the legislative component of government that enacts laws specifying penalties for certain violations from the judiciary that along with a jury passes judgments and assigns penal sentences. That division of legal labor created a sharp contrast between the classical age of monarchical punishment in which penalty was highly centralized and the progressive era of modern criminal justice reform. Along with torture as policy, the unlawful enemy combatant designation offers evidence of a reversal of reform. Militarized penality in war on terror imitates the classical age when trials where strictly controlled by sovereign power, reproducing insurmountable asymmetries between the accused and the accuser. Such laws against law is recognized by legal scholars, defense attorneys, and some legislators who voice fierce criticism over the legality of the unlawful enemy combatant designation and the military-style tribunals installed to prosecute them (Amann 2004; Katyal and Tribe 2002).

The Military Commissions Act of 2006

Over past several years, there have been several conflicting court decisions over the constitutionality of the unlawful enemy combatant designation alongside the treatment, interrogation, and prosecution of those detained. In a definitive decision in 2004 the U.S. Supreme Court ruled on three overlapping cases challenging the government's authority over enemy combatants, including the use of indefinite detention and refusing them access to federal courts. Declaring that "a state of war is not a blank check for the president" the High Court ruled that those deemed enemy combatants both in the United States and at Guantánamo Bay have the right to contest their detention before a judge or other neutral decision maker (Greenhouse 2004, A1; see *Hamdi v. Rumsfeld; Rasul v. Bush*). In response to the Supreme Court's decision, the White House rerouted its approach by developing a plan and procedure to classify and try terror suspects who could be deemed unlawful enemy combatants. Nevertheless, in 2006 the Supreme Court in *Hamdan v. Rumsfeld* invalidated the system of military commissions Bush had established for trying terrorism suspects, concluding that tribunals required Congressional authorization. The court also required that suspects be treated in accordance with a provision of the Geneva Conventions, Common Article 3, which prohibits cruel and inhumane treatment, including "outrages upon personal dignity." The *Hamdan* ruling also raised questions over the legality of the Bush administration's secret CIA detention program while "making clear that the abusive interrogation techniques used by the CIA violated the United States' obligations under international law and that CIA operatives could be held criminally liable for such abuses" (Human Rights Watch 2006a, 1).

Reacting to that ruling, Congress set out to assemble a tribunal system believed to be congruent with decision of the Supreme Court. After months of debate, Congress passed the MCA of 2006, a measure that Bush quickly signed into law (Stolberg 2006a). Under the revised proceedings, the government—specifically, the executive branch and the military—enjoys numerous built-in advantages in determining whether a suspect fits the classification of unlawful enemy combatant. As we shall demonstrate, the MCA reconfigures and recentralized penal power in the war on terror in ways that gut due process and meaningful judicial oversight; in fact, the MCA created few differences from its predecessor that Bush ordered into effect in November 1, 2001. Likewise, the new law poses serious threats to international human rights by preventing suspects from filing suit via the writ of habeas corpus to challenge the legality of their detention or to raise claims of torture and other abuses (see Swanson 2004). Human rights advocates complain that MCA tribunal system does not meet the fair trial provisions required by the Geneva Conventions and extant human rights law (see Kacprowski 2004; Paust 2005).

In light of the scope and significance of the MCA, it is important to outline some of its specific features, particularly as they relate to a new economy of penal power. Originally envisioned to dispense battlefield justice, military commissions functioned as criminal courts conducted by the U.S. military and strive to emulate courts-martial. The MCA resembles and also departs from that model by granting the government authorization to prosecute certain noncitizens before a military tribunal. As Human Rights Watch reports,

> The new commissions differ from the old commissions in two important respects: the new commissions' rules provide that defendants cannot be convicted based on evidence that they cannot see or rebut, and that defendants can appeal all convictions to a civilian appellate court.[5]
>
> Nonetheless, the MCA contains some of the same troubling provisions included in the old commissions' rules. The relaxed rules on hearsay and evidence obtained through coercion mean that defendants could be convicted based on second-hand summaries of statements obtained through coercive interrogations—without any opportunity for the defendant to confront his accusers. In addition, beyond the procedures and rules of evidence that it explicitly mandates, the new legislation allows the secretary of defense to establish further rules and procedures at odds from their courts-martial equivalent if the Secretary of Defense considers reliance on courts-martial rules and procedures to be "impracticable." (2006a, 3)

Under the MCA, the government can try any non-U.S. citizen determined to be an unlawful enemy combatant. Interestingly though, only a handful of detainees at Guantánamo Bay are expected to be tried under the MCA, leaving hundreds others there in a legal black hole: subjected to indefinite detention without charge, stripped of their habeas rights, and without ever being permitted to review the evidence against them. As further evidence of counter-law in the war on terror, the MCA creates military trials against civilians that previously would have been kept under the direction of criminal courts, including terrorism cases. By doing so, it allows the commissions to permit lax rules and procedures that undermine due process and rights to fair trial while being able to sentence the convicted to life imprisonment or even death. (see chapter below on torture for details on MCA allowing coercive interrogations.)

From its origin, the unlawful enemy combatant was a legal construct created solely by the executive branch along with the U.S. Department of Defense that intended to push the legislature and the judiciary to the sidelines as the White House pursues its war on terror. Under the laws of war (international humanitarian law) combatants defined as belonging to an armed force are distinguished from civilians; however, civilians engaging in hostilities also can be treated as combatants and suffer the same consequences: subject to being lawfully attacked and killed as well as captured. The MCA expands the definition of "combatant" to include those who have "purposefully and materially" supported hostilities against the United States, even if they have not participated hostilities themselves, thereby recasting civilians as unlawful enemy combatants. "These definitions have essentially been invented by the administration and Congress. They have no basis in international law and undermine one of the most fundamental pillars of the Geneva Conventions—the distinction between combatants, who engage in hostilities and are subject to attack, and non-combatants" (Human Rights Watch 2006a, 6; O'Connell 2005).

Adding to the highly centralized form of penal power in the war on terror, the MCA strips noncitizens the right to file a claim for habeas corpus to challenge the legality of their detention before an independent court or to seek relief from inhumane conditions of confinement, abuse, and even torture. It is estimated that as many as 200 pending habeas cases brought on behalf of the Guantánamo detainees (and a handful of detainees in Afghanistan) could be summarily dismissed. Court stripping provisions run contrary to international law guaranteeing that victims of human rights violations have a right to relief and access to independent courts to contest the legality of their confinement and issue complaints of abuse and torture: the United States is obligated to comply with the International Covenant on Civil and Political Rights (ICCPR) and the Convention against Torture (CAT).[6] Adding to an emerging culture of impunity within the war on terror, the MCA effectively prevents any person from ever filing claims under the Geneva Conventions in lawsuits against the United States or its personnel (Human Rights Watch 2006a).

The new law affords the president the latitude to interpret the "meaning and application" of the Geneva Conventions, merely reiterating presidential powers to interpret U.S. treaty. Still, the MCA clearly points out that the president's interpretation carries no more weight than any other executive branch regulation, and is subject to being overruled by federal court. Human rights experts, nevertheless, are concerned that the MCA seems to endorse President Bush's view that he has the unreviewable authority to interpret and redefine the terms of the Geneva Conventions (see Jinks and Sloss 2004; Katyal and Tribe 2002). The MCA clearly marks a legal shift from the use of the criminal courts to military tribunals in the war on terror. At the bill signing, Bush was joined by senior members of his war cabinet: Vice President Dick Cheney, Defense Secretary Donald H. Rumsfeld and General Michael V. Hayden, director of the CIA. The new legislation is hailed by key Republican lawmakers who are considered the authors of the MCA, Senators John W. Warner, Lindsey Graham, John McCain, all of whom has close ties to the U.S. armed forces (Stolberg 2006a).

Although the MCA obviously was backed by the majorities in the House and Senate, criticism by influential Democrat Party leaders has been made public. "Congress had no justification for suspending the writ of habeas corpus, a core value in American law, in order to avoid judicial review that prevents government abuse," said Senator Patrick J. Leahy of Vermont, the senior Democrat on the Senate Judiciary Committee (Stolberg 2006a, E2). More than 500 habeas suits are pending in federal court, and justice department officials indicated that they would move swiftly to dismiss them under the new law, prompting challenges by civil liberties lawyers, who regard the habeas-stripping provision as unconstitutional. Only days old, the MCA had already spawned one legal contest with many others likely to be filed (Stolberg 2006a; see Human Rights Watch 2007; Labaton, 2007).[7]

Recentralizing the Economy of Penal Power

Although it is true that the humanitarian values of eighteenth century reformers played a key role in diminishing the use of cruel and barbaric forms of punishment, Foucault (1977) also takes into account another theoretical explanation. In what he observed to have been a dual function of penality, Foucault noted that creating a rational and more certain system of dispensing sentences not only was believed to deter certain kinds of property offenses but also erected limits on the arbitrary power of the monarchy. As Garland puts it, "Penality was being adapted in to the emerging structures of modernity" (1990, 142). The adaptation of penal power to the conditions of late modern society are found in Ericson's (2007) examination of counter-law, or laws against law that enhances more administrative measures of social control while displacing criminal law (see Agamben 2005; Butler 2004). In doing so, counter-law sets out to reduce the types of uncertainties produced by due process and judicial appeals. Many of the tactics used by the Bush team in war on terror mark a recentralization of the economy of penal power that echo previous forms of punishment in the classical age. That apparent reversal ought not be viewed as a historical shift backward; rather, by thinking forward it represents a reconfigured form of penal power in which contemporary political actors seem willing to adopt so as to harness some of the uncertainty of late-modern society, with special emphasis on controlling terrorism.

Whereas another chapter deals with the phenomenon of "governing through terror," (also see Mythen and Walklate 2006; Simon 2007) at this stage of the analysis it is important to acknowledge the parallels between counter-law measures in late modern society and absolutist forms of penal power in the classical age. To reiterate, the political theology during the ancièn régime entitled the divinely ordained monarchy to interpret any crime as an attack on the sovereign, resulting in an unleashing of military sources with an unrestrained power. While surely expressive in terms of its symbolic value, such militarized forms of vengeance also served instrumental purposes by exacting virtual total control over the accused. Beyond the linguistic metaphor, war and militarization provide legal justification for such tactics as the opening of Guantánamo Bay to hold unlawful enemy combatants. Likewise, recent developments evident in the MCA reinforce—and embolden—the president's authority as political executive and military commander-in-chief, creating a sense that democratic imperatives are being undermined in favor of a more absolutist form of penal power (Katyal and Tribe 2002). It is fitting here to remain mindful of Ericson's (2007) notion of counter-law as it sheds light on the newly administrative types of governance. More to point of this analysis, it also is important to emphasize that the MCA and similar authoritarian tactics in the war on terror demonstrate a more militarized form of counter-law. Militarized laws against law serve clear organizational objectives, for instance the streamlining of the prosecution of terror suspects or simply warehousing them indefinitely without having to bring charges or submit them to a trial. Equally important though, that reshaping of the legal also fortifies penal power in the executive seat of government where the president (and the secretary of defense) claims to have the need for greater control and military flexibility in the war on terror.

Much like Ericson's understanding of counter-law that erodes due process and constitutional safeguards while enhancing administrative (civilian) proceedings, the MCA exhibits a militarization effect on the legal sphere, transforming cases of terrorism that previously would have been prosecuted under criminal law into cases for handled by military tribunals. The militarized form of counter-law resembles penal power in the classical age insofar as Bush, the commander-in-chief, refuses to interpret acts of terrorism as the criminal offenses they clearly are. Rather, the President's approach to political violence seems to suggest that terrorism is an attack against the sovereign, in legal parlance "acts of war . . . under the jurisdiction of the military" (Pious 2006,

223–224). Bush claims to possesses the sole discretion (without any judicial review) to designate a person as an unlawful enemy combatant; that charge can be levied against anyone and that person could be detained indefinitely anywhere in the world. Without any established definition of "international terrorism," or any requirement of "probable cause," guilt by association rather than concrete acts of hostility could serve as the basis for detention and trial. All judges, prosecutors, and military defense lawyers would be appointed solely by the commander-in-chief. "In the tribunals the penalties would be set by the president (though he could not change a not guilty verdict) and could include the death penalty, with the penalty being carried out in secret" (Pious 2006, 227). Moreover, the Department of Defense has indicated that it retains the authority to hold indefinitely all those it considered to be dangerous, even those acquitted in their tribunal (Seelye 2005). Many provisions of the MCA and similar militarized tactics in prosecution and detention hark back to the ancièn régime as described by Foucault:

> The entire criminal procedure, right up to the sentence, remained a secret: that is to say, opaque, not only to the public but also to the accused himself . . . In the order of criminal justice, knowledge was the absolute privilege of the prosecution . . . it was impossible to know the identity of his accusers, impossible to know the nature of evidence, impossible to have a lawyer . . . The secret and written form of the procedure reflects the principles that in criminal matters the establishment of truth was the absolute right and the exclusive power of the sovereign and his judges . . . the king wished to show in this that the "sovereign power" from which the right to punish derived could in no case belong the "multitude." (1977, 35)

Again, the point here is not to argue that enhanced presidential powers in the war on terror, especially by way of a distinctly militarized form of counter-law, is the same as royal power in the classical age. A deeper, Foucauldian analysis reveals that while the sovereign went to great lengths to amplify his message of power, most notably in the public spectacle and other ceremonies and rituals, the absolutist form of power couched in contemporary presidential authority is at once firmly pronounced then muted. That type of governance is typical of the way counter-law becomes increasingly administrative by not drawing too much public attention to the manner in which it undermines due process and other democratic checks and balances. Nonetheless, striking similarities exist between prosecutorial tactics in the ancièn régime and the counter-law measures instituted in the war on terror, prompting us to consider the extent to which the economy of penal power is becoming recentralized within the presidential hierarchy.

CONCLUSION

With echoes of the risk society in the backdrop, the Bush administration says it is justified in establishing the military tribunal system, citing reasons of national emergency. The president claims that displacing the criminal courts with military ones is necessary because sleeper cells of terrorists are poised to infiltrate civilian courts, leaving prosecutors, judges, and jurors vulnerable to physical harm. Because the public nature of criminal courts may threaten to expose intelligence methods, sources, and agents, closed military tribunals also are said to be required to protect national security. To that end, Bush argues that he has the constitutional authority to establish military commissions by fusing his power as commander-in-chief with his oath of office to defend the constitution, citing precedents from Civil War, World War II, and the Korean War. Similar special military tribunals have been instituted in the past, most interestingly the commission convened by President Andrew Johnson to try persons suspected of conspiracy in the assassination of Lincoln. Still, such military tribunals are rare, and, with the exception of the Lincoln case, commissions are intended to be used as temporary measures in the absence of regular courts-martial (Fisher 2005; Pious 2006). The war on terror is different from conventional armed conflicts in several ways, in particular its temporal frame in which there is no clear end in sight. Therefore, the MCA and other military tactics are likely to become permanent fixtures in the U.S. government's playbook on counter-terrorism.

Under the ancièn régime, monarchical authority was contained in the lettres de cachet, permitting the king's power to uphold local hierarchies in ways that averted legal accountability (Farge and Foucault 1982). Reminiscent of the classical era, detention as ordered solely by the executive branch of government has become a site for enforcing undemocratic and unaccountable political decisions. Consider the controversy over the harsh treatment and detention of Haitian refugees in Miami in the 1980s and early 1990s. Those practices are characterized by Jonathan Simon as reflecting "the demands for social order maintenance outside the bounds of democratic decision-making. That was the classic function of royal imprisonment as well" (1998, 600). Similar criticisms surfaced in the indefinite detention of Mariel Cubans whereby Judge John Noonan of the U.S. Court of Appeals for the Ninth Circuit, in 1994, ruled that the government's fixation on the dangerousness of the Mariel prisoners constituted a serious threat to democracy. Noonan, too, observed the similarities between monarchical traditions and contemporary detention practices:

> The infamous *lettres de cachet* of the King of France, a device for confining persons on the royal say-so, began as an extraordinary political measure and eventually became a routinized method of preserving order,

employed in thousands of cases. As was the case in France, the discretion exercised in imprisoning without trial is in the name of high authority but actually delegated to much lower employees of the government. Our government does limit this easy administrative method of confining person to one small segment of the population. Some evils are too great for any margin to be given them. The practice of administrative imprisoning persons indefinitely is not a process tolerable in use against any person in any corner of our country. (*Berrera-Echavarria v. Rison,* 21 F. 3d 314, 318 [1994]; see Simon 1998, 601, Welch 2002)

Of course the use of seemingly monarchical—absolutist—power in the war on terror is difficult to overlook in view of the Bush administration's commitment to counter-law: encompassing such tactics as the unlawful enemy combatant designation, the misuse of immigration law, and torture, all of which proceed with little or no Congressional or judicial oversight (see Bradley and Goldsmith 2005; Chemerinsky 2005, Welch 2006c). Armed with the royal say-so, Bush claims to possess the sole discretion to designate virtually anyone anywhere in the world as an enemy combatant: subjecting that person to a military tribunal likely to spiral down a legal black hole with few, if any, avenues for exit. Human rights advocates have expressed grave concerns over military tribunals that have the potential for creating a new class of *desaparecidos* (the "disappeared"), who completely vanish from the free world. With an eye on past "disappearance" campaigns waged by governments in Latin America in the 1970s, international attorneys point to the importance of enforcing the Inter-American Convention on the Forced Disappearance of Persons and the International Covenant on Civil and Political Rights (see Jinks and Sloss 2004; Paust 2005).

The European Union has taken notice of questionable detention practices in the war on terror and has warned member states not to extradite persons to the United States if there is a reasonable risk that it will lead to human rights abuses against that individual (see *Chahal v. United Kingdom* 1996). In fact, Spanish government officials in November 2001, indicated to the United States that it would refuse to extradite eight men suspected of involvement in the 9/11 attacks without guarantees that their trials would not be transferred from civilian courts (Pious 2006). As this discussion suggests, militarized tactics that contribute to a highly centralized form of penal power go beyond prosecution, figuring also into matters of detention (Amann 2004). So that we may explore in greater depth the controversy over confinement in the war on terror, the next chapter extends our Foucauldian analysis to Guantánamo Bay.

CHAPTER 4

Guantánamo Bay

As he was being reassigned from the detention center at Guantánamo Bay (GITMO in Pentagon parlance), the former warden Mike Bumgarner was blamed for the suicides resulting from his attempted institutional reforms that loosened the restrictions on prisoners. He reflected on this tour of duty: "We tried to improve their lives to the extent that we can—to the point that we may have gone overboard, not recognizing the real nature of who we're dealing with," he said. "I thought they had proven themselves. I'm ashamed to admit it, but I did not think that they would kill themselves" (Golden 2006a, EV16). The experiment to reform Guantánamo Bay had failed, giving way to a more coercive penal discourse. Shifts in that direction were evident in December 2006 with the opening of Camp 6, a new $30 million facility modeled after a county jail in southern Michigan. GITMO has certainly tightened up, moving three-fourths of the 400 prisoners into maximum security cells. Commander of the Guantánamo task force, Rear Admiral Harry B. Harris Jr., said hardened measures reflected the changing nature of the prison population and his conviction that all of those now held here are dangerous men: "They're all terrorists; they're all enemy combatants. I don't think there is such a thing as a medium-security terrorist" (Golden 2006b, EV2). Still, military planners contend that GITMO is drifting away from interrogations toward the long-term (or indefinite) detention of men who, for the most part, would never be charged with any crime (Amann 2004).

INTRODUCTION

In the wake of 9/11, GITMO has emerged as a unique and highly controversial experiment, prompting a penological question: what kind of prison is it exactly? While attempting to prepare a response to that question, it is useful to turn to an area of theoretical criminology that draws on critical perspectives. In *Power, Discourse and Resistance: A Genealogy of the Strangeways Prison Riot*, Eamonn Carrabine offers a valuable template for understanding the manifold purposes of incarceration. Moreover, he sheds light on the relevance of discourse, a term that points to "a system of thought that informs practice. It refers to both a framework of belief and a guide for appropriate conduct. As such the various discourses serve to 'incorporate' the agencies of the powerful within the project of imprisonment" (2004, 38; see also Bosworth 1999; Bosworth and Carrabine 2001; Carrabine 2000). Much like the work of Carrabine and a host of critical sociologists, this project is influenced by Michel Foucault's (1977) writings on prison, and at an even deeper level by Friedrich Nietzsche (1996 [1887]) whose genealogical method skeptically investigates all phenomena for their signs, symbols, and meaning of power (see Adler and Longhurst 1994; Garland 1990).

In brief, Foucault (1977) points to two modes of exercising power over individuals that are now apparent at GITMO. The first modality relies on the imposition of negative gestures including rejection, banishment, and exile, particularly as they manifest in long-term imprisonment and indefinite detention. In the second, power is demonstrated through the pursuit of instituting perfect order by way of meticulous classification and control, notably in the social sorting of prisoners and unlawful enemy combatants (see Cousins and Hussain 1984, 189). To illustrate how those modes of power shape penal technologies, Foucault goes to great lengths to decipher the function and meaning of the panopticon, Bentham's classic cylinder prison design. Nowadays, virtually all supermax prisons are panoptic because, even though they do not conform to a circular architecture, the wide use of surveillance cameras serves what Foucault describes as a "principle that power should be visible and unverifiable" (1977, 201).[1] While the panopticon, or "utopian vision machine," has become a model and metaphor for clarifying the role of surveillance in a highly technological society, it is at the sharp end of the panoptic spectrum where its power is most extreme (Lyon 2006; Virilio 1994). Indeed, the growing literature on supermax prisons reflects Foucault's fascination with institutionalization and the demand for control (King 1999; Miller 2007; L. Rhodes 2004; Ward and Werlich 2003).

Attempting to know fully the internal workings at GITMO, however, poses a problem because it is for the most part an institution that remains inaccessible except for highly monitored visits by select members of the media, civilian and military attorneys, and human rights organizations (Amnesty International 2005; Conover 2003; Human Rights Watch 2004, 2005). Despite numerous official obstacles, together those sources do provide a window that invites us to look into some revealing aspects of that prison. Interviews with former detainees conducted by journalists in conjunction with public statements issued by political and military figures also contribute to a discursive basis for interpreting the purpose of GITMO and its practices. From its inception, GITMO has imbued a shadowy persona reminiscent of novels by Franz Kafka, himself inspired by Nietzsche (Smith 1996). In *The Trial*, a nightmarish scenario unfolds with an ordinary man seized by the authorities to face a tribunal without being apprised as to what he was being charged with and why

(Kafka 1999). Similarly, when Shafiq Rasul arrived at GITMO from Afghanistan on January 16, 2002 shackled in a "three piece suit" (handcuffs attached to leg irons), he asked the government officials facing him in an interrogation room, "Where am I?" To which he was told, "We can't disclose that information" (Rose 2004, 86). In light of its emphasis on high security and tight control, it is tempting merely to place GITMO onto the expanding roster of supermax penitentiaries; however, that would be a missed opportunity. As this work demonstrates GITMO is an unusual institution. Considering its Kafkaesque, even existential traits compounded by indefinite detention, one corrections expert bluntly described GITMO as "prison plus" (Rose 2004, 67).

This analysis of GITMO takes decidedly critical stance because it is concerned with the ways in which power is embedded within the institution and inside its practices. Attempting to answer the penological question concerning precise nature of GITMO, the project sets out to integrate an examination of prison discourse with Foucault's thoughts on rationalities guiding institutional practices. It is assumed that a key to unveiling the composition of GITMO lies not only in what political actors and prison administrators claim to be its purpose but also in how those objectives are pursued inside the institution: that is, its technologies. Suggested here, GITMO exists as a unique Foucauldian phenomenon in ways that do not entirely resonate in other supermax prisons. That phenomenon also creates a penal paradox for GITMO. On the one hand, GITMO adheres to techniques normalization aimed at transforming detainees into beings who are docile, obedient, and useful for generating "enormously valuable intelligence" for the expanding war on terror. On the other, such penal technologies coupled with harsh interrogation (and torture), repressive conditions of confinement, and few prospects for release, produce resistances that undermine the expressed purpose of GITMO; it replicates Foucault's conclusions about the overall failure of prisons. To comprehend how each of those components of GITMO contributes to its deep sense of irony, we must delve into the available descriptive and conceptual evidence. The discussion begins with a brief overview of Foucault's contribution to penology so as to establish a starting point for this analysis.

Foucauldian Penology

While exploring the emergence of penal technologies—specifically the methods or "know-hows" of deploying punishment—it is important to recognize a key point from the perspective of Foucault. That is, the birth modern prison does not refer to the actual introduction of incarceration since the practice of internment had been in existence across Europe previously in the seventeenth century. Rather, Foucault insists that the birth of the modern prison lies in its transformations in two areas. First, modern prison became a systematic method of punishing both minor and major crimes. Second, the penal regime in the modern prison is remarkable for its commitment to classification, separation, and the deliberate use of isolation; likewise, the institution contained different housing units for prisoners assigned to different categories, furthering the social sorting process. In the case of GITMO, one could argue that it merely another supermax prison. Such a swift conclusion, however, would miss the finer points that distinguish GITMO from other high-security facilities. GITMO is an unusual institutional entity: it is neither a standard supermax prison reserved civilian prisoners, nor a brig used to hold military personnel convicted of crimes while serving in the armed forces. Instead, GITMO is a facility that remains closely aligned to a form of presidential power that makes grand claims about its military authority in justifying the detention and interrogation of so-called unlawful enemy combatants.

Foucault draws attention to two processes that contributed to emergence of the modern prison. First is the demise of the public spectacle and the vanishing of the theatrical component of punishment, pushing penality back behind the walls of the institution away from open view. The second process involves a shift in punishment's intended target: from bodily pain to the deprivation of liberty as envisioned by reformers inspired by the Enlightenment and its value of humane treatment of convicts. Such reform also was driven by utilitarianism and the ultimate goal of deterring crime. Whereas public torture and executions certainly served to set an example of what the consequences of crime could be, so did imprisonment but in a different way: "neither by spectacle or show of force. It simply deters by spreading knowledge that the condemned is deprived of his liberty, his rights" (Cousins and Hussain 1984, 171). Reversing the direction from deterrence as an outward trajectory of imprisonment to an inward track, Foucault delves into the internal mechanisms of the modern prison, attending closely to the significance of power. Departing from the sheer force conveyed in the public spectacle, Foucault contends that penal power in prison is founded on continuous surveillance and the tasks of monitoring, classifying, and documenting through copious note taking and detailed record keeping. In contrast to the spectacular bursts of power delivered by public torture and execution, the protocol of the modern prison distributes power regularly and evenly; by doing so, the emphasis is placed on training and disciplining the convict, turning its subject into an object of knowledge (Foucault 1977, 77–78). By transforming subjects into objects, Foucault also points crucial attention to the prisoner's personality (i.e., mind, psyche, "soul," or "seat of habits") in ways that inform new penal technologies which in turn produce an even greater effect on the body.

Among the lasting imprints that Foucault has had on penology is his willingness to reach beyond the idea that the modern prison was the product of legal reformers intent on civilizing punishment. Committed to understanding how that shift in penality relates to power, Foucault claims that the modern prison is distinctive for its development of disciplinary techniques aimed at organizing convicts into units then focusing specifically on their individual composition, thereby facilitating the process of transforming them into a beings who are docile, obedient, and useful. That goal explains in part why the prison protocol borrows from similar techniques contained in similar institutions such as the military, schools, hospitals, and factories because they too are geared toward producing the same effect from training. That transformation is carried out by exercising power through—not against—individuals. By concentrating on that particular process Foucault remains faithful to his claim that we live in disciplining society rather than a disciplined one; as we shall examine later, prisons often fail in achieving discipline and in fact create resistance that further undermines its intended goals (see Burchell, Gordon, and Miller 1990).

In sum, Foucault finds that disciplinary techniques in the form of hierarchical observation, normalizing judgment, and examination are deployed in an array of social settings; however, unlike students in a school or workers in a factory who return home afterwards, prisoners are not subject to periodic control but to a form of domination that is constant and continuous. Indeed, Foucault's view of that type of social control closely mirrors that of Goffman (1961) and his analysis of total institutions (see also Clemmer 1958; Sykes 1958). Once in prison though, the prisoner's offense is less important than "who" (as subject) and "what" (as object) the offender actually is: his makeup, personality, and a constellation of psychological and physiological traits. It is the "delinquent," as Foucault puts it, who is characterized as "a biographical unity, kernel of trouble" representing "a type of anomaly" (1977, 254). It is the construction of the "delinquent" that provides a starting point for criminology, particularly the positivist approach embracing science. That particular perspective of criminology issues "scientific" claims about the "delinquent" that form the basis of "knowledge" about who—and what—the "delinquent" actually is. That ethnology of criminals differs from the viewpoint from the judiciary that passes sentences based largely on the nature of the offense and not necessarily the "essence" of the lawbreaker (Foucault 1977, 101–103; 105). Foucault contends that it is inside prison—equipped with its penal technologies—that the "delinquent" is actually constructed, a process carried out by a criminological "science" geared toward establishing the "truth" that exists in the links between the criminal and his crime (see Foucault 1980, 1989).

Penal Discourse and GITMO

GITMO is part of a larger naval installation (Guantánamo Bay Naval Base, Cuba) located on 45-square-mile strip of land on the southeast tip of

Cuba that the United States has leased in perpetuity since 1903, following the Spanish-American War (Golden 2006a). For decades, the naval base has enjoyed a relatively quiet existence until the events of September 11 when the U.S. Department of Defense put into motion plans to utilize sectors of the base for the expressed purpose of detaining and interrogating terrorist suspects. There the U.S. military has held upwards of 600 detainees (nearly 300 in 2008), many of whom were captured in Afghanistan in the early phases of the war on terror following the attacks on the World Trade Center and the Pentagon. The U.S. government insists the detainees are terrorists affiliated with the Taliban or Al-Qaeda (i.e., unlawful enemy combatants) and pose an imminent threat to national security. On those grounds, the White House contends that it has the authority to detain them indefinitely; some selected detainees are eligible for military tribunals but not civilian criminal courts (Lewis 2004). Aside from the legal controversies that surround GITMO to be addressed in this chapter, there exist important institutional dimensions of the detention camp that deserve mentioning so as to provide a visual outline of the penal setting.

GITMO is a joint military prison and interrogation camp under the leadership of the Joint Task Force of Guantánamo (JF-GTMO). In January 2002 when the first contingent of detainees arrived, GITMO was still, literally, a work in progress. At the time, marines had just completed a makeshift prison: Camp X-Ray consisting of dozens of rows of steel-mesh cages, ringed by a perimeter of razor-wire fence, and exposed to the harsh elements of the Caribbean (D. Rose 2004). Eventually, detainees were transferred to newly constructed cell blocks, leaving Camp X-Ray to be slowly swallowed by the jungle. At present, GITMO comprises three detention sectors: Camp Delta (with detention camps 1–6), Camp Echo (a 612-unit detention center that stands as part of Camp Delta), and Camp Iguana (a smaller, low-security compound located about a half mile from the main detention area). More recent renovations are evident in Camp 6. Altogether the detention complex is commonly referred to by the military as GITMO (and at times called by its former name, Camp X-Ray). The security force consists mostly of U.S. Army military police and U.S. Navy Master-at Arms (Pious 2006). Visiting journalists have been granted tours of some of the detention units accompanied by explanations that some parts of the camp are easier to manage than others. For example, Tim Golden (2006a, E16) describes Camp 4 as a newer wing where level 1, or "highly compliant," prisoners were allowed to live in communal barracks, serving their own food and moving freely in and out of small recreation yards. Some detainees are held in Camp 1, for level 2, or "compliant," detainees while a handful are held in Camp 5, the maximum-security area.

Moving into more conceptual territory, it is important note that we shall be departing slightly from a standard use of the term "discourse" as referring to passages of spoken and written statements. This analysis is similar to that of Carrabine (2004), who gravitates to a more Foucauldian notion of the concept, emphasizing how it structures knowledge and organizes the ways in which things are done. Foucault (1972, 49) insists that discourse is not merely constellation of signs but also a practice "that systematically form the objects of which they speak" (see also G. Williams 1999). We should avoid viewing penal discourse as some exotic linguistic device since it stems from work of Karl Mannheim (1991), who influenced criminology with his sense of phenomenology (i.e., sociology of knowledge). Although exactly how many different penal discourses exist is debatable, there is some agreement that a total of six serve to capture a broad range of claims and practices (Adler and Longhurst 1994; Carrabine 2000, 2004). Three of those discourses pertain to the ends of incarceration (rehabilitation, normalization, and control) and the remaining three to the means (bureaucracy, professionalism, and authoritarianism). The means essentially point to the technologies or methods of carrying out the objectives of the ends, or the rationalities and justification of imprisonment. It is important to realize that those discourses are not fixed but are rather dynamic, subject to being continually produced and challenged both within the prison and in society at large. Nowadays we maintain an ongoing conversation over what prisons are for, in a macrosociological sense and what the prison experience is like, in a microsociological one (Carrabine 2004).

In determining what type of penal institution GITMO is, it is helpful to reflect on the prevailing discourses, in particular normalization and control as the ends. Equally important, attention is turned to authoritarianism as the means since it represents a form of government technology aimed at how the institution is run by the personnel, including guards and administrators.[2] Because establishing and keeping control precedes normalization, let us first address that form of penal discourse. Control by its very nature refers to complete order as determined by the rigid rules geared toward a smooth operation of the prison, dealing with disruptions in a swift and firm manner. Indeed, control often implies a heavy-handed approach to custodial management. The mere mention of the name GITMO brings to mind images of a harsh—even brutal—show of force and tight control. Moreover, that extreme degree of control is notable for its militaristic thrust; for all their strong-armed tactics, other supermax prisons are still paramilitary in their organization. In the early days (January 2002) of GITMO, unlawful enemy combatants were transported from the worldwide "battlefield" of the war on terror via military aircraft to a makeshift prison built by marines called Camp X-ray:

> A dozen rows of steel-mesh cages, open to the elements, ringed by a razor-wire fence. On arriving, the detainees had been led into a compound and

photographed as they waited to be processed. Shackled hand and foot, dressed in orange jumpsuits, still wearing the black-lensed goggles, surgical masks, headphones, and taped-on gloves which they had been forced to don at the start of their twenty-seven hour flight, the detainees knelt in the Gitmo dust, as crew-cut servicemen loomed in threatening poses over them. Within a few days, the US Defense Secretary, Donald Rumsfeld, would regret allowing these pictures to be released: to have done so, he said, was 'probably unfortunate.' The front-page headline used with the photos in Britain's conservative Daily Mail typified responses outside the United States. It consisted of a single word: "TORTURE!" (Rose 2004, 2)

Formal military tactics deployed for purposes of control are backed up with claims by U.S. politicians that those prisoners were the "worst of the worst," a common trope echoing of "superpredators" described by conservatives supporting the need for supermax prisons (Bennett and DiIulio 1996; Human Rights Watch 1997, 2000). Even so, widely circulated quotes from military leaders add a heightened alert over the particular "dangerousness" of detainees at Guantánamo Bay. In the words of General Richard E. Myers, chairman of the Joints Chiefs of Staff, those prisoners, given half the chance, "would gnaw through hydraulic lines in the back of a C-17 to bring it down" (Rose 2004, 2; see Foucault 1988). The cages of Camp X-ray eventually were replaced by a permanent structure called Camp Delta, but, like other supermax prisons, the conditions of confinement are spartan at best. The cells consist of prefabricated metal boxes painted a faded green, somewhat larger than king-size bed (56 square feet). The control discourse manifests in the physical environment of each cell which has in it a hard steel wall-mounted bed, two-and-a-half feet wide. There is an Asian-style toilet, a hole in the floor that faces an open grill in the door where guards are expected to pass by every thirty seconds. A single water tap is situated so close to the floor that the prisoner must kneel down. The Pentagon reports that the spout is located low so as "to accommodate Muslim foot-washing needs" (Rose 2004, 60; see Amnesty International 2005). Complimenting the control discourse that penetrates the physical environment are symbols of 9/11 scattered around GITMO. Hanging in the makeshift office where guards are permitted to send email is a poster of the Twin Towers captioned "Are you in a New York state of mind? Don't leak information—our enemy can use to kill US troops or more innocent people" (Rose 2004, 58; see Garland 2006).

Control discourse is facilitated by means of authoritarianism that is "based on militaristic lines of regulation" (Carrabine 2004, 40). GITMO, like supermax prisons, frequently relies on coercive tactics in managing the population, especially against prisoners who try to buck the system. In such instances, GITMO's punishment squad—the Extreme Reaction Force

(ERF)—is activated for purposes of "cell extraction," a no-nonsense control tactic also used in civilian prisons for removing a recalcitrant prisoner from his cell to be placed in solitary confinement known as "Romeo Block" where they would remain naked (or half-naked) for days or even more than a week. Former prisoners report that those "ERF-ings" had become so common that it found a place in the GITMO jargon. Detainees who had been "ERF-ed" for even minor rule infractions (e.g., having an extra drinking cup in their cell) claim that they were subjected to having their Koran mishandled, their private parts grabbed and pepper-sprayed by a team of guards in riot gear; in the process, prisoners' eyes have been poked, their heads flushed in their toilet, forcibly kneeled on, kicked, and punched prior to being dragged out their cell in chains then having their beards, heads, and eyebrows shaved (Amann 2004; Conover 2003; Rose 2004). Whereas civilian prisons are required to have disciplinary hearings to determine whether solitary confinement is warranted, such proceedings do not exit in GITMO. Of course, what is being described here are counter-resistance tactics intended to reassert control over stubborn prisoners, an issue that will be explored in detail in a forthcoming segment. Nevertheless, such strong-armed measures demonstrate how closely GITMO fits the control penal discourse, perhaps even in its ideal type.

In general, civilian supermax prisons maintain a highly defined commitment to the control discourse, without any pretense of rehabilitation or normalization. That marks a key point of departure for penal discourse at GITMO. Although closely embracing control as its purpose, it also ventures into the realm of normalization. Normalization technologies at GITMO, however, differ from other prisons that seek to bring conduct into line, making them suitable candidates to reenter society. Although GITMO does not set out to prepare detainees to return to free world—perhaps many will be kept indefinitely—there is a transformation process that is acutely utilitarian: that is, changing unlawful enemy combatants into beings who are docile, obedient, and useful for the expressed objectives of producing intelligence aiding America's war on terror. Rather than rushing into an analysis of interrogation, however, it is important to keep a close eye on GITMO as an institution predicated on several forms of penal technology that in one way or another contribute to the transformation process. By examining closely the normalization discourse embedded in the penal technologies at Guantánamo Bay we gain further insight into its own logic and operating principles.

PENAL TECHNOLOGIES

Foucault became well known for his unique way of posing questions that go beyond "who" is punished and "why," directing critical attention at the process, or "how," individuals are punished. In doing so, he offers insights on the strategies of disciplinary techniques (see Foucault 1991a). Foucault discovered two fundamental techniques embedded in the modern prison: (1) the division, distribution, and arrangement of bodies and (2) an established routine governing their activities throughout the day. The former points to spatialization and the later to temporality insofar as time is divided into segments, allowing periods in which detailed activities occur. Foucault, however, adds that the process avoids fragmentation by integrating those facets of corrective technology. "Discipline is (not) simply an art of distributing bodies, of extracting time from them and accumulating it, but of composing forces in order to obtain an efficient machine" (1977, 64). The overarching aim is toward constituting a productive force whose sum is greater than its parts. Moreover, domination is formally established when it is incorporated into a hierarchy: a vertical alignment that creates and sustains asymmetries of power. The notion of hierarchies figures prominently in Foucault's work, contributing to a catalogue of disciplinary techniques that are mobilized, or put into motion, by three means: hierarchical observation, normalizing judgment, and examination.

Hierarchical Observation

Disciplinary techniques rely not only on mere monitoring—or keeping track of individuals—but rather on a form of intense observation that is hierarchical in structure; as a result, it becomes coercive and intrusive, attending to minute details of individual conduct (Foucault 1977, 170). By its very nature, observation involves vision. Therefore, because the disciplinary task is to improve observation so as to enhance power, the boundaries and field of vision are greatly expanded. In prison, for example, the "optics" are widened by architecture (e.g., the panopticon) and electronic devices (e.g., surveillance cameras). The panopticon serves as a coherent model of geometry in the form of its circular design, but it also speaks to the role of spatialization insofar as prisoners are arranged in their individual cells in which guards can easily view them.

Not to be lost in Foucault's analysis is his reference to a military camp that serves as an almost ideal type of "observatory."[3] As prisons move up the scale in terms of their security level, so does the degree of observation. GITMO, like other supermax institutions, imposes intense and continuous monitoring of detainees, a feature that is enhanced by bright lights even in cells while prisoner struggle to sleep. Two features, however, separate GITMO from its supermax counterparts. First, GITMO is not merely based on the military model: it *is* the military model, replete with a bona fide military organization and various camps where detainees are held, Camp Delta, Camp Echo, and the former Camp X-ray. By contrast, other supermax prisons are paramilitary, at best. Second, given its penal discourse on normalization, GITMO's spatial environment is planned in ways to facilitate the interrogation process, a purpose that is absent in other supermax institutions committed solely to tight control. Foucault goes on to conclude that the military camp is a diagram of power that operates by means of general visibility, becoming an underlying principle for urban development, along with an array of institutions such as asylums, schools, and prisons. That "spatial nesting" then becomes hierarchized by way of "embedded" surveillance. Whereas architecture often boasts its external form to be seen from afar, Foucault notes that, for instance in the case of the prison, the function of architecture is to reverse the observation by imposing close supervision upon those confined inside. In doing so, such architecture along with compartmentalizing prisoners into cells carries power right to them, making it possible to know them, and alter them. The disciplinary institution, therefore, served as a machinery of control like a microscope (as well as a telescope) focused on prisoners and their conduct, making possible to observe and record all their activities. The ideal "optic" or "perfect eye" is one that sees everything constantly and at once; hence, panoptic (Lyon 2006).

The observation, however, is monitored not by some neutral machine but by a "specialized personnel" who claim to have "expertise" or even "scientific expertise" that aids their ability to "know" the subject. In prison, guards are afforded such power by their administrators within the hierarchy that reproduces an air of superiority and command, thereby creating and reinforcing the trajectories of power that ultimately transform the prisoner from a subject (who) into an object (what). The process, however, is not complete until the prisoner, much like all objects of surveillance (e.g., patients, pupils, workers) internalize the gaze and modify their conduct according to the demands of the penal regime, conforming to rules and allowing themselves to be transformed into docile, obedient, and useful subjects. Along the way, prisoners who are compliant are rewarded and those who are not are punished (Foucault 1977, 191).

GITMO is staffed by military personnel who claim to have expertise in dealing with its special population. Even more to the point, the interrogation program (and some say the entire prison) is run by so-called experts who claim to possess special—even "scientific"—knowledge on extracting confessions. The GITMO Joint Task Force has two main divisions: The Joint Detention Group and the Joint Interrogation Group. The detention group has the responsibility over all aspects of over incarceration while the interrogation group handles the interrogation process. Still, the groups work in tandem and guards are brought into the transformation technology, as General Geoffrey Miller says, "to set the conditions" for interrogation, by "softening-up" the detainees (Rose 2004, 87; Human Rights Watch 2004, 2005). As we shall see below, there is also an incremental token economy system at GITMO aimed at distributed rewards and punishments. Nonetheless, it is the observation component that is paramount in this part of Foucault's analytical scheme. As one guard at GITMO explained, "You got to pay attention to detail. Observe things" (Rose 2004, 55). Guards nevertheless approach their task of observation in ways that reflect Foucault's notion of biopower whereby the prison provides a regime to facilitate the "knowing" process of whom the individual actually is. For instance, rather than accepting prisoners' outward characteristics at face value as being genuine, the gaze is filtered through a lens of suspicion. According to one guard: "There are some detainees who seem pretty nice . . . [but] there is only one way do this job. You got to go in there with the idea that they are terrorists, every single day. You have to have that mindset: that they are here for a reason" (Rose 2004, 56).

Normalizing Judgment

Discipline refers to enforcement of established (or desired) norms of behavior. To that end, specific techniques are introduced in prisons (and other institutions such as schools, factories, etc.) for correcting transgressions and minimizing deviations, a process that Foucault calls normalization, or the bringing of proper conduct into line (1977, 177). It is important to note that penal regimes operate beyond the direct governance of the law, essentially becoming self-contained and autonomous in the ways they carry out institutional management. Prior to being designated to prison, convicts are undergo some form of "judicial judgment" of their status as lawbreakers either through the courts or in the case of unlawful enemy combatants, some type of tribunal or administrative review. Nonetheless, the process of judgment also continues within the penal regime. Correctional staff, guards, and administrators all possess the power to discipline prisoners when their conduct is determined to be in violation of institutional rules, or merely "out of line." That infra-penality, "a partitioned area that the law left empty" is at the center of normalizing judgment within all disciplinary regimes, giving way to the dispersal of "judges of normality," for example, the "teacher-judge" in educational settings, "social worker-judge" in the welfare state, and the "guard-judge" in prisons. "It is on them that the universal reign of the normative is based" (Foucault 1977, 304). Along with infra-penality, normalizing judgment as a modality of disciplinary power contributes to how daily routines and everyday behavior in prisons are shaped, specifically with respect to time (tardiness, absences, interruptions of tasks), activity (inattention, negligence), speech (idle chatter, insolence), the body (irregular gestures, poor hygiene), and sexuality (impurity, indecency). Even the slightest violations of any of those norms could be met with minor physical punishment and deprivations and petty humiliations (Foucault 1977, 177–178).

Since the 1970s, U.S. courts have retreated from their "hands-off" dictum, thereby imposing more judicial oversight over the operation of prisons and their treatment of convicts. As a result, correctional administrators must contend with the prospects of legal actions and law suits resulting from breaches of court-ordered reforms. Prisons nevertheless enjoy what Foucault calls "infra-penality," which provides administrators and staff with the autonomy to manage the institution as they see fit, as long as it conforms to the rule of law. In 2004, the U.S. Supreme Court struck down the government's policy of denying GITMO detainees access to federal courts (*Hamdi v. Rumsfeld*; *Rasul v. Bush*). That decision, however, said little about how prisoners would be treated within the institution, giving the military administrators at GITMO a free hand in how they wish to deal with the population. To be clear, GITMO, even in its short history has undergone a series of changes with respect to how it is managed. One particular warden was been criticized for "coddling" detainees (Brigadier-General Rick Baccus) while another is accused of brutality (Major-General Geoffrey Miller) (Harbury 2005; Hersh 2004). As we shall discuss, warden Bumgarner has been characterized in the media as a reform-minded administrator committed to upholding the Geneva Conventions and the humane treatment of detainees, a plan that was met with considerable controversy (Golden 2006a).

Normalizing judgment furthers the enforcement of specific institutional rules governing the prison. Whereas some rules are grand in their purpose and scope, such as prohibiting physical attacks on staff and other inmates, others are remarkable for being meticulous: aimed at even the slightest infraction, such as fussy or intrusive inspections of the body and one's belongings. Moreover, it is just not only the scale of rule enforcement but also its constancy that adds to the overall thrust of control. While discipline might be superficially viewed as petty or even arbitrary, Foucault contends that it is driven less by repression and more by the objective of inculcating a "reformed" attitude, behavior, abilities, and skills. That normalization process targets not so much "signs and representation as movements of the body, gestures, and attitudes" (Cousins and Hussain 1984, 188). Because the ultimate goal is to transform the prisoner into an individual who is docile, obedient, and useful, the primary disciplinary technology minimizes its use of blunt force and maximizes forms of correction that are economical and subtle, including for example, incremental rewards (and deprivations) contained in a token economy and behavior modification schemes, or what Foucault describes as a "micro-economy of perpetual penalty" (1977, 181).

In light of his Weberian propensity toward ideal types, Foucault frequently describes prisons that seem to exist in model alone, making it difficult to locate a quintessential prison for transformation. GITMO, much like similar supermax facilities, does not spare it use of physical force against detainees; still, that tactic serves to undermine long-term transformation. Nevertheless, Foucault's attention to rules and their enforcement does throw some light onto the microeconomy of perpetual penalty and its role in normalizing judgment as well as examination. With a firm commitment to authoritarianism, GITMO strives to become a smooth, efficient machine with little tolerance for disruption. "There is only on rule that matters," said a former detainee. "You have to obey whatever the U.S. government personnel tell you to do" (Rose 2004, 69). With the threat of strict punishment looming overhead, prisoners at Camp Delta are required to adhere to the Detainee Standards of Conduct that contains a list of thirteen rules, including the following:

- Detainees WILL NOT be disrespectful to any U.S. Security Forces personnel or other detainees.
- Detainees WILL follow the orders of U.S. Security Forces at ALL times.
- Detainee units can and WILL be searched at any time.
- Detainees WILL NOT harass, annoy, harm or otherwise interfere with the safety or operation of the detention facility.

Foucault's eye for recognizing spatialization and the arrangement of objects in the normalization process is relevant to GITMO considering the degree to which even the most minute detail is placed under close inspection. Consider Rule 9 of the Standards of Conduct:

Detainees WILL at all times display their comfort items in the front of their unit in the following order:

a. Soap
b. Shower shoes
c. Toothpaste
d. Toothbrush
e. Small Towel
f. Water bottle

In his later work, Foucault returns to the significance of rules especially as they pertain to a more defined conception of power that acknowledges the role of political actors and agencies in exercising control. That idea is important considering rules since such "prohibitions" simply do not spring out of thin air; rather, they are constructed by and enforced by specific persons and groups. As Foucault notes. "Power acts by laying down the rule" (1978, 83), adding, "All modes of domination, submission, and subjugation are ultimately reduced to an effect of obedience" (85). At GITMO, as is the case in all prisons, rules and their enforcement lend organizational structure to the institution while maintaining control over its population.

Examination

A similar means of mobilizing disciplinary techniques is found in examination, a procedure aimed at determining the condition of the prisoner while documenting progress toward a defined objective. By combining the techniques of hierarchical observation and normalizing judgment, the examination "establishes over individuals a visibility through which one differentiates them and judges them" (Foucault 1977, 184). Such assessment ultimately reveals "the truth" about the prisoner, extracting knowledge by locating "individuality into the field of documentation" (189). It is within the protocol that meticulous note taking and record keeping occurs, enhancing an administrative regime embodied in bureaucracy (see Weber [1920] 1978, 1985). Through written progress reports and files containing an array of documented traits and characteristics, the individual becomes "formalized" within power relations, contributing to a "new type of power over bodies" (Foucault 1977, 191). Through the process of examination, an individual becomes a case, an object for clinical study and scientific gaze. "It is the individual as he may be described, judged, measured, compared with others, in his very individuality; and it is also the individual who has to be trained or corrected, classified, normalized, excluded, etc." (Foucault 1977, 191). In light of the power embedded in description, the individual, or case study, can be controlled and actively dominated; rather than archiving the person as a "monument for future memory" he or she becomes a written "document for possible use" and "object of power" (p. 191).

In sharp contrast to other supermax prisons that make few claims toward normalization, GITMO situates itself deep inside the war on terror, providing a unique venue where intelligence is gathered through "expert" interrogation methods. As one observer notes, "Harvesting intelligence through prisoner interrogations has become Guantánamo's principle raison d'etre" (Rose 2004, 80). Examination figures prominently within the interrogation project since it strives to determine who certain detainees actually are and what they know, developing what can be described as case studies. At Guantánamo Bay, those case studies indeed take on a clinical gaze reflected in Major-General Geoffrey Miller's choice of words: "I think of Guantánamo as the interrogation battle lab in the war against terror" (Rose 2004, 81). Under Miller's tutelage beginning in January 2003, interrogation become more frequent and intense, a departure from General Baccus's authority, when interrogations were relatively infrequent and low key. Former detainees Asif Iqbal and Shafiq Rasul said they were interrogated five times in 2002 and none in the last half of that year; after Miller took charge, they were interrogated more than 200 times over a 15-month stretch (Rose 2004; Human Rights Watch 2004).

Moreover, the methods—or technologies in Foucault parlance—were modified dramatically. Miller merged the Joint Detention Group consisting of the guards with the Joint Interrogation Group comprising interrogators, translators, and analysts. As incoming guards were oriented to GITMO, Miller's staff made PowerPoint presentations instructing them how to "coordinate prisoner treatment" with the intelligence experts. In doing so, guards would understand that distributing privileges and punishments in living units would facilitate the interrogation sessions. According to one source, "It stressed that close cooperation between guards and interrogators is the surest way to achieve greater intelligence findings" (Rose 2004, 88; Conover 2003). Lieutenant-Commander Charles Swift, a military defense attorney, was blunt when he complained that the interrogators and not the custodial staff were in effect running GITMO, having the final word as to how detainees would be treated: "You could be a model prisoner, your behaviour can be impeccable, but if you are not cooperating with the interrogators, you're going to be treated like the very worst inmate" (Rose 2004, 88). To aid interrogations that would sometimes last as long as twenty continuous hours, a long list of techniques are frequently deployed: dietary manipulation, sleep deprivation (or "adjustment" to refer to reversing the sleep cycle from night to day) isolation (as long as thirty days), shackling in uncomfortable positions ("stress and duress"), exposure to extreme heat and cold as well as to loud noise/music, strobe lights, and unpleasant smells. There is also an array of physical, psychological, and cultural tactics intended to heighten fear and anxiety among Muslim males, such as death threats aimed at them and their families, nudity, sexual humiliation, and the use of dogs. Another cultural technique involved depriving Muslim detainees of their Koran, or in widely reported incident of flushing it down a toilet (Amnesty International 2005; see Harbury 2005; Hersh 2004). Much attention also has been focused on the more extreme techniques that human rights lawyers characterize as torture, for example, "waterboarding" that induces suffocation and the sensation of drowning (Stout 2008). All along, guards and interrogators would be led to believe that they were immunized from being prosecuted for torture or war crimes since their actions were supposedly authorized by the president of the United States as commander-in-chief (Danner 2004; Greenberg and Dratel 2005).

The clinical approach adopted at GITMO affirms Foucault's thesis on how power is designed to pass through the body and not necessarily against it. Rather than merely deploying blunt force at all times, the interrogation techniques at GITMO take a "scientific" approach that attends to individual differences in ways that facilitate transformation. Upon visiting GITMO in 2003, the International Committee of the Red Cross noted that medical files detailing the mental health of prisoners were shared with interrogators so that they could develop "interrogation plans," a violation of medical ethics ensuring patient-doctor confidentiality. Interrogators have also been consulting with psychologists contracted by the military in efforts to improve psychological operations (McCoy 2006). The individualistic approach was further enhanced by Miller's assembling of "tiger teams" (five-member intelligence units) committed to the gung-ho bravado of their commanding officer. While still in intelligence training centers prior to being stationed at GITMO, Miller would address the in-coming interrogators by videophone:

> I tell them: the tiger never sleeps at Guantánamo Bay. These young people were so talented and so committed to winning the mission, that before long, our tiger teams will know more about you and your family than you know yourself, and the events that led you into terrorism. We are very, very good at interrogation. (Rose 2004, 110)

This conforms with Foucault's (1977) observation that prisons enjoy considerable autonomy from the judiciary and other agencies of oversight. Moreover, precisely how programs are carried out by prison wardens and their staff of so-called experts also is quite autonomous, allowing them to improvise with various techniques and modifying—even simplifying—them as they see fit (Foucault 1991, 80–81). Adjusting penal strategies so as to optimizing their effectiveness is an ongoing process, particularly in the face of prisoner resistance to many tactics. As we shall explore in the next section, coercive techniques—including torture—not only fail to produce credible confessions but also are met with considerable resistance, thereby precipitating greater counter-resistance and an endless cycle of repression and rebellion.

PRISONER RESISTANCE AT GITMO

Although penal discourse might seem rational—and at times persuasive—often there remain deep problems in the ways in which technologies are administered; as mentioned, they frequently backfire and create resistance. That paradox produces challenges for virtually all correctional institutions to one degree or another. However, tactics that are more coercive in nature tend to bring about greater refusal and rebellion which consequently are countered with even harsher authoritarian measures (King 1999; Rhodes 2004). Those dynamics clearly undermine the disciplinary goal of transforming prisoners into beings who are supposed to become docile, obedient, and useful. For Foucault (1977) that limitation poses an obstacle for his analysis and brings into question whether other disciplinary enterprises are doomed to fail elsewhere, especially without the benefit of a highly controlled environment, as is the case with prisons. Recognizing that drawback rooted in his reliance on Weberian ideal types, Foucault later concedes that prisoners do stubbornly resist disciplinary technologies and that penitentiaries usually resemble a "witches' brew compared to the beautiful Benthamite machine" (1991, 81; 1980). Foucault's revised position falls back in line with Nietzsche ([1887] 1996) who also noted that punishment generally undermines improvement, injecting resistance.

Resistance at GITMO takes on many forms, including collective rebellion, hunger strikes, and mass suicides. Not only are those manifestations of refusal of interest but so are the ways administrators and staff at GITMO respond, especially when they exhibit an even a stronger commitment to harsh methods. As early as October 2002, a memo documented interrogator's frustration that they were not achieving results; although they had been deploying a range of coercive techniques, prisoners were still putting up stiff resistance. Rather than questioning whether those detainees were actually terrorists and perhaps instead innocent persons (e.g., victims of false arrest motivated lucrative bounties), military officials toughened interrogation tactics along with other aspects of the conditions of confinement.[4] Eventually, new incoming wardens had to deal with problems created by coercive techniques, harsh conditions of confinement, and the fact that many of detainees would probably be held indefinitely. Consider the tour of duty of Colonel Mike Bumgarner who took over as the warden of Guantánamo Bay in April 2005. He received his marching orders from the overall commander of the military's joint task force at Guantánamo, Major-General Jay W. Hood, who provided some simple instructions: keep the detainees and his guards safe and prevent escapes. Furthermore, Hood suggested that Bumgarner "study the Third Geneva Convention, on the treatment of prisoners of war, and begin thinking about how to move Guantánamo more into line with its rules" (Golden 2006a, EV1). Although he knew the conventions well, Bumgarner thought to himself, "How do you deal with an individual whom the president of the United States and the secretary of defense have called the worst of the worst?" (EV1). Still, he did not have much time to ponder international law since he was focused on the 530 prisoners, most of whom were classified as "noncompliant," including some who had assaulted guards.

> In older parts of the camp, the detainees would sometimes bang for hours on the steel mesh of their cells, smashing out a beat that rattled up over the razor wire into the thick, tropical air. Occasionally they would swipe at the guards with metal foot pads ripped from their squat-style toilets, declassified military reports say. The detainees rarely tried to fashion the sort of shanks or knives made by violent prisoners in the United States. But they did manage to unnerve and incite the young guards, often by splattering them with mixtures of bodily excretions known on the blocks as "cocktails." (Golden 2006a, EV2)

Despite those frequent disruptions, Bumgarner had been aware that many of the detainees were not the hardened terrorists the Pentagon officials had claimed, although he did believe that many of them were dangerous. Soon he began to engage some of the more influential detainees as a means gaining greater control of the prison in face of growing resistance. In his initial message to the detainees, he said, "Look, I'm willing to give you things, to make life better for ya, if y'all will reciprocate." What he asked in return was "Just do not attack my guards" (Golden 2006a, EV3). While reaching out to the prisoners, he also began to make other modifications of the penal environment, including installing clocks on the cellblock walls, so that prisoners could anticipate their prayer sessions. In response to complaints about the tap water, bottled water was distributed at mealtime, and authorities even went so far as to remove the stars-and-stripes labels along with the brand names Patriot's Choice and Freedom Springs. Those nominal though seemingly genuine acts of respect did not go far given the overall repressive nature of GITMO. Within two months, some prisoners went on a hunger strike, demanding better living conditions, proper treatment of the Koran by guards, and a cease to the playing of the "The Star-Spangled Banner" over distant loudspeakers during or right after the evening call to prayer. But, more important, they insisted for fair trials or freedom. The unusually large number of prisoners then on hunger strike involved worried the medical staff.

As resistance began to take hold, Bumgarner retained his personal style of management, focusing on a particularly influential detainee, Shaker Aamer (a.k.a., The Professor) who was initiating several civil disobedience campaigns. "You're either gonna start complying with the rules," Bumgarner recalls warning him, "or life's gonna get really rough." The warden did not mean to threaten physical force, only to emphasize strongly that "Aamer's few privileges—like, say, his use of a toothbrush—hung in the balance" (Golden 2006a, EV4). In his discussions with Aamer, he found common ground on how to make GITMO a more "peaceful place." That is: bring the institution in line with the Geneva Conventions and encourage staff to treat the detainees with respect, citing an annoying practice of referring to prisoners in transit as "packages": "We are not 'packages'," a detainee told the warden, "We are human beings" (Golden 2006a, EV6).

The warden's approach to institutional management, however, was not widely shared among his staff. Many guards were reluctant to have lengthy dialogues with detainees, let alone expressing an interest in the Geneva Conventions for dealing with "a bunch of terrorists." More to the point, operatives in the Joint Interrogation Group "were furious" over Bumgarner's hands-on style and willingness to exchange privileges for good behavior. As the "experts," interrogators always felt that they ought to be in charge of that particular system of rewards and punishments. But Bumgarner did not budge, insisting that his job was to run the prison as he saw fit (see Jacobs 1977 on wardens and their management styles):

Bumgarner set about trying to solve the problems he saw. He instructed members of the guard force to stop referring to the detainees as "packages."

On compliant blocks, he had guards start turning down the lights between 10 P.M. and 4 A.M. and stop moving prisoners during those hours to allow the detainees to sleep. To avoid disturbing their prayers, he ordered guards to place yellow traffic cones spray-painted with a "P" in the cellblock halls at prayer times. He asked his aides to see that "The Star-Spangled Banner" recording would be played at least three minutes before the call to prayer. (Golden 2006a, EV7)

The warden did find support among some of his senior staff who realized that establishing compliance at GITMO was key to institutional management, and not any different from civilian jails and prisons regardless of their security level. Still, there was a big difference: at GITMO, there is no such thing as tacking on a few more years to the sentence for bad behavior. Indefinite detention loomed large, undermining short and long term compliance. As one guard noted, compliance at GITMO brought only prayer beads, packets of hot sauce, and a slightly thicker mattress, but not early parole. Detainees understood that as well as the fact that the prison itself was operating outside the orbit of international law. "There were no rules and no law. Any guard could do whatever they wanted to do" complained one detainee (Golden 2006a, EV8).

Over time, detainees felt a greater solidarity sharing a common adversary in the form of GITMO. Devising ingenious ways to communicate, some prisoners tossed messages attached to long threads from their clothing with wads of hardened toothpaste into nearby cells; others shouted into the plumbing to talk between floors. Their frustration with being detained, mistreated, and denied fair trials fueled a newfound sense of purpose. In 2002, a handful of hunger strikers were force-fed; however, in 2005 the large numbers (fifty-six) of such resisters prompted officials to rethink their approach, even considering detainee complaints. Aamer, the Professor, told Bumgarner that the hunger strikers were demanding the following: ending to the secret abuse project of Camp 5; bringing the detainees to trial or returning them to their home country; and improving medical and living conditions. The warden tried to keep the negotiations on institutional issues within his grasp (e.g., observing parts of the Geneva Conventions) and convinced the Professor to end his strike and persuade the others to do so. When the Aamer, accompanied by Bumgarner, visited the units housing hunger strikers, the cells erupted with applause: "He was treated like a rock star," Bumgarner recalls. "I have never seen grown men—with beards, hardened men—crying at the sight of another man." He paused, searching for an analogy. "It was like I was with Bon Jovi or something" (Golden 2006a, EV8). Eventually, most hunger strikers suspended their protests and disciplinary tensions eased becoming an interlude that Bumgarner would call the "period of peace." During that time, the warden revamped the reward system governing "comfort items" that was viewed as arbitrary; detainees also would be issued tan uniforms replacing the orange jumpsuits. Even more significantly, a detainee council was allowed to convene, addressing institutional grievances but that experiment was quickly terminated when detainees were found passing notes. So too was the "period of peace." Soon disturbances and a riot followed, prompting a heavier custodial presence and the shutting off of water and electricity. Hunger strikes resumed; this time detainees focused on their legal status rather than living conditions. Grown tired of seeking compliance through negotiations, the staff resumed their tough custodial stance. Rules once again became stricter; guards even resorted to switching on noisy fans to drown out prisoners trying to shout to one another from their cells.

For a while guards gained the impression that there renewed toughness was contributing the overall control of the prison; however, hunger strikers soon were back in session. When medical staff realized that hunger strikers were able to manipulate the feeding tubes by reversing the flow of nutrients, they resorted to harsher tactics. Participating in a hunger strike was to be treated as a "disciplinary" matter, and like all rule infractions, it would be met with force—namely, restraint chairs in which prisoners would be strapped down for a painful feeding protocol. Human rights lawyers condemned the use of restraint chairs but officials at GITMO felt that they were necessary and produced firm results, gaining the upper hand in resistance. But that feeling did not last long as prisoners resulted in mass suicide attempts, ingesting hoarded medication. When guards swiftly searched the housing units for medication and other contraband, detainees rioted, prompting guards to fire rounds of rubber bullets and pepper spray. Once again, some prisoners took desperate measures: on July 9 (2005), three committed suicide by hanging themselves in the back corners of their cells. Although each of the deceased had been involved in hunger strikes, their medical files revealed no signs of depression or psychological problems (Risen and Golden 2006). Military leaders went on the offensive and hours after the suicide, in a news conference the new GITMO commander, Admiral Harry Harris, described them as an act of "asymmetric warfare" (Golden 2006a, EV16).

Taking cues from Nietzsche and Foucault, Carrabine (2004, 59) furthers his genealogical investigation of the origins of prisoner resistance by concentrating on the "complex intersection of a number of different and competing forces." Whereas his analysis is both in-depth and far-reaching, he does embrace an important concept that helps us understand resistance and disorder at GITMO: fatalism. That concept, however, cuts both ways. In one direction, fatalism suggests that convicts tend to accept inevitably their fate as prisoners and grudgingly—ritualistically—go along with the institutional demands rather than forcefully upending the penal regime (see Durkheim

[1897] 1966; Lockwood 1992). Reversing that concept, fatalism also translates into "desperation" which "provokes the will to commit 'new infractions' to provide a 'dramatic reassurance that he can still make things happen.' In other words, desperation refers to a crushing sense of hopelessness that in turn prompts a feeling that there is nothing left to lose" (Carrabine 2004, 139; Matza 1964, 188–191). By citing Matza, Carrabine introduces an almost existential motivation that should not be overlooked, especially given the Kafka-esque nature of GITMO (see also Cohen and Taylor 1992, 1981).

While cultivating in detainees a deep sense of despair and fatalism—in both of its forms—GITMO is still viewed as an institution with a particular penal purpose. Recent pronouncements by military leaders speak to a discourse committed to control and even normalization. According to General Hood, many young Arab detainees held at GITMO "were beginning to see the light. They hadn't been radicalized at Guantánamo. Rather, as conditions at the camp had improved, their preconceptions about Americans had worn away. 'They discover, 'You guys aren't so bad.' I think the hard-core people have lost ground over the last four years. They are clearly losing ground'" (Golden 2006a, EV15). In an equally revealing pronouncement, Hood added,

> We are going to establish the most world-class detention facilities, and we are going to show the world that we're doing this right. Every provision of the Geneva Conventions related to the safe custody of the detainees is being adhered to. Today at Guantánamo—and, in fact, for a long time— the American people would be proud of the discipline that is demonstrated here. (Golden 2006a, EV15; see Wright 2006)

Looking into the claims of effectiveness at GITMO, however, there remain serious doubts and questions about what it has actually achieved.

PERPETUATING FAILURE

Despite devoting enormous attention to the prison and its intricate methods of normalization, Foucault (1977, 1991a) is left with the realization that the entire penal project is a failure, even though it continues to survive. The prison persists in large part because it serves broader political purposes having to do with the distribution of power and domination over certain individuals and groups. Foucault is not alone with that perspective; throughout contemporary history, reformers and penologists have cited the defects of prison. Nevertheless, because its advocates believe that there are strong merits in good penitentiary practice and such strategies for crime control ought to be reasserted, the prison has not been abandoned (Garland 1990; Rothman 1971, 1980). Foucault, by contrast, argues further that the prison persists because of its immersion into a wider disciplinary apparatus inseparable from modern society. According to his own reasoning, Foucault insists that failure of prison produces a form of success in the realm of social control aimed at the "delinquent" (or "dangerous") class; in the end we left with a perpetual struggle that ensures the existence and maintenance of a criminal justice system (1977, 271; 1988). Indeed, the persistent threat of criminals is met with public calls for coercive measures, a demand the state is willing to fulfill.[5]

While relaxing a functionalistic logic, the war on terror and in particular GITMO ought to be understood within a deeper theoretical context. Because the threat of terrorism is very real and continues to reverberate in American society, the idea of an institution located safely on the other end of a foreign island is often welcomed by the general public as it searches for ways to reduce collective anxiety in a post–9/11 world (Welch 2006b; Ericson 2007). For many in the mainstream, GITMO offers emotional security by providing a seemingly pragmatic solution not unlike other punitive sentiments (e.g., "lock 'em up and through away the key"). Furthermore, GITMO serves potent symbolic purposes, offering "evidence" that the US government is "doing something" in the war on terror as well as "getting tough" with terrorists. With those social psychological and political considerations in full view, it is important to explore the internal failings at GITMO along with its wider external problems that undermine counterterrorism strategies, both of which fuel the paradox of GITMO.

A close reading of the chronology of GITMO demonstrates that many of those being held are not the "worst of the worst" as the Bush administration proclaims. There is considerable evidence of innocent persons being arrested elsewhere and transported to the prison; some were apprehended at the hands of those hoping to cash in on the lucrative bounties offered by the US government (Amnesty International 2005; Human Rights Watch 2004, 2005; Rose 2004). The fact that many detainees have been released strongly indicates that they were wrongly placed at GITMO in the first place. This bizarre scenario is not merely a benign problem of "mistaken identity" but is, rather, a serious ethical matter with strong implications to human rights (see Butler 2004, Gregory 2004). Among other things, wrongful detention points to the importance international law that entitles all persons arrested to a fair trial along with an array of due process guarantees. It is clear that those fundamental procedures would reduce the number of errors in the pursuit of terrorists. Such mistakes, it should be noted, also threaten national security since it means the government is wasting its time and energy on the wrong persons; clearly, those resources could be better used in worthy investigations.

In terms of the penal technologies in the form of interrogation methods used at GITMO, there are good reasons to doubts claims of effectiveness. At the top of operations at GITMO for a considerable stretch of time was General Geoffrey Miller, whose background does not entail any real experience interrogation; in fact, he had never filled an intelligence post in his career until he was stationed at GITMO. Other military personnel have commented on Miller's lack of expertise. According to Lieutenant-Colonel Tony Christino, Miller "does not appear to be well-qualified either to direct strategic interrogation efforts or to asses the value of intelligence derived from such efforts" (Rose 2004: 83). Likewise, Milton Beard, former CIA chief in Sudan and Afghanistan, also questions why Miller was selected to oversee GITMO and its intelligence mission. Nevertheless, Miller exercised considerable leverage in terms of how GITMO would conduct interrogations; he developed the controversial tiger teams, a select unit of interrogation specialists believed by many to be too young and inexperienced to handle intelligence duties. In his visits to GITMO, Rose says it is not difficult to spot the interrogators, who, instead of military uniforms, wear polo shirts, lightweight shoes, khakis, or even shorts, "and most of them look surprisingly young—well under the age of thirty" (Rose 2004, 79). Shafiq Rasul, a former detainee wondered about the use of such youthful interrogators and how naïve some of their questions seemed (e.g., assuming Rasul's hometown, Tipton, England, was a good place to buy surface-to-air missiles): "You'd look at these guys in their shorts and polo shirts and think, 'This guy's an interrogator? He's only twenty years old!'" (109).

While more seasoned intelligence screeners were assigned to duty in Afghanistan, less experienced interrogators were shipped to GITMO. Miller defended his youthful tiger team, even though seven of ten were reservists and many had just graduated from "tiger team university" (at Fort Huachuca) upon completing a twenty-five-day course on interrogation. For many on the tiger team, GITMO would be their first job involving counter-terrorism. Still, Miller insisted that their inexperience was an asset and since the field of intelligence was a young person's game, they would benefit from remaining flexible and not fixed to old tactics. Lieutenant-Colonel Christino argued otherwise saying that inadequate training and inexperience would produce poor results. Compounding matters, tiger teams relied on interpreters (or "terps") rather than interviewing suspects in their native language. Given that detainees at GITMO are interrogated by such poorly prepared staff and relying solely on translators raises questions over actual value are those suspects, creating the impression that they might very well be small fries rather than big fish. By contrast, consider the case of Abu Zubaydah whom the CIA held in a secret location (in Thailand). To interrogate Zubaydah (believed to be a close associate of Osama bin Laden), a highly experienced agent was flown thousands of miles from Kuwait so that the questioning would be lead in not only Arabic but Zubaydah's local dialect. Senior interrogators who met with journalist David Rose revealed that their work depends greatly on painstaking preparation. Underscoring Foucault's observations on biopower and how in-depth knowledge (e.g., personal biography) helps to determine who (or what) the individual actually is, an experienced intelligence agent replied, "The person who has the advantage is the one who really knows his subject. I would normally spend a minimum of ninety days doing a 'PI'—a preliminary inquiry on a subject—learning everything about him, before asking a single question. If warranted, I would dig deeper with subpoenas, wiretaps, etc. Sometimes this could even take a year or two before you get to the interview stage" (Rose 2004, 111; Harbury 2005).[6] Revelations about use of inexperienced interrogators and interpreters prompt some who work in the intelligence field to wonder whether GITMO might be a "front" adding that captured al-Qaeda ringleaders are held in secret prisons scattered around Southeast Asia, Eastern Europe, Afghanistan, and "floating interrogation cells" in the Indian Ocean (Hersh 2004; Gregory 2004). Of course, questions remain about the relative value of testimony being extracted from either low-level operatives, let alone innocent persons, held at GITMO. More to the point, there is a large and convincing body of literature that indicates that coercive interrogation methods—including torture—produce unreliable confessions because the person in extreme pain will say just about anything to reduce the suffering (see S. Cohen 2006; Harbury 2005). Adding to the paradox, such unreliable evidence also confounds efforts to reveal truth as well as to proceed with a criminal prosecution since the courts have a tendency of not allowing such testimony (see McCoy 2006). Against that set of knowledge, Miller still insists, "I believe that we understand what the truth is . . . They [tiger teams] can identify the truth of any statement made with a high degree of accuracy" (Rose 2004, 125).[7]

It is clear that external problems for GITMO also contribute to its failure as an effective tool in counterterrorism strategies. At the center of any well regarded criminal justice campaign is its perceived legitimacy; crime control and counterterrorism tactics that appear out of step with human rights are bound to erode public support (see Welch 2006a). As the war on terror becomes increasingly globalized, there is a wider audience that looks to what the U.S. government is doing and condemning many of its current practices that violate international law. Contrary to popular and political reasoning, trampling the rights of people does not contribute to national security; rather, they undermine it. Moreover, solid counterterrorism policies and practices are contingent upon good international relations. Former national security advisor Zbigniew Brzezinski (2004) observes that America's safety is dependent on international security. As the link between national sovereignty and national security dissolves, America's domestic security increasingly is in the hands of others. Brzezinski emphasizes that an effective counterterrorism platform requires that the problem be understood in its proper historical and political context. At the root of every act of terrorism is a political conflict. Cooperation within the international community on matters of counterterrorism is particularly important for the United States given that anti-Americanism is at an all-time high around the world. Fueling such resentment is the widely shared view that the US government ignores principles of international law and human rights, especially in the case of GITMO (Knowlton 2005). Loud calls to shut down GITMO are heard within the United States and abroad. In Britain, America's closest ally in the war on terror, attorney general Lord Goldsmith, called for GITMO to be closed, saying camp's existence was "unacceptable" and ran counter to the U.S. tradition as a "beacon of freedom, liberty and of justice" (Cowell 2006, EV1; see Sciolino 2006).

Foucault suggests that the panopticon serves as a more general model for ordering society by exercising power in ways that improve surveillance that in turn facilitate normalization and conformity. Ideally, the panopticon, according to Foucault, offers positive rather than negative transformations; indeed, it was designed to arouse little resistance to the power of surveillance (1977, 218). By sharp contrast, GITMO, despite all its penal technologies aimed at transforming prisoners into docile, obedient, and useful subjects toward generating "enormously valuable intelligence," is a repressive institution not only in its day-to-day operations but also in its disconnection from a democratic world where prisoners have access to courts, inspiring hopes of a fair trial and perhaps even release. GITMO it is a unique prison intimately tied to a form of presidential power that in the sphere of the war on terror has proven to be militaristic and absolutist: rather than civilian and in accord with a separation of governmental powers (see Agamben, 2005; Butler 2004). With those developments in full view, a critical understanding of GITMO coincides with other Foucauldian ideas. Discussing the production of delinquency, Foucault proposed that there was an "attempt to impose a highly specific grid on the common perception of delinquents: to present them as close by, everywhere present and everywhere to be feared . . . aimed at maintaining a permanent state of conflict" (1977, 286; 1988a). Quite easily, one can insert the word terrorist (or unlawful enemy combatant) into that statement and conclude that social construction of their "dangerousness" serves to the perpetual and potentially endless war on terror (see Gregory 2004).

CONCLUSION

Admittedly this chapter covers a good deal of territory, but it is keen to realize the potential for Foucault's contributions in a post–9/11 world. Here several Foucauldian concepts were introduced to sharpen a critical interpretation of GITMO. Foucault's approach to studying penal practices concentrates on methods, technologies, and the know-how; and his aim was to deepen analysis while also examining discourse surrounding the rationalities ("ways of thinking") that claim to justify certain penal technologies. Foucault's work is appreciated for recognizing "the interplay between a 'code' which rules ways of doing things (how people are to be graded and examined, things and signs classified, individuals trained, etc.) and a production of true discourses which serve to found, justify and provide reasons and principles for these way of doing things" (1991a, 79). He remained interested in how individuals govern themselves and others by "the production of truth," referring not to entities that can be determined as factual but rather the establishment of domains in which "the practice of true and false can be made at once ordered and pertinent"(1991a, 79).

Reaching beyond matters of penal discourse and technologies, the last segments of the paper draw attention to resistance and the failure of prisons in general and of GITMO in particular; still, there are a few final conceptualizations that allow us to situate further those concerns within a Foucauldian perspective. Unlike the "legislative instance" (authorized to write laws) and "judicial instance" (empowered to sentence convicts), the prison is driven by the "penitentiary instance," which possesses a supplementary disciplinary power that Foucault characterizes as "sovereign." He even goes so far as to argue that the courts merely pass a "prejudgment" on the convict but the actual judgment occurs during imprisonment while the prisoner is subjected to close and constant evaluation to determine who the subject—and later the object—really is (1977, 247). Foucault reveals a notable paradox in the "penitentiary instance." Prison reformers in the eighteenth century created legal codes so as to remove arbitrary judicial power; apparently, that distribution of power became reconsolidated as penal power governed by the prison. "It seems as if they took away the arbitrary discretion from the hands of judges and princes only to entrust it to those who administer and supervise legal punishment" (Cousins and Hussain 1984, 194; Foucault 1977, 231–232, 247; see Ericson 2007).

Although that paradox certainly applies to the relative autonomy enjoyed by prisons in Western societies, those institutions nevertheless are subject to some oversight and accountability. As the exception, GITMO possesses absolute autonomy internally with respect to its daily operations and interrogations that continue with virtually no monitoring for human rights abuses (with the exception of occasional nonbinding visits by the International Committee of the Red Cross). GITMO's internal autonomy also is invigorated by its external autonomy in the form of a presidential power that claims to have unreviewable authority to designate certain persons as unlawful enemy combatants and banish them to indefinite detention (even leading to the death penalty). To be clear, both the internal and external autonomies of GITMO are vitalized by the sovereign, manifesting in a presidential authority that continues to resist balancing or separating powers in the war on terror (Agamben 2005; Butler 2004). Advisors in the Bush administration seek legal refuge for the president under the umbrella of military authority that they argue provides the executive with broad and sweeping powers, as the title commander-in-chief implies. As then Deputy Assistant Attorney-General John Yoo insisted in a written consultation for the Pentagon's general counsel William J. Haynes a few days before GITMO officially opened, "Restricting the President's plenary power over military operations (including the treatment of prisoners) would be constitutionally dubious" (January 9, 2002; Greenberg and Dratel 2005). Of course, that high degree of militarization in the war on terror also is seen more recently in the controversial (and legally dubious) MCA of 2006 designed to "try" some detainees held at Guantánamo Bay (Human Rights Watch 2006a).

For the most part, GITMO exists and operates away from the rule of law, including international treaties and conventions intended to protect the rights of all persons held under lock and key. That realization prompts us to question the so-called progressive chronology of prisons that suggests over time punishment becomes more just and humane. It is true that GITMO is a unique institution and not representative of most "reformed" prisons, even though it does share many repressive characteristics with supermax prisons. Nonetheless, penologists ought to recognize that like all prisons, GITMO is based on a form of modern power in which punishment functions as a form of "political technology" aimed at controlling and dominating certain populations (Foucault 1977, 23–24). As we suspend our belief in a progressive history, GITMO—along with the escalating reliance of incarceration and frequent use supermax prisons—stems of a larger paradox that Stuart Hall (1988) calls "regressive modernization."

CHAPTER 5

Torture

AMID REPORTS THAT MENTAL health specialists were involved
in prisoner abuse scandals at Guantánamo Bay and Abu Ghraib prison in Iraq,
the American Psychological Association in 2007 scrapped a measure that
would have banned members from assisting interrogators at Guantánamo Bay
and other U.S. military detention centers. The APA's policy-making council
voted against a proposal to prohibit its psychologists from taking part in any
interrogations at U.S. military prisons "in which detainees are deprived of adequate protection of their human rights" (Associated Press 2007a, EV1). Still,
the association approved a resolution that reaffirmed the association's opposition to torture and restricted members from taking part in interrogations that
involved any of more than a dozen specific practices, including sleep deprivation and forced nudity; psychologists who participate in those practices could
be expelled and lose their state licenses to practice. Moreover, the group went
on to claim that presence of psychologists would help insure interrogators did
not abuse prisoners. "If we remove psychologists from these facilities, people
are going to die," said Army Colonel Larry James, who serves as a psychologist
at Guantánamo Bay (Associated Press 2007a, EV2). To which another psychologist countered, "If psychologists have to be there so detainees don't get killed,
those conditions are so horrendous that the only moral and ethical thing is to
leave" (Associated Press 2007a, EV2).

INTRODUCTION

Since revelations of torture and prisoner abuse at Abu Ghraib and
Guantánamo Bay, there has been a deluge of opinions on the ethics of interrogation in the war on terror. An important aspect of the torture debate focuses
on legal questions over the harsh treatment of suspects and prisoners
(Greenberg and Dratel 2005; Lewis 2004). Nevertheless, other areas of knowledge also deserve careful consideration; for instance, a close look at key sociohistorical developments in torture and interrogation exposes a deeper lineage
of the controversy. At the onset, it is tempting to turn to the scholarly literature
on torture which delves into ancient and medieval practices believed to be
extinct and replaced with more humane forms of punishment, notably the

prison (Foucault 1977; Garland 1990; Langbein 1977). Even though the reemergence of torture since 9/11 speaks to manifestations of power discussed in those works, accounts of contemporary history dating back to the Cold War provide a more suitable starting point for interpreting modern torture (Danner 2004; Harbury 2005; McCoy 2006). Also rather than merely tracing a social history of torture in descriptive terms, it is useful to construct a genealogy that delivers insight into the ways in which power is transmitted from one agency to another. Much like the previous chapter, this analysis of torture is inspired by the work of Michel Foucault and at an even deeper level by Friedrich Nietzsche, whose genealogical approach skeptically examines all phenomena for their signs, symbols, and significance of power ([1887] 1996; see Adler and Longhurst 1994; Garland 1990).

Embarking on an analysis of modern torture, we explore the process in which unthinkable acts of brutality become "necessary" forms of policy and practice. In doing so, a sociohistorical approach is informed by taking into consideration the role of discourse as it shapes the dialogue and meaning of torture, interrogation, and treatment of prisoners (Welch 2007d). Much of the prevailing discourse by political actors regrettably entails formulating slick denials and legalistic justifications for abusing suspects in pursuit of gaining information on terror plots and extracting confessions. Given the obvious threat to human rights, Stan Cohen (2006, 2005) favors of a second history of torture that chronicles the pattern of rationalizing tough interrogation techniques contained in a new paradigm for torture (see Gearty 1997, 2005a). A second history of torture prompts us to examine critically the influence that discourse imposes on practice since it is rife with language intended to both stoke and assuage fear (e.g., "the ticking time bomb" [Dershowitz 2002]). Likewise, such discourse has a desensitizing effect, leading otherwise morally committed persons to accept harsh tactics as a "lesser evil" against more ominous risks to national security (Ignatieff 2004). Since 9/11, torture has been imbued with a sense of impunity because those who order and carry out such atrocities are unlikely to face criminal prosecution for war crimes. There is nevertheless nothing new about that form of immunization, as this work suggests. Locked into a genealogy of modern torture is a persistent claim that tough tactics are vital to protect the state from potent sources of destruction, whether communism or terrorism. Alfred McCoy points to degrees of political, professional, and public complicity in American-style torture:

> In this heated controversy, all of us, proponents and opponents of torture alike, have been acting out a script written over fifty years ago, during the depths of the Cold War. Indeed, a search for the roots of Abu Ghraib in the development and propagation of a distinctive American form of torture will, in some way, implicate almost all of our society—the brilliant scholars

who did the psychological research, the distinguished professors who advocated its use, the great universities that hosted them, the august legislators who voted funds, and the good Americans who acquiesced, by their silence, whenever media or congressional critics risked their careers for exposes that found little support, allowing the process to continue. (2006, 6)

Contextualizing such direct and indirect involvement in torture, the chapter begins with a theoretical overview of discourse as it interacts with governmentality. As we shall see, key to understanding that linkage is the translation process whereby power is transmitted from one station in the hierarchy to next. Along the way, political rationalities and governmental technologies prepare a path for torture, transforming the unthinkable into practice. While discussing the emergence of modern torture in the Cold War era, special attention is devoted to the scientific forces driving behavioral research and how its findings on physical and psychological pain became the foundation for a new paradigm of torture. Those origins are important as we uncover the genealogical roots of torture in a post–9/11 world.

Translation, Governmentality and Discourse

In pursuit of a critical interpretation of power as it operates in the context of prisons, Carrabine (2000, 2004) explores on a trilogy of interrelated concepts—namely, translation, governmentality, and discourse. Such an integrated approach not only bridges micro- and macrolevels of penology but also clarifies the ways in which action, belief, and conduct are structured according to specific contours of power, thereby advancing a social theory of imprisonment. Carrabine's intention is "to offer a way of thinking that brings the sociology of the prison into a more theoretically comprehensive account of strategies of domination and regulation, without falling victim to limited understandings of how imprisonment is experienced at particular times and places" (2000, 312). Turning to a "sociology of translation" (or "actor-network theory"), Carrabine asserts that the traditional dichotomy between the micro (i.e., individuals and psychology) and macro (i.e., institutions and economic history) is superficially bracketed, impeding insight into the construction and maintenance of power relations. As a remedy, the micro- and macroplanes of penology ought to be approached from the same analytical perspective which considers how domination is continually produced. Such a process is described along lines of translation, defined as the way "we understand all the negotiations, intrigues, calculations, acts of persuasion and violence, thanks to which an actor or force takes, or causes to be conferred on itself, authority to speak or act on behalf of another actor or force" (Callon and Latour 1981, 279). As a result, the relationship between power and structure is forged by networks, alliances, points of resistance, and relative durability, thereby enabling the keepers of the prison to exercise power over the kept. The notion of translation is useful because it permits us to envision a process by which agents translate phenomena into resources which become the propelling force in networks of control (Clegg 1989). In his research, Carrabine interprets the practice of incarceration as a translation of networks that constitute both agency and structure, thus throwing light on the vitality possessed by powerful actors in penal environments (see Bosworth and Carrabine 2001).

Furthering the micro/macro framework, Carrabine taps into the literature on governmentality (Burchell, Gordon, and Miller 1991; Garland 1997a; Rose and Miller 1992). In doing so, he proposes a conceptual vocabulary that helps us comprehend what prisons are *for* (i.e., political rationalities) and *how* imprisonment practices are carried out (i.e., governmental technologies). Foucault's *Prison and Discipline* (1977) is criticized for its failure to make clear linkages between the microphysics of power and its relations to the state and larger society; consequently, it seemed as if the production of docile bodies remains detached from broader valences in the disciplinary project (see Garland 1997b). As if in riposte, Foucault (1978, 1991) hones his conception of power with an important formulation. While not gravitating to a theory of state (e.g., a Marxist critique), he defends his bottom-up perspective as superior to the deductive top-down trajectory of power, remaining focused on the nature of power at the lowest levels. Foucault argued that methods of analysis aimed at local arenas could be replicated for studying the ways in which populations are governed in the territories of nation-states. Moreover, changes in the practice of government ("the conduct of conduct") have enormous significance in the project of modernity, particularly given its rationality or system of thinking about who can govern whom.

Political rationalities further clarify micro/macro connections that offer moral justifications of certain methods of exercising power (Rose and Miller 1992). Equally important are government technologies that refer to an array of programs, calculations, techniques, and procedures through which authorities embody so as to express or give life to the ambitions of government.[1] It is precisely at this juncture of conceptualization that Garland hooks into the significance of translation: "Power is not a matter of imposing a sovereign will, but instead a process of enlisting the cooperation of chains of actors who 'translate' power from one locale to another" (1997, 182). Power in that sense is not a monolithic entity centralized by the state but a force that is dispersed throughout local arenas that in turn often meets the expressed objectives of authorities situated further up the chain. Nevertheless, such dispersal is animated by discourse, understood as a system of thought that informs and guides practice. Keeping our sites on penology, Carrabine expands on that notion of discourse as a tool to decipher ways of thinking about incarceration. "As such, the various discourses serve to 'incorporate' the agencies of the powerful within the project of imprisonment—that is, civil servants, governors, staff, and so forth articulate these ideas and practices" (2000, 316). Adding clarity to the underlying assumptions of discourse embedded in translation, Carrabine concurs with Giddens who purports that human subjects have "as an inherent aspect of what they do, the capacity to understand what they do while they do it" (1984, xxii). Even though actors may not possess a fully mapped out conception of the discursive structure, as Carrabine contends, they are able and often willing to act on the beliefs and justifications rooted in political rationales and government technologies. It is precisely at those points of contact where translation occurs.

As discussed previously, Carrabine adopts a Foucauldian notion of discourse, emphasizing how it structures knowledge and organizes the ways in which things are done. Foucault (1972, 49) insists that discourse is not merely a constellation of signs but also a practice "that systematically forms the objects of which they speak" (see Williams 1999). Whereas it is debatable as to exactly how many different penal discourses exist, there is some consensus that a total of six encompass a wide range of claims and practices (Adler and Longhurst 1994). To reiterate, three of those discourses pertain to the *ends* of incarceration (i.e., rehabilitation, normalization, and control), and the other three to the *means* (i.e., bureaucracy, professionalism, and authoritarianism). The *means* point to the technologies or methods of carrying out the objectives of the *ends*, or the rationalities and justification of imprisonment. It is crucial to note that those discourses are not fixed but rather dynamic, subject to being continually produced and confronted both within the prison and in larger society. Although a sociology of torture does not conform neatly to the aforementioned six penal discourses, it does benefit from deciphering various claims about the practice of torture, including its political rationales (i.e., ends) and government technologies (i.e., means). By examining contemporary discourse on torture, we are able to interpret the process of translation and how it serves to channel power from one locale to another. Moreover, it is through a genealogy of modern torture that we are able to understand the role of translation that uses discourse to transform the unthinkable into the thinkable, which, in turn, becomes the basis for policy and practice.

The Origins of Modern Torture

Historians find that from 1950 to 1962, the U.S. government enabled the CIA to pursue its fascination with mind-control research, believing that it could prove to be a crucial weapon in the Cold War. Billions of tax dollars were funneled into numerous experiments aimed at studying the effects of hallucinogenic drugs, electric shock, and sensory deprivation, creating a massive scientific campaign that McCoy calls "a veritable Manhattan Project of the mind" (2006, 7; Simpson 1994). Those developments are especially noteworthy in a genealogy of torture. Unlike traditional forms of torture that implemented physical tactics aimed at the body, modern torture—as cued by science—relied more on psychological techniques. Among its innovations, the science of torture boasted the creation of "no-touch torture." Following years of experiments, torture scientists discovered that physical pain, regardless of its intensity, generated resistance, thereby undermining attempts to extract information or a confession from the subject. By contrast, a new psychological paradigm of torture advocated by the CIA integrated "self-inflicted pain" with "sensory deprivation" into a technique that was perceived as being superior to the traditional physical model. Scientists argued that subjects capitulate more readily to interrogation when they feel responsible for their own suffering since the synergy of physical and psychological trauma unfastens personal identity. Indeed, the iconic image of a hooded Iraqi prisoner standing on a box with arms extended to electrical wires offers compelling evidence of a CIA method geared toward both sensory deprivation (i.e., the hood) and self-inflicted pain (i.e., extended arms) (McCoy 2006; Watson 1978; Welch 2008b).

The translation of torture methods from agencies to practitioners is easily found in the publication of a document titled the *Kubark Counterintelligence Interrogation* manual (CIA 1963). It is in that instruction book that "no-touch torture" was codified for purposes of teaching interrogators modern—scientifically informed—tactics not only believed to be effective but also difficult to detect since the scars remained deep inside the psyche (Doerr-Zegers et al. 1992). Such translation was swift and global insofar as modern torture techniques devised by the CIA with the support of key members of the scientific community were propagated initially through the U.S. Agency for International Development's (US AID) Office of Public Safety to police departments in Asia in the 1960s then into Latin America after 1975. The CIA's torture paradigm was circulated by the U.S. Army Mobile Training Teams in the 1980s throughout Central America. Whereas those programs were decidedly covert, the political rationale was not: modern torture would serve national security by battling the putative threat of communism (Feitlowitz 1998; Hinton 2006; Huggins, Haritos-Fatouros, and Zimbardo 2002; Kahn 1996).

For the most part, torture was put back in the toolbox at the end of the Cold War while the U.S. government resumed its public stance supporting human rights principles (e.g., participating in the World Conference on Human Rights in Vienna [1993], and ratifying the UN Convention against Torture). During the 1990s, even CIA counterinsurgency missions were drastically reduced. After the attacks on September 11, however, relatively dormant political rationales attached to national security would once again lead to the use of modern torture as a prominent technology in the war on terror. Rather than rushing to investigate tough interrogation tactics in a post–9/11 world, it is useful at this stage of the analysis to consider other developments that inform a genealogy of modern torture. Key sociohistorical moments clearly demonstrate the significance of discourse and how elements of power are translated from agencies to individual practitioners. In the following subsections, we closely examine with some depth interrogation as a "scientific project" and how that knowledge is transmitted into specific methods of interrogation. Finally, we look critically at modern torture as it has reemerged since September 11.

A Science of Interrogation

In drawing a genealogy of modern torture, events following the Second World War figure prominently since the Cold War produced a climate of heightened mistrust—and paranoia—between the Soviet regime and the United States. Seeking an edge in power, both the KGB and the CIA embarked on massive mind control experiments they believed would lead to detecting espionage. Similar to nuclear physicists who spearheaded groundbreaking research on weaponry, psychologists too gained considerable prestige because it was believed that they possessed the key to unlock human consciousness (Fisher 1977). Bonds linking the intelligence community and the military establishment with academic psychologists were strengthened not only by a shared nationalism but also through financial funding. After World War II, the Office of Strategic Services in Washington also recruited German scientists who had conducted Nazi experiments involving psychology and human physiology. At that phase of "torture science," drugs, especially LSD, became a major interest because it was purported to improve interrogations aimed at identifying spies and double agents (e.g., Operation Paperclip; see Cockburn and St. Clair 1988; McCoy 2006). Much like the inquisitions in medieval Europe, the extraction of confessions is of chief importance to the interrogator. Enter prominent psychologist Irving Janis who had an extensive background on cognitive research developed by the Soviet military in the 1940s. Janis proposed that confessions (even false ones) could be produced with a combination of sophisticated hypnosis techniques, drugs, and electric shock (Janis 1949; see Bowart 1978). With rumors that the Soviets had already cracked the code for "brain washing" the CIA rushed to channel more funding into experimental psychology that might give the United States an advantage in "brain warfare" (Marks 1979; see Lifton 1961). To reiterate, those activities occurred amid the Cold War's ecology of fear and hysteria, reinforcing widespread worries over national security.

Of particular significance is the formulation of a CIA mind-control program known as MKUltra, a notorious plan of behavioral research that first relied on bizarre experiments featuring hallucinogenic drugs and hypnosis (from 1950 to 1956) before moving toward more mainstream studies on cognitive psychology (until 1963). That body of knowledge would ultimately become the "scientific" basis of a definitive interrogation manual compiled in 1963, an instructional booklet that would serve to transmit the science of interrogation into forms of practice in the field. As follows, the direct lines of translation are easily traced within the structure of MKUltra.

> The MKUltra researchers were given extraordinary powers. At the program's outset, [Richard] Helms proposed, and Director [Allen] Dulles agreed, that 6 percent of the budget for the [CIA] agency's TSD [Technical Services Division] could be spent 'without the establishment of formal contractual relations.' Helms noted that talented academic and medical researchers 'are most reluctant to enter into signed agreements of any sort which connect them with this activity since such a connection would jeopardize their professional reputations.' " (McCoy 2006, 28; Senate, Foreign and Military Intelligence, Book I, 404–405, see Senate 1977)

Under the umbrella of MKUltra, the CIA infiltrated important institutions in civil society, including prestigious universities and hospitals where medical researchers would conduct drug and sensory deprivation experiments on unwitting human subjects, in an effort to advance the "science" of interrogation (Cameron 1956; Weinstein 1990). Although much of the financial infrastructure for mind-control research rested on government funds, private foundations also contributed (e.g., the Ford and Rockefeller foundations; see Simpson, 1994). Not to be overlooked is the role of the APA, particularly its Division of Military Psychology, which served as crucial network by linking university professors with Pentagon dollars. Unlike ethical constraints placed on psychiatrists, such as the Hippocratic Oath, psychologists enjoyed the type of flexibility that government, military, and clandestine agencies appreciated (Dunlap 1955). Indeed, the synergy of government resources with eager investigators would propel the "science" of interrogation as it set out to break new ground in the fields of cognitive and behavioral research, all of which was bounded by a shared sense of service to national security. CIA contracts were awarded to such prominent psychologists as Albert Biderman, Irving L. Janis, and Harold Wolff, each contributing to a deeper and more clinical understanding of self-inflicted pain (Haggbloom 2002). Adding to the "science" of interrogation (and torture) during that period was the work of a young psychologist at Yale named Stanley Milgram.

In what can be described as a notable link in the chain of translation, Milgram's (1964) studies demonstrated that any ordinary person is capable of inflicting physical pain on another human being, provided it is done so according to the instructions, orders, or commands of an authority figure. Indeed, along with the use of self-inflicted pain, the CIA torture paradigm would benefit from Milgram's findings on obedience (Blass, 2004). At the Yale University Interaction Laboratory, Milgram recruited "ordinary" townspeople to participate in a so-called learning study. In brief, each volunteer was seated before an electronic console that read "Shock Generator Type ZLB" and told that when the "student" located in another room failed to correctly answer a test item, the "student" would be administered a shock. When the "student" was hit with mild shock, he let out a groan of discomfort and as higher voltage was delivered, he would respond with a violent scream. Although the "student" was not actually being shocked and merely pretending to be in pain, the "ordinary" person believed that an electrical current was administered as punishment for committing errors in the "learning" test. More to the point, Milgram reported high rates of compliance. In fact, when the "student" could be heard but not seen, 65 percent of volunteers switched the controls to the full 450 volts, supposedly reaching the fatal maximum level. Many volunteers clearly exhibited nervousness and trauma as the degree of voltage escalated, but they remained committed to the task under the instruction of a "legitimate" authority figure, the experimenter wearing a white lab coat.

The study concluded that the volunteers were not driven by a sadistic need to punish the "student." Rather, those "ordinary" persons were responding obediently to social convention structured along lines of authority (Milgram 1974; see Kelman and Hamilton 1989). As McCoy puts it, "At the end of each simulated-torture session, ordinary New Haven citizens walked out of the Yale laboratory with a check for $4.50 and the disturbing knowledge that they, like Gestapo interrogators, could inflict pain and even death on an innocent victim" (2006, 48). Implications to translation and the training of coercive interrogation methods are evident, particularly in light of the ways in which the CIA torture paradigm was disseminated to other nations dealing with the "threat" of communism. Soon Milgram's laboratory findings would spread to the field. Police officers in Asia and Latin America began learning and cooperating with harsh—even brutal—techniques aimed at "breaking" suspects for purposes of extracting information pertinent to national security. At that point in history, a genealogy of modern torture had graduated from the scientific inquiry, moving into the realm of practice.

Translating Science into Practice

In the early 1960s, the CIA, equipped with "scientific" knowledge about human reactions to sensory deprivation, shifted toward a more fundamental design for interrogation, thereby shunning other primitive forms of inflicting pain (Senate 1977). Nevertheless, the particulars of interrogation required a vehicle to be transmitted to practitioners. Enter the 1963 handbook known as *Kubark Counterintelligence Interrogation*, an instructional volume that would deliver the "know-how" for the next four decades, spreading to a long roster of countries where the CIA was operating. Written in a clinical—even cool—tone, *Kubark* remained committed to psychological principles governing effective questioning protocols, citing the theory of inducing regression of the personality. As the effects of disorientation (i.e., time and place) establish a weaker state, the subject becomes needy and dependent on a stronger, even authoritative figure. Moreover, because the new paradigm of interrogation is geared toward efficiency, the process is accelerated by the use of isolation and sensory deprivation techniques (e.g., hooding and "sleep adjustment"). Similarly, confusion is achieved by delivering nonviolent blows on the psyche (e.g., personal insults and sexual humiliation). The overarching objective of those psychologically informed methods is to maximize the destructive force of self-inflicted pain. According to *Kubark*, "It has been plausibly suggested that, whereas pain inflicted on a person from outside himself may actually focus or intensify his will to resist, his resistance is likelier to be sapped by the pain in which he seems to inflict upon himself" (1963, 94). In setting the ideal conditions for interrogation, the subject, once sufficiently disoriented, can be placed in a state of self-inflicted pain by a method as simple as enforced standing with arms extended (see Biderman and Zimmer, 1961).[2]

Kubark scans a range of psychological literature on isolation and sensory deprivation, becoming the foundation for the CIA's new paradigm for torture. But as a mere document it remained static; for its content to be actualized, it required a theater where actors could follow its script. That theater, in military parlance, was South Vietnam. Before entering Saigon and other strategic locations, CIA agents and interrogators underwent intensive three-week programs at its training center, The Farm, near Williamsburg, Virginia. Leaving the controlled environment of the laboratory far behind, intelligence operatives would soon train South Vietnamese police and military officers in the cruel art of torture under actual field conditions. In light of the nature of military theaters, compounded by the fierce mission to root out insurgency, the textbook lessons of *Kubark* would be complemented—or corrupted—by the use of physical violence, especially when impatient interrogators grew increasingly frustrated by seemingly ineffective psychological methods (Bowden 2003; Danner 2004). Serving as its front, the CIA operated through the Office of Public Safety (a division of US AID) between 1962 and 1974, and by 1971 a global anticommunist program had trained more than one million police officers in forty-seven countries, including 85,000 in South Vietnam (Klare 1972; McCoy 2006). The CIA-OPS program disseminated the new paradigm of interrogation that would become synonymous with brutality and gross human rights violations. Amnesty International (1975) reported that torture was commonly used by police in twenty-four of the forty-nine nations that sponsored OPS police training. Some of the CIA methods also were taught academically at the International Police Academy in Washington. Upon its own investigation, Congress found evidence of torture lessons contained in student graduation theses.[3]

As the war in Vietnam escalated, the CIA itself also departed from its purely psychological model for interrogation. Determined to fight terror with terror, the agency untapped its 1965 counter-terror program that paid teams to carry out assassination, kidnapping, intimidation, and a host of physical abuses. Attempting to conceal its obvious mission, the program's personnel was renamed the Provincial Reconnaissance Units (Marchetti and Marks 1974). By the late 1960s, the CIA had expanded its "counter-terror" efforts with the notorious Phoenix program; given its deep financial pockets coupled with no oversight, it evolved into a covert murder machine (Valentine 1990). Still, Phoenix maintained the CIA's ongoing interest in psychological and physiological techniques, even transporting American psychiatrists with electroshock equipment to the theater. In one particular episode, psychiatrists failed to "break" their subjects after administering more than sixty shocks a day for a week; when the experiment was halted, interrogators disposed of the expired prisoners and the doctors returned to the United States (Cotter 1967). Similarly, when a CIA research team (featuring a neurosurgeon brought to South Vietnam) also failed to manipulate the behavior of Vietcong suspects after implanting into their brains tiny electrodes, the prisoners were shot by Green Beret troopers and their bodies burned (Cockburn and St. Clair 1998; Thomas 1988). By the time Congress began discovering the horrors of the Phoenix campaign in the 1970s, it is estimated that more than 20,000 Vietcong suspects had been killed. Many of those fatalities were victims of a "pump-and-dump" apparatus that would brutalize Vietcong suspects during interrogations and when the subjects died, their remains were simply disposed of. Despite those revelations, CIA director William Colby defended the agency and its covert operations as "an essential part of the war effort" that was "designed to protect the Vietnamese people from terrorism." As further evidence of the translation process, Colby remarked that although Phoenix was initiated by American agents, the program was transferred to the Vietnamese National Police and remained under its control (House of Representatives 1971).

As the Phoenix program, along with the conflict in Southeast Asia, faded from public and political memory, its paradigm to integrate physical and psychological methods would resurface as U.S. agents relocated to South and Central America in the 1970s and 1980s (Parry 1997). Anticipating that expansion, army intelligence as early as 1965 had developed Project X as "an exportable foreign intelligence package to provide counterinsurgency techniques learned in Vietnam to Latin American countries" (Department of Defense 1991). While a genealogy of torture in those regions deserve a close examination of precisely how the CIA disseminated its interrogation model, constraints here on text limit us to merely recognize that much like the Phoenix program, techniques were taught via resident instruction courses and training manuals (translated into Spanish).[4] Moreover, Phoenix-like tactics, including the use of sodium pentothal (so-called truth serum) in interrogation sessions, kidnapping adversary family members, physical brutality, and execution, would be exported to South and Central America (Kahn 1996; Harbury 2005). Indeed, the pattern of human rights atrocities in ten Latin American countries would "bear an eerie but explicable resemblance to South Vietnam (McCoy 2006, 71). Despite numerous Congressional inquiries and a steady stream of books documenting CIA complicity in torture in Latin America, the agency and its torture paradigm would survive, even lie dormant until the next national security emergency, September 11 (Danner 2004; Fagen and Garreton 1992).

TORTURE IN A POST–9/11 WORLD

The attacks on September 11 prompted the White House to view terrorism as an imminent threat to national security; consequently, its official response would be a unique form of warfare aimed at nonstate actors. Among the weapons used are revived interrogation methods as well as torture for purposes of correcting the information deficit since U.S. intelligence has had but scant knowledge of Al-Qaeda and its operations (Clarke 2004; Scheuer 2004). As the details of White House decision making emerged, it became clear that the Bush Administration was formulating a torture policy in ways that would immunize its the authors and architects along with those who order and administer it. In effect, that impunity shielded governmental actors and operatives from prosecution, even in cases where there exists credible evidence of war crimes. In *The Torture Papers: The Road to Abu Ghraib*, Greenberg and Dratel (2005) reveal how Bush advisors prepared a legal defense for the use of torture. To reiterate, the legal narrative contained in official memos exhibits three aims that would facilitate the unilateral and unfettered detention, interrogation, abuse, judgment, and punishment of prisoners: "(1) the desire to place the detainees beyond the reach of any court or law; (2) the desire to abrogate the Geneva Convention with respect to the treatment of persons seized in the context of armed hostilities; and (3) the desire to absolve those implementing the policies of any liability for war crimes under U.S. and international law"(Dratel 2005, xxi).

Among the revelations in *The Torture Papers* is the now infamous White House definition of torture, contradicting the standard interpretation established in the Convention against Torture that ratified by the United States in 1994. A memorandum by Jay S. Bybee, assistant attorney general to Alberto R. Gonzales (then White House counsel and later attorney general) altered the definition of torture, arguing, "Physical pain amounting to torture must be equivalent in intensity to the pain accompanying serious injury, such as organ failure, impairment of bodily function, or even death" (Greenberg and Dratel 2005, 172–214; Danner 2004).[5] Efforts by the White House to sidestep its obligations under the Convention against Torture and the International Covenant on Civil and Political Rights (ICCPR), along with federal statutes prohibiting torture, worry the human rights community. Compounding matters, several government officials have stated publicly that they endorse interrogation tactics that appear to constitute torture. While being questioned by the Senate, Porter J. Goss, then the director of the CIA, was confronted by Senator John McCain (R–AZ) who spent five years as a prisoner of war in Vietnam. When McCain asked Goss about the CIA's reported use of "waterboarding," in which a prisoner is made to believe that he will drown, Goss replied only that the approach fell into "an area of what I will call professional interrogation techniques"(Jehl 2005a, A11; see Herbert 2005; Stout 2008). As a clear paper trail of legal arguments favoring torture, *The Torture Papers* are nothing less than revealing. As previously noted, "Rarely, if ever, has such a guilty governmental conscience been so starkly illuminated in advance" (Dratel 2005, xxi). Further evidence of translation in formulating policy is found in the "corporatization" of government lawyering in which the White House policy architects begin with an specific goal and work backwards without benefit of a moral anchor that could prevent their client's descent into unconscionable conduct (Dratel 2005; see Greenberg 2005).

In search of other ways to skirt its obligation to uphold bans on torture, the Bush administration resorted to extraordinary renditions by which detainees are transferred to another government as a means of outsourcing interrogation and torture (e.g., Egypt, Jordan, Morocco, and Syria; Grey 2006). Given its global reach, the procedure of rendition requires that aircraft stop in other countries for refueling. Since American military aircraft are not allowed to land in many sovereign states, the CIA contracts the services of private charters that are able to shuttle without creating suspicion of wrongdoing. (Shane, Grey, and Williams 2005,A1). Amid reports that the U.S. government was outsourcing torture, President Bush assured the world that "torture is never acceptable, nor do we hand people to countries that do torture" (Mayer 2005, EV1). Bush's denial contradicts evidence that more than 100 suspects have been rendered to other nations with the expectation that they will be abused and tortured (Harbury 2005; Priest and Gellman 2002). Moreover, renditions are a matter of policy carried out by "the CIA under broad authority that has allowed it to act without case-by-case approval from the White House or the State or Justice Departments," according to current and former government officials (Jehl and Johnston 2005, A14).[6]

In addition to extraordinary renditions, harsh interrogation methods involving physical abuse were making a comeback in the wake of 9/11. Several of the national security officials interviewed by reporters of the *Washington Post* defended the use of violence against captives as just and necessary. An unidentified FBI agent told reporters, "It could get to that spot where we could go to pressure" (Priest and Gellman 2002, A1). While arguing that torture ought not be "authorized," Robert Litt, a former Justice Department official, suggested it could be used in an "emergency" (Williams 2001, 11). Similarly, a government operative who has supervised the capture and transfer of accused terrorists quipped, "If you don't violate someone's human rights some of the time, you probably aren't doing your job" (Priest and Gellman 2002, A1). Just how closely the CIA torture paradigm would be emulated in the war on terror would be realized as evidence of harsh interrogation and physical abuse surfaced at Guantánamo Bay and Abu Ghraib, as well as at Bagram Air Force base in Afghanistan.

Guantánamo Bay: The New Interrogation Laboratory

Compounding the legal questions surrounding unlawful enemy combatants and their military tribunals, human rights organizations criticize the institutional conditions at Guantánamo Bay, issuing allegations of torture, abuse, and mistreatment against detainees. Former detainees have told the press that American soldiers at GITMO beat and humiliated them, even holding guns to their heads during interrogations; other reports include the chaining and shackling prisoners for as long as fifteen hours at a time, feeding them food rations that were ten years past their expiration dates, and providing foul drinking water. One detainee reported that he was beaten after refusing to be injected with an unknown substance (N. Lewis 2004; Tyler 2004a; Waldman 2004). In May 2005, a high-level military investigation into accusations of detainee abuse at Guantánamo Bay concluded that "several prisoners were mistreated or humiliated, perhaps illegally, as a result of efforts to devise innovative methods to gain information," including acts in which female interrogators forcibly squeeze male prisoners' genitals (Lewis and Schmitt 2005, 35) In memorandums that were never meant to be disclosed publicly, the FBI reported that they had witnessed questionable interrogation methods. One agent observed, "On a couple of occasions, I entered interview rooms to find a detainee chained hand and foot in a fetal position to the floor, with no chair, food or water. Most times they had urinated or defecated on themselves and had been left there for 18, 24 hours or more" (A. Lewis 2005b, EV1). The abused detainee was Mohamed al-Kahtani, a Saudi who is suspected of being the planned twentieth hijacker on September 11, 2001, was logged in great detail. Kahtani was interrogated for as long as twenty hours at a stretch, and at one point he was put on an intravenous drip and given three and a half bags of fluid. When he requested to urinate, guards told him to do so in his pants, which he did. FBI agents, reporting on the mistreatment of Kahtani, said a dog was used "in an aggressive manner to intimidate" him. According to the log, Kahtani's interrogator told him that he needed to learn, like a dog, to show respect: "Began teaching detainee lessons such as stay, come and bark to elevate his social status to that of a dog. Detainee became very agitated" (A. Lewis, 2005b, EV1).[7]

Prisoner abuse at GITMO should not be viewed apart from its overall institutional mission. From its inception the prison was designed to provide a specialized venue where intelligence is gathered through "expert" interrogation methods. Recall that, while in charge of the prison, Major-General Geoffrey Miller boasted, "I think of Guantánamo as the interrogation battle lab in the war against terror" (Rose 2004, 81). Under Miller's direction beginning in January 2003, interrogation became more frequent and intense. As mentioned previously, Asif Iqbal and Shafiq Rasul said they were interrogated five times in 2002 and none in the last half of that year; then after Miller took charge, they were interrogated more than 200 times over a fifteen-month period (Rose 2004; Human Rights Watch 2004). As noted, Miller significantly revamped the prison's organization to facilitate interrogation by merging the Joint Detention Group consisting of the guards with the Joint Interrogation Group comprising interrogators, translators, and analysts. As incoming guards were oriented to GITMO, Miller's staff made PowerPoint presentations advising them how to "coordinate prisoner treatment" with the intelligence experts. Therefore, guards were told that distributing privileges and punishments in living units would improve the interrogation sessions. To aid interrogations that would sometimes last as many as twenty continuous hours, a long list of techniques have been frequently deployed: dietary manipulation, sleep deprivation (or "adjustment" to refer to reversing the sleep cycle from night to day) isolation (up to thirty days), shackling in uncomfortable positions ("stress and duress"), exposure to extreme heat and cold as well as to loud noise/music, strobe lights, and unpleasant smells (Amnesty International 2005).

Also used are a host of physical, psychological, and cultural tactics designed to heighten fear and anxiety among Muslim males, such as death threats aimed at them and their families, nudity, sexual humiliation, and the use of dogs. Another cultural technique involved depriving Muslim detainees of their Korans, or in widely reported incident of flushing it down a toilet (Amnesty International 2005). The "clinical" approach to interrogation also extended to the unethical use of medical information; interrogators have also been consulting with psychologists contracted by the military in efforts to improve psychological operations (Associated Press 2007a; see also chapter 4). As modern torture took form at GITMO, other sites would undergo similar restructuring so as to support the mission of interrogation. Soon harsh physical and psychological techniques used at GITMO would be exported to other prisons where U.S. military and intelligence operations, most notably Iraq. When Major-General Geoffrey Miller was transferred from to Abu Ghraib it became clear that his regime of abuse and tough interrogation methods would follow (Hersh 2004; Rose 2004).

Abu Ghraib: Images of Imported Techniques

In late 2002, the *Washington Post* published detailed accounts of American intelligence officers who had resorted to abuse and torture of detainees held at Bagram Air Force base in Afghanistan (Priest and Gellman 2002). Even though the story appeared front page, it generated little public or political interest. Then, some fifteen months later, the horrors of Abu Ghraib were exposed. A significant difference between the two otherwise similar reports of abuse and torture was the availability of explicit photographs. Within days of the breaking story, graphic visual evidence circulated around the globe. Pictures of naked Iraqi prisoners, simulating sex acts, taunted by dogs, and stacked in human pyramids confirmed suspicions that the U.S. military was operating outside the orbit of international law, relying on abuse and torture to extract information or merely as a means of punishment and humiliation (Sante 2004; Sontag 2004). The photographs offer irrefutable evidence of abuse and torture at the hands of U.S. military and intelligence personnel, further revealing specific techniques of self-inflicted pain, sensory deprivation, and sexual humiliation. Perhaps that is the reason why there was so much concern to control the spin of the scandal. The government and military quickly issued the standard "bad apples" explanation to counter growing realization that abuse and torture was systemic (*New York Times* 2004a). Adding to the controversy over Abu Ghraib is the degree of impunity. Blame for the abuse of detainees would be put solely on a handful of reservists featured in the photographs and not on ranking military leadership or key policymakers in the intelligence community. As columnist Bob Herbert phrased it, "Under Commander in Chief, George W. Bush, the notion of command accountability has been discarded. In Mr. Bush's world of war, it's the grunts who take the heat. Punishment is reserved for the people at the bottom. The people who foul up at the top get promoted. There was no wholesale crackdown on criminal behavior" (2005, A25).[8]

In 2005, as political figures in both parties were hoping the Abu Ghraib scandal fade from public embarrassment, it became known that other incidents of detainee abuse occurred in Iraq before and even during the Abu Ghraib investigation. Three former members of the Army's elite 82nd Airborne Division say soldiers in their battalion at Camp Mercury near Fallujah routinely beat and abused prisoners to help gather intelligence on the insurgency as well as to amuse themselves. Captain Ian Fishback tried to report the allegations to his superiors for seventeen months; failing that he sent some of his allegations in letters to top aides of two senior Republicans (Human Rights Watch 2005; Schmitt 2005). One sergeant while serving as a detention guard acknowledged abusing prisoners at the direction of military intelligence personnel. The similarities to Abu Ghraib are striking. Detainees were also stacked, in human pyramids (but fully clothed) and forced to hold five-gallon water jugs with outstretched arms or do jumping jacks until they lost consciousness. "We would give them blows to the head, chest, legs and stomach, and pull them down, kick dirt on them. This happened every day" (Schmitt 2005, A1, A6).

Also in 2005, as the Pentagon persistently denied that prisoner abuse was systemic or widespread even more evidence of brutality was made public. Reports from the war in Afghanistan indicate that some forms of abuse and torture were also linked to interrogation procedures. The case of a prisoner known only as Dilawar captures the cruelty imposed on Afghans suspected of terrorism and insurgency. Dilawar was hauled from his cell at the detention center in Bagram, Afghanistan to answer questions about a rocket attack on an American base. When he arrived in the interrogation room, an interpreter who was present said, his legs were bouncing uncontrollably in the plastic chair and his hands were numb. He had been chained by the wrists to the top of his cell for much of the previous four days. Days after his death (and that of another prisoner) in 2002, "military coroners determined that both had been caused by 'blunt force trauma' to the legs. Soon there after, soldiers and others at Bagram told the investigators that military guards had repeatedly struck both men in the thighs while they were shackled and that one had also been mistreated by military interrogators" (Golden and Van Natta, 2005, A12). The aforementioned revelations clearly contradict claims by the Bush administration that detainee abuse by U.S. military abroad has been infrequent, exceptional and unrelated to policy. Rather, it suggests that a paradigm of interrogation involving torture has been replicated at various prisons under U.S. command since 9/11.

Conclusion

Summarizing his theoretical work on discourse, governmentality, and translation, Carrabine positions his observations on power into a wider framework of social theory. He proposes that state power in the form of its penal system designed to regulate or transform prisoners stem from a "composition of actors, devices and strategies, in relatively durable associations through discursive alignments to achieve particular ends" (2000, 318). The mobilization of relatively stable networks is realized through the translation of thought and action from "centres of calculation." Such translation implies movement, spanning time and space while enrolling agency of particular projects. Indeed, it is the constellation of networks that enables calculated action upon conduct into a diversity of locales. Whereas Carrabine asserts that the penal system ought to be envisaged as an effect of such networks, a similar argument can be made for the practice of modern torture because there exists a translation of thought and action contained in political rationalities and governmental technologies. Modern torture is largely justified as a necessary means to protect national security, especially in a post–9/11 world in which nonstate actors possess the will and capabilities to wreak havoc.

Certainly much of the ritualistic abuse of prisoners documented at Abu Ghraib and Guantánamo Bay can be understood as expressive punishment resulting from the frustration of captors and their emotional need to scapegoat persons perceived as terrorists or insurgents. Methodical torture on the other hand tends to be more instrumental since harsh interrogation techniques are believed to be important tools in the war on terror in gaining information about terror plots and extracting confessions. That uncritically accepted purpose opens some analytical space to consider again Foucauldian insights into power. Foucault (1977) suggests that the practice of the penitentiary is aimed at transforming prisoners into docile and useful beings so that upon release they can adapt to the demands of the political economy driven by wage labor. Such transformation is established by a range of technologies in prison, including continuous observations, examinations, and exercises. Similarly, the practice of modern torture not only strives to make terror suspects docile but also useful in the production of intelligence needed to battle terrorism.

Techniques embodied in modern torture derive from scientific and behavioral research, setting the tone for a seemingly clinical—albeit cruel—approach to interrogation. The "science" of torture reveals a preoccupation with inflicting psychological and physical pain with the stated objective of "breaking" the subject. "Scientific" torture also is a modern government apparatus that speaks to the nature of power contained in the state. Foucault (1977, 1980) described criminology as a clinical science of individual differences that emerged in the nineteenth-century penitentiary as a means to implement its disciplinary practices, including the continuous monitoring of each convict and modifying the tactics according to individual reactions and deviations. Foucault argued that particular strand of positivistic criminology has always been closely aligned to the disciplinary power that shaped it (see Cole 2001; Garland 1992; Rodriguez 2006). Incorporating Foucault's critique of clinical criminology into a genealogy modern torture, we see a sharper connection between a network of scientists and interrogators and state power that both vitalizes and legitimizes their practices. In conclusion, the thrust of this chapter draws on significant sociohistorical developments during the past fifty years that have spawned the reemergence of modern torture in a post–9/11 world. Attending to discourse, translation, and governmentality, we gain a better understanding of the process by which unthinkable acts of brutality become "practical" forms of policy and practice. Such a process reflects Foucault's notion of a "strategic envelope," referring to the horizons of thought and action that make certain governmental ambitions possible (1978, 100; see Garland 1997).

PART THREE

Expanding Range

CHAPTER 6

Ordering Iraq

IN *IMPERIAL LIFE IN THE EMERALD CITY: INSIDE IRAQ'S GREEN ZONE* (2006) Rajiv Chandrasekaran provides an in-depth tour of the American reconstruction and those in charge. To ensure the "right" personnel were selected for the job, close scrutiny over their political lives remained a top priority, particularly with respect to party loyalty. Chandrasekaran reports that commitment to the Bush team and Republican Party political agenda— including their views on *Roe v. Wade*—served as a key criterion for being hired by the Coalition Provisional Authority (CPA) often by way of contacts in the Pentagon (e.g., James O'Bierne) and its liaisons with conservative think tanks. Even before the invasion took place, the Bush administration was assembling a long list of desirable candidates. For example, Frederick M. Burkle Jr. was assigned to oversee Iraq's health care system. His credentials were impeccable: a master's degree in public health and postgraduate degrees from Harvard, Yale, Dartmouth, and Berkeley; two bronze stars for military service in the navy, as well as field experience with the Kurds in northern Iraq after the 1991 Gulf War. In the first week of the formal reconstruction, Burkle was informed that he was being replaced because a senior official at US AID said the White House wanted a "loyalist" in the job. His replacement was James K. Haveman Jr. His résumé included "running a Christian adoption agency that counseled young women against abortions. He spent much of his time in Iraq preparing to privatize the state-owned drug supply firm—perhaps not the most important priority since almost every hospital in the country had been thoroughly looted in the days after Hussein was overthrown" (Goldfarb 2006a, EV2; see Kaplan 2004a, 2004b).

INTRODUCTION

Central to crimes of power in a post–9/11 world is the war in Iraq. Countering claims that the invasion was both justified and legal, it is important note that only the United Nations can authorize military action to disarm an aggressor, to ensure that disarmament is the real objective rather than a particular nation's political or commercial interests (Beyani 2003; see Allen 2004; Keen 2006, 15). Upholding that interpretation, United Nations

Secretary General Kofi Annan said that he believed that the war was "illegal" and not valid under international law terms. "Well, I'm one of those who believe that there should have been a second resolution [because] it was up to the Security Council to approve or determine" what the "consequences should be" for Iraq's noncompliance with earlier resolutions. "I have stated that it was not in conformity with the Security Council—with the U.N. Charter." Reiterating his point, Annan replied, "It was illegal, if you wish. From our point of view and from the charter point of view it was illegal" (Tyler 2004b, A11; see Jehl 2005a; Welch 2006a).[1] Given its historical significance to the rule of law, Kramer and Michalowski draw on the Nuremberg Charter in reminding us that wars of aggression are the most reprehensible and destabilizing of all state crimes, constituting the 'supreme international crime' " (2005, 446; Kramer, Michalowski, and Rothe 2005). As evidence that the Bush administration abused its power and misled the world as to why it was going to invade Iraq is the so-called 10 Downing Street memo. The secret British document reported on July 23, 2002 that Bush had decided to "remove Saddam, through military action," which suggests that the White House was intent on war with Iraq earlier than it acknowledged (Jehl 2005a, A10).[2]

Recent books by Richard Clarke (2004), former terrorism advisor, and Paul H. O'Neill (see Suskind 2004), former treasury secretary indicate that Bush had decided to invade Iraq by summer of 2002. Moreover, other evidence suggests that, long before the attacks of September 11, a coterie of neocons had been planning to return to Iraq for a Desert Storm Part 2 (Armstrong 2002; see Tenet 2007). Altogether there appears that a colonial project in Iraq had been in the making for some time (Ali 2003a, 2003b; Keen 2006). A critical analysis of power embedded in the war on terror prompts us to turn attention to the invasion and occupation of Iraq, especially because those developments are laden with historical, cultural, and economic elements characteristic of late modern imperialism. To situate properly both time and space, there is much to learn from the field of human geography, most notably the book *The Colonial Present*. In that study, Derek Gregory draws a complex genealogy of American and British investments in Iraq from World War I, through the Iran–Iraq war (1980–1988) to the Gulf War (1990–1991). It is now common knowledge that the story does not end there. In the aftermath of 9/11, the White House (and the Blair government) resumed its war in Iraq as "yet another front in the endless and seemingly boundless 'war on terror' " (Gregory 2004, 13; see Ikenberry 2002).

Delving into an examination of colonialism, it is helpful to say a few words about that troubling subject. Colonialism refers to "the extension of a nation's sovereignty over territory and people both within and outside its own boundaries, as well as the beliefs used to legitimate this domination" (Bosworth and Flavin 2007, 2). As a form of social and economic system that consumes resources and dominates labor, colonialism also penetrates culture in ways that project a racial superiority of the conqueror; in doing so, it strives to legitimize the exploitation, mistreatment, and discrimination of the colonized (L. Ross 1998). Edward Said (1993, 9) distinguishes between imperialism and colonialism: the former points to the practice, theory, and attitudes of a "dominating metropolitan center ruling a distant territory," whereas the later symbolizes the implanting of settlements there. Imperialism and colonialism operate in tandem to advance empire which marks the control of the political sovereignty of one state by another (see Chowdhry and Beeman 2007). In his work, Gregory prefers to speak about the colonial present rather an imperial one because he wants to retain the active sense of the verb "to colonize" in order to direct attention to the "constellations of power, knowledge, and geography . . . [that] continue to colonize lives all over the world" (2004, xv).[3] Likewise, this chapter sets out to decipher key developments in the occupation and reconstruction of Iraq, particularly as they interact with political, economic, and military modalities of power. Setting the stage, the discussion begins with an overview of what is meant by the term *ordering*.

POWER AND ORDERING

As a human geographer, Gregory finds inspiration from Foucault and in particular his *The Order of Things: An Archaeology of the Human Sciences* in which he offers deep insights into the ordering of space. It is within such ordered space where perceptual grids facilitate language allowing us—without hesitation—to think, speak, and name specific objects and ideas.

> Order is, at once and the same time, that which is given in things as their inner law, the hidden network that determines the way they confront another, and also that which has no existence except in the grid created by a glance, an examination, a language; and it is only in the blank spaces of this grid that order manifests itself in depth as though already there, waiting in silence for the moment of expression. (Foucault 1970, xxi)

In the context of European modernity, widely accepted perceptions have contributed to a proliferation of spacings and partitions, including the clinic, the asylum, and the prison. Even more to the point of colonialism, the production of spacings lend themselves to territories exterior to Europe that contained people who would be depicted as "others." Although Foucault did not write about colonialism at great length, he did lecture on the topic later in his career (2003). He observed how European colonial models not only were transported elsewhere but also had a boomerang effect on the mechanisms of power in the West; in effect, those paradigms would then be practiced by the West on itself (2003; see Gregory 2004, 263–264; 1995).

The establishment of order whether in the form of institutions (e.g., prisons) or colonialism is made possible through a social construction process whereby those entities are fabricated, but Foucault reminds us that their existence is not entirely false. Rather, those regimes of "order" become validated by spinning their own sense of truth that, of course, generates real material consequences. Gregory writes of the tendency within modernity to create its colonial other as a way to produce and privilege itself: "This is not to say that other cultures are supine creations of the modern, but it is to acknowledge the extraordinary power and performative force of colonial modernity" (2004, 4). The social construction process fabricates two potent narratives: the first are stories that "the West" tells itself about itself; the second are stories about the colonial other, an alterity that gives back "the West" an image of itself (Gregory 2004; see Dussel 1995; Said 1978). Because the reciprocated image of "the West" is a conveyed as a benevolent one that takes credit for spreading its "glorious creativity" to distant lands, the momentum of empire mediates its own destructive forces, apologetically known as a "white man's burden," or what Niall Ferguson calls a "savage war of peace" in reference to America's post–9/11 militarism (2001, 35; Kagan, 2006, 2004; Wheatcroft 2006).

A return to Foucault provides an opportunity to reflect on the recent ordering of Iraq in a post–9/11 world (see Welch 2008b). It is apparent that the term *order* has more than one meaning. Order refers to an arrangement of objects denoting neatness within a distinct spatial context or geography. Often times, order also means a desirable condition of society, particularly in pursuit of reducing crime, chaos, and other forms of disorder. In another sense of the word, order implies a command, or a linguistic device aimed at telling people what to do. Certainly, an order can also resemble a request such as in a restaurant, but that's really a polite way of telling others what one wants. Those varied meanings of order certainly pertain to Iraq, old and new. After the First World War, Iraq was created out of three provinces of the Ottoman Empire at the direction of the British government. After the 2003 invasion, a new Iraq has been created along with the need to instill order so as to provide public safety as well as a friendly environment for international investors, a task that has become easier said than done. Despite all the extravagant claims that the newly elected Iraqi government is steering its own destiny, the dominating presence of the U.S. military and foreign business interests suggests that Iraqi political leaders—and the Iraqi people—are operating under a larger set of commands beyond their control. Looking at Iraq from that perspective, there is much to discern about its current order and its relation to colonial discourse and material imperatives emanating from outside the region (see Banks 2007; Rabinow 1986; Thomas 1989).

Inherent to critiques of colonialism are efforts to understand the alignment between culture and power as mutually reinforcing (Said 1993; Thomas 1994). For instance, culture is not merely a reflection of the world but is involved in "the production, circulation, and legitimation of meanings through representations, practices, and performances that enter fully into the constitution of the world" (Gregory 2004, 8; 1995). Here the linkage between culture and power can be further illuminated by drawing on three concepts discussed previously: translation, governmentality, and discourse (see chapter 4). The conceptual chore is to integrated micro- and macrolevels of sociology in order to recognize the manner by which action, belief, and conduct are structured according to a shape—or geometry—of power. Turning again to a sociology of translation (or "actor-network theory"), the conventional division between the micro (i.e., individuals and psychology) and macro (i.e., institutions and economic history) should be unbracketed, giving way to a holistic vision of power relations as they maintain domination. Analyzing power and knowledge, Foucault (1988, 135–136) concentrates on social practices to determine who had been given the right to speak what counted as the truth. In the realm of colonialism, domination and control are facilitated by translation whereby negotiations, persuasion, and even violence can be traced to an authority who claims to speak or act on behalf of another actor or force (Callon and Latour 1981, 279; see Carrabine 2000). As a result, power, structure, and culture are forged by networks and alliances. Although points of resistance are common, the colonial project delivers relative durability that sustains domination (see Bosworth and Flavin 2007; Chowdhry and Beeman 2007). The concept of translation offers a glimpse into the process by which agents transmit phenomena into resources, becoming a notable force in networks of control (Clegg 1989).

Writings on governmentality similarly shed light on the importance of political rationalities and governmental technologies (Burchell, Gordon, and Miller 1991; Garland 1997; Rose and Miller 1992). Foucault's (1978, 1991) later ruminations on power suggest that methods of analysis situated at local arenas can be replicated for studying the ways in which populations are governed in the territories of nation-states. Moreover, changes in the practice of government ("the conduct of conduct") have enormous significance in the project of modernity—including colonialism—particularly in light of its rationality or system of thinking about who can govern whom. Exposing micro/macro connections, we witness political rationalities that furnish moral justifications for exercising power. Likewise, there exist government technologies that refer to a host of programs and procedures through which authorities embody so as to animate the ambitions of government. From that perspective, colonialism is made possible by recruiting the cooperation of chains of political, economic, and military actors who transmit power from one locale to another. To be clear, power in that sense is not monolithic; rather, it operates as a force that is dispersed throughout local vicinities that in turn often meets the expressed objectives of authorities stationed further up the hierarchy.

Dispersal is fundamental to the way power is distributed to other sectors of the colonial enterprise; moreover, that influence is rendered through discourse, which serves as a system of thought that informs and navigates practice (Foucault 1988). Whereas dispersal suggests an outward movement of power, discourse is a unifying activity in which beliefs and justifications are shared, even consolidated into a cohesive force. Through discourse, willing actors get "on board" a project that requires the participation of an array of players both within government and out: for example, in the case of Iraq, foreign investors and contractors, all of whom contribute to a synergy that makes colonial ambitions possible. The articulation of ideas and practices, however, does not mean that there isn't room for improvisation (and corruption), but through discourse embedded in translation, cooperating participants possess an understanding of what they are doing while they are doing it (Giddens 1984, xxii). Translation of power occurs precisely at points where political rationales (i.e., ends) and government (i.e., means) technologies make contact because, from a Foucauldian viewpoint, discourse structures knowledge and organizes the ways in which things are done. To recapitulate, discourse as a dynamic entity is not merely a constellation of signs but also a practice "that systematically forms the objects of which they speak" (Foucault 1972, 49).

By taking a hard look at discourse underpinning the colonization of Iraq, we gain a capacity to decipher the process of translation and how it serves to channel power from one locale to another. In the backdrop is Foucault's bottom-up method of replicating power relations at the locale level, demonstrating how the phenomenon unfolds in the governing of populations within territories of nation-states. From there, other scholars have delved into workings of imperialism and globalization especially along lines of dominant discourse (Gregory 1994; Said 1993). Jameson (2003) issues a bold view of what he calls the Americanization of the world, arguing that technology has produced a new transnational cybernetic, a term that implies not only a system of communication but also one of control. Gregory takes exception to Jameson's notion of a world economic system benevolently regulated by the United States, comparing it to Joseph Conrad's (1926) "Geography Triumphant" in which the world had been measured, mapped, and made over not only in the image of science but also of capital. Among his observations, Gregory notes "the middle passage from imperialism to globalization is not as smooth as he (Jameson) implies, still less complete, and the 'new transnational cybernetic' imposes its own unequal and uneven geographies" (2004, 12). Gregory calls for alternative ways of mapping the turbulent times and spaces in which we live with special emphasis on studies that narrate the war on terror as a series of stories unfolding far from America: most notably in Iraq, as well as in Afghanistan and Palestine. The attacks of September 11 have a complex genealogy that reaches back to the colonial past, says Gregory, and those events have been used by

Washington (as well as London and Tel Aviv) to advance a brutal colonial present—and future. In the passages to follow, the focus will remain on the ordering of Iraq with careful attention to its political, economic, and military maneuverings. Indeed, a critique of those developments deepens not only our understanding of power but also the dynamic nature of governmentality, translation, and discourse in a post–9/11 world.

COLONIAL RECONSTRUCTION

Especially since the 2003 invasion of Iraq, evidence of American imperialism leading to state crimes has become increasingly apparent (Kramer and Michalowski 2005; Kramer, Michalowski, and Rothe 2005; see Kauzlarich 2007; Kauzlarich, Mullins, and Matthews 2003; Mullins, Kauzlarich, and Rothe 2004). As mentioned in chapter 2, the U.S. government has been harshly criticized for its willful disregard of international humanitarian law, or law of armed conflict. Most notable are the following violations of IHL: (1) the failure of the occupying power to secure public safety and protect civilian rights in the wake of widespread looting and violence along with a host of home demolitions and arbitrary arrests leading to detentions (Amnesty International 2004); (2) indiscriminate responses to Iraqi resistance have contributed to a greater number of civilian casualties (Normand 2004; Parenti 2004); (3) war crimes involving the abuse and torture of Iraqi prisoners (Harbury 2005; Hersh 2004). The fourth breach of IHL to be discussed here pertains directly to the illegal transformation of the Iraqi economy since the Fourth Geneva Convention (1949) clearly bans occupying powers from restructuring the economy in their own vision (see Greider 2003; Krugman 2004). As American forces gained control over Iraq, the state-dominated economy has been overhauled and retrofitted to accommodate the imperatives of a market economy committed to lassez-faire, neoliberal free trade, supply-side tax policy, privatization, and foreign ownership (Juhasz 2004; Klein 2003b, 2007). Indeed, those political and economic transformations throw crucial light on the nature of colonialism in Iraq contoured along Foucauldian notions of discourse, governmentality, and the translation of power.

The term *reconstruction* widely used by the U.S. government in its attempt to rebuild Iraq has a deeper resonance; *to reconstruct* also suggests the remaking of a previous image or in this case a colonial past when distant world powers dictated control over a political and economic order. Commenting on the reconstruction of Iraq, comparisons were made to other colonial occupations; echoing the colonial past, Kurtz (2003) proposed that the United States follow the British India model (see Dodge 2003; Gregory 2004). As we shall see in this section, the reconstruction of Iraq according to an economic plan outlined by American policymakers illuminates the colonial present. Moreover, the U.S. occupation of Iraq allows us to reflect on the dual meaning of the word *order*. implying both a stable formation of society as well as a command emanating from another source of power.[4] With special emphasis on recent economic transformations, Iraq has the design to become a colonial other of the United States, or, according one Middle East analyst, "America's Iraq" (Schama 2003). That observation does not mean, however, that the colonial project is complete nor does it suggest that the Americanization of the Iraqi economy will succeed in the long term (Jacques 2006; Rose 2006). Political violence, insurgency, and sabotage should be not separated from the forms of resistance aimed at challenging both the American occupation and the new lassez-faire market economy predicated on privatization and the influx of foreign investment (Anderson 2004).[5] As security deteriorated in 2003, outside financiers had become cautious about investing in Iraq. In response, Bremer announced that his first priority of Operation Iraqi Prosperity would be to restore confidence of foreign investors: "The most important questions will not be [those] relating to security but to the conditions under which foreign invested will be in invited in" (MacKinnon 2003, 24; see Bremer 2003, 2006). Adding to the economic chorus of the neocons, Paul Wolfowitz (in March 2003) explained to a Senate Committee that Iraq "can really finance its own reconstruction and relatively soon" (Farley and Wright 2003, 36).

Contributing to a critical examination of those developments, some criminologists have delved into the significance of state crimes as they occur within the framework of the political economy in a post–9/11 world (Haveman and Smeulers 2008; Kramer and Michalowski 2005; Welch 2006a). In his probing work on economic war crime in Iraq, Dave Whyte (2007) goes to great lengths to unveil key financial shifts in the remaking of the Iraq, offering evidence of corruption so significant that it raises more questions surrounding the legality—and legitimacy—of the American occupation. Much of that corruption is rooted in the lassez-faire ideology (i.e., neoliberalism) that promotes the moral worthiness of profit seeking as it strives to minimize state-sponsored regulation of the market place (Tombs 2001). To cut through "red tape," lassez-faire enthusiasts prefer to construct policies that create relatively unregulated spaces for commerce; as a result, with little or no oversight those economic environments become zones for corruption and fraud (Rawlinson 2002). To understand precisely how the new Iraqi economy became rife with corruption, it is important to attend to the activities of the CPA—arguably a colonial entity—during its first fourteen months in office. During that stretch of time,

> the CPA issued 100 legally binding administrative orders by decree. Together, the orders formed the foundations of Iraq's new economy, criminal justice system and political structure. Those orders erected the pillars of a neo-liberal economy: the abolition of state production and commodity

subsidies; the eradication of import tariffs and trade barriers (Order 12); the deregulation of wage protections and the labour market (Order 30); tax reform (Order 37); monetary reform and reforms in the banking sector (Orders 18, 20, 40, 43, 74 and 94); the establishment of international trade rules based on the World Trade Organisation (WTO) model (Orders 54, 81 and 83); and the privatization of state enterprises (Orders 39, 46 and 51). The regime was founded on the principle of "trickle down" economics: the idea that wealth can be created and development stimulated by creating favourable terms of investment for private capital. (Whyte 2007, 181)

Perhaps most telling from a colonial standpoint was Order 39, which "promotes and safeguards the general welfare and interests of the Iraqi people by promoting foreign investment through the protection of the rights of foreign investors in Iraq" (quoted in Gregory 2004, 244). The order allows full foreign ownership over state-owned assets encompassing more than 200 state-owned enterprises (e.g., banks, mines, factories); consequently, Iraqi electricity, telecommunications and pharmaceuticals industries were dismantled. Foreign ownership of those industries and financial institutions means that profits can be taken outside of Iraq (Eviatar 2003, A37). Those transformations have not gone unnoticed: in the British courts opponents have argued that Order 39 marks an illegal occupation of Iraq under the Hague and Geneva treaties (Corporate Pirates 2005a, 2005b).[6] Specifically, Article 55 of the Hague regulations prohibits the privatization of a nation's assets while under an occupied military power. Cognizant that Order 39 was clearly in violation of international law, the CPA did not complete the sale of Iraqi state enterprises. As evidence of power translation in which willing actors respond to imperatives emanating from further up the hierarchy (Carrabine 2001), however, the CPA did provide a blueprint for privatization to be enacted by future Iraqi governments, especially those supportive of American economic interests (Eviatar 2003; Klein 200b3; 2004a).[7] That prophecy was fulfilled particularly by former Iraqi exiles involved in the U.S.-backed Iraqi Reconstruction and Development Council, whom the local people viewed with suspicion, especially those appointed as advisors to key Baghdad ministries operating as "carpetbaggers" and "pawns of the Bush administration" (Gregory 2004, 228). In the words of U.S. Deputy Secretary of Defense Paul Wolfowitz, "It is an enormously valuable asset to have people who share our values, who also understand what we're about as a country" (Cockburn 2003, 28; Jehl 2003). In the runup to establish a provisional national assembly, members of the CPA expressed reservations about open elections. An advisor to the Authority revealingly remarked, "If you move too fast, the wrong people might get elected," prompting the lament "colonial politics as usual" (Hiro 2004, A1; Scheer 2004, 39).

Similar economic changes paved the way for "product dumping" in which an influx of foreign commodities forced thousands of local Iraqi companies out of business. Within days of Order 12 being passed by the CPA, surplus chicken legs from Tyson (a U.S.-based corporation) were shipped to Iraq, depressing the market price of chicken down to $1.25 a kilo: five cents below what Iraqi producers could sustain (Colliers 2003). That form of sudden or "shock" capitalism reached deep into the population, contributing to the 70 percent unemployment within a new economic structure that lacked crucial forms of social welfare (Kramer and Michalowski 2005). Oddly, Iraq remains dependent on imported refined petroleum products because its refinery capacity has not been restored fully after years of deterioration during UN sanctions and damaged further by U.S. military strikes (as well as sabotage by insurgents) (Special Inspector General for Iraq Reconstruction [SIGIR] 2005b). A frustrated filling station attendant complained, "Of all things we never thought we'd be without gasoline in Iraq" (Wong 2003, A1).[8] Columnist Naomi Klein issued a strong rebuke to the American-style reconstruction, writing, "It is robbery, mass theft disguised as charity; privatization without representation. A people, starved and sickened by sanctions, then pulverized by war, is going to emerge from this trauma to find that their country has been sold out from under them (2003b, 32).[9] Of course, after the invasion of Iraq and the toppling of Hussein's government, the nation's political and economic status was in transition and that is why it is important for an occupying power to adhere to the rule of law. The Hague and Geneva rules are intended to protect the democratic sovereignty of populations under occupation by imposing limits on what an occupying power can actually do before a democratic government is established (Wheatcroft 2006). As Keen (2006), Kramer and Michalowski (2005), and Whyte (2007) point out, the CPA acted beyond its limits in ways that have had a lasting impact on the political and economic durability of Iraq and its dependency on external market forces and foreign investors (see Bremer 2006; Hogan, Long, Stretesky, and Lynch 2006; Long, Hogan, Stretesky, and Lynch 2007).

As noted throughout this book, the suspension of law has become a hallmark in the way the United States has administered its war on terror (Agamben 2005; Butler 2004; Ericson 2007). Not only has the departure of the rule of law enabled the United States to reconstruct Iraq in its own image—a colonial other—but it has also undermined significant mechanisms governing accountability. To expedite reform, the CPA established its own methods of distributing revenue from the Defense Fund for Iraq (DFI), thereby producing opportunities for corruption (Harriman 2005, 2006). Some members of Congress found it remarkable that the CPA shipped nearly $12 billion in cash to Iraq (between May 2003 and June 2004) mostly in huge, shrink-wrapped stacks of $100 bills. The House committee investigating the matter calculated that the shipment weighed 363 tons and had to been flown in on wooden pallets aboard giant C-130 military cargo planes. Congressman Henry Waxman (D–CA) wondered, "Who in their right mind would send 360 tons of cash into a war zone? That's exactly what our government did" (Shenon 2007, EV2). Former American civilian administrator in Iraq, Paul Bremmer who stepped down from his post in June 2004, said the CPA had to bring tons of U.S. dollars into Iraq because the country had no functioning banking system. Government auditors, however, have repeatedly criticized the American and Iraqi governments for failing to monitor the money once it reached Iraq. There is strong speculation that some of the cash was pilfered by contractors and military personnel and some believe that some of the money might have ended up with the insurgent groups now battling American troops (Shenon 2007, EV2). In a similar story, the U.S. Government Accountability Office in 2007 estimated that upwards of 100,000 and 300,000 barrels a day of Iraq's declared oil production over the past four years are unaccounted for and could have been siphoned off through corruption or smuggling to aid the insurgency. At an average of $50 a barrel, the discrepancy was valued at $5 million to $15 million a day. "That's a staggering amount of oil to lose every month," said Philip K. Verleger Jr., an independent economist and oil expert. "But given everything else that's been written about Iraq, it's not a surprise" (Glanz 2007a, EV4).

ORDERING IMPUNITY

Adding to mounting evidence that the American government deliberately undermines accountability, formal legal immunity was extended to all U.S. personnel for activities pertaining to the reconstruction of the Iraqi economy. On the same day the CPA was granted authority by United Nations Security Council Resolution 1493, President Bush authorized Executive Order 13303 that shielded any U.S. national from prosecution or another other judicial proceeding from any wrongdoing with respect to the DFI and all Iraqi proceeds. Such legal immunity provides shelter for those engaging in corruption, theft, and embezzlement involving Iraqi oil. Likewise, the CPA issued Order 17 that extended impunity to members of the coalition military forces, foreign missions, and contractors operating in Iraq (Kelly 2004; Whyte 2007). Still, before the CPA was dissolved there appeared to be an opportunity to inspect the authority's financial activities but regulatory agencies were stonewalled, thereby hindering audits by SIGIR (2005a, 2005b, 2006) and the International Advisory and Monitoring Board (IMAB 2005a, 2005b; see Iraqi Revenue Watch 2003, 2004a, 2004b, 2004c, 2004d; Lawson and Halford 2004).

Had careful monitoring been in place during the tenure of the CPA, serious forms of corruption could have been detected, perhaps even prevented. Even so, despite the lack of cooperation on part of the CPA, independent auditing persisted, uncovering financial dealings that occurred in the absence of an adequate system of accounting. KPMG Bahrain (2004) discovered thirty-seven contracts (involving more than $180 million) had been distributed for which no records could be located, blatantly violating UNSCR 1483 stipulations that required a transparent level of administration for the CPA (Catan 2004).

The reconstruction under the tight control of the CPA transferred DFI funds mostly to U.S. contractors.[10] Moreover, under Bremer's stewardship, a CPA executive order blocked the allocation of reconstruction funds to non-coalition partners. Commentators wasted little time mocking what they called "Iraq, Inc." noting that corporate disputes over funding resembled "a pair of undertakers burning down a house, then squabbling over who gets the job of making the coffins" (Steel 2003, 30; Chatterjee 2004; Usborne, Cornwall, and Reeves 2003). A notable member of the "coalition of the billing" is Kellogg Brown and Root (KBR), a subsidiary of Halliburton, where Dick Cheney served as CEO prior to becoming Bush's vice president. A closer look into the roles of Cheney, Halliburton, KBR, and the Bush administration in the reconstruction of Iraq reveals an even more troubling picture (Dean 2004; Keen 2006; Rothe 2006). In 2000, Cheney resigned from Halliburton with a retirement package on a future contract estimated at more than $62 million. Although he sold approximately 660,000 shares of stock (worth $36 million), Cheney continued to retain 433,000 stock options rather than placing those holdings in a blind trust (CBS News 2003; Cook 2003). Senator Frank Lautenberg (2003) issued a congressional report finding that deferred salaries and holding stock options while serving as vice president violated federal ethics standards that bar elected officials from having a financial interest in a private corporation. As Halliburton continued to earn reconstruction contracts for Iraq, Cheney maintained his denial that he was financially benefiting: "I have absolutely no influence of, involvement of, knowledge of in any way, shape, or form of contracts let by the Army Corp of Engineers or anybody else in the Federal Government" (NBC "Meet the Press" 2003; see Hartung 2004).

Even long before Bush-Cheney took office, Halliburton and its subsidiaries (e.g., KBR) have had a long record of violating conditions of government contracts, including blatant overcharging, kickbacks, and cost overruns. During the Clinton administration, eligibility requirements for contractors were strengthened, even barring some companies that had committed infractions in the past. Under those new rules, Halliburton and its associated firms were no longer eligible for government contracts; however, on April 1, 2001, the Bush administration overturned one regulation (65 FR 80255) and replaced it with another (66 FR 17754). As a result, Halliburton and other companies with past violations regained their standing to earn contracts. For Halliburton and KRB, it was business usual. In 2003, the defense department discovered that those companies had overcharged the U.S. government for 57 million gallons of gasoline (worth $61 million) delivered to the Iraq under a no-bid contract (Kelley 2003; Southern Studies 2003/2004). Among other evidence of over-charging and wrongdoing, Halliburton has been cited for bilking the military for dining services, purchasing unnecessary and excessive products, and seek-ing payment for labor never performed; compounding matters, the company also has been implicated in the controversial UN oil-for-food program (Ivanovich 2004; Waxman 2004). The reconstruction effort has proven tremendously profitable for Halliburton since it is "the biggest contractor to the U.S. government in Iraq earning three times as much as Bechtel, its near-est competitor . . . earning $3.9 billion dollars from the military in 2003" (Chatterjee 2004, 39; see Rothe 2006).[11]

Within a zone of little or no regulation, the CPA awarded (mostly American) contracts by utilizing two basic schemes. First, the CPA issued con-tracts according to a no-bid procedure: it has been estimated that 73 percent of contracts worth $5 million were authorized noncompetitively, including KBR's $1.4 billion contract to reconstruct the oil infrastructure (Iraq Revenue Watch 2004d; Tyler and Bonner 2003). In the second scheme, bids were issued under short notice periods, giving insiders who had prior infor-mation of the contract a notable advantage (Whyte 2007). The design of the contract process also featured other mechanisms that promised to funnel even greater funds from the DFI into the deep pockets of contractors: including cost-plus incentives (i.e., merit pay) with scant scrutiny to determine whether the performance goal (e.g., deadline) was met (SIGIR 2005B); overcharging (a maneuver used by KBR to extract an additional $108 in "unresolved costs"; see Willis 2005); the employment of "ghost workers" of nonexistent employ-ees on payrolls that inflated costs (Mekay 2004). The CPA also contributed to an ecology of bribery in which a common method of securing a contract was to issue payoffs upwards of $300,000 (Harriman 2005; SIGIR 2006), thereby institutionalizing corruption in pursuit of maximizing profits (Scheer, Scheer, and Chaudhry 2003). While Whyte (2007) and Kramer and Michalowski (2005) point to enormous evidence of economic war crimes, specifically in violation of UNSCR 1483, it is unlikely that high ranking officials in the CPA and U.S. government would be prosecuted. Even though there have been some "token enforcements" against persons charged with fraud (Willis 2005), there remains a deeper culture of impunity that merely fuels illegal and uneth-ical financial schemes in the reconstruction of Iraq (Christadoulou 2006; Christian Aid 2003; Green and Ward 2004).

The Reconstructed Present

Like other colonial projects, traces of the past are retained in their current form. The prevailing economic infrastructure of the new Iraq was laid firmly by the CPA (Chandrasekaran 2006). To be sure, revamping the previously state-controlled economy so that it would accommodate foreign investment and privatization schemes remained at the center of the CPA's mandate (Goldfarb 2006a, 2006b). Greater reliance on privatization goes beyond plans to expand a market economy from within Iraqi society but also to external entities in the form of military and military-support operations. Since the end of the Cold War, the Pentagon has continued spreading contracts for such jobs as providing security, interrogating prisoners, cooking meals, fixing equipment and constructing bases that were once reserved for soldiers. By the end of 2006, more than 100,000 government contractors were employed in Iraq (not counting subcontractors); that figure is approaching the size of the U.S. military force stationed there and is 10 times the number of contractors that deployed during the Persian Gulf War in 1991. The actual presence of contractors clearly surpasses the Pentagon's previous estimate, which said there were 25,000 security contractors in Iraq (Merle 2006; see Avant 2005).[12]

A key problem with the vast number of contractors working in Iraq—especially in the role of providing security—is the lack of clear oversight since most of those working for private firms go about their business under the radar of the U.S. government. The huge influx of contractors into Iraq "further demonstrates the need for Congress to finally engage in responsible, serious and aggressive oversight over the questionable and growing U.S. practice of private military contracting," said Representative Janice D. Schakowsky (D–IL), who has been critical of the military's reliance on contractors (Merle 2006, D1; see Newburn 2007). But again efforts to obstruct accountability within a free market economy are a chief component of the neoliberal agenda aimed at minimizing government regulation. In the United Kingdom, the Blair government stands accused of reneging on pledges to control private security companies operating in Iraq because it wants to "privatise the war" as part of its exit strategy (Sengupta 2006, EV1). Humanitarian groups, members of Parliament, and international lawyers have called for tighter controls on "mercenaries." John Hilary of War on Want's, an antiwar charity expressed worries that the U.K. government is planning to privatize the occupation in Iraq by allowing "mercenaries" to reap huge profits.[13] At the same time, the U.K. (and U.S.) government have failed to enact laws to punish their human rights abuses, including firing on Iraqi civilians. "How can Tony Blair hope to restore peace and security in Iraq while allowing mercenary armies to operate completely outside the law?" (Sengupta 2006, EV2). Recall that under the CPA's Order 17 all non-Iraqi military personnel and private military contractors were immunized from prosecution for acts performed within terms of their contract by Paul Bremer (see Pincus 2007).

While a committee in the House of Representatives was still trying track down billions of missing dollars in cash shipped to Iraq after the American invasion (mostly in huge, shrink-wrapped stacks of $100 bills; see Shenon 2007) as well as billions of barrels of missing oil (Glanz 2007a, May 12), there are other concerns over accountability, including the billing procedure utilized by contractors. At the center of one investigation is KBR, a company that has been subjected to numerous investigations for billions of dollars in contracts it received for work in Iraq. More recent inquiries focus on allegations that it systematically misused federal rules to withhold basic information on its practices from the U.S. government. Overall, KBR has amassed contracts for more than $20 billion for such services as providing housing, food, fuel, and other necessities for American troops as well as for restoring that country's crucial oil infrastructure. Whereas KBR has been penalized in that past for contract violations, this marks the first time the federal government has weighed in and accused it of systematically engaging in a practice aimed at veiling its business practices in Iraq. The practice in question is the use of the term "proprietary information" that is protected by Federal Acquisition Regulations (FAR). KBR, however, routinely stamped nearly all of the data it collects on its work as proprietary so as to impede deliberately not only the investigations into the company's activities but also things as simple as managerial oversight of the work, constituting an abuse of FAR within the procurement system (Glanz and Norris 2006, EV1). A special inspector general charges that "KBR is not protecting its own data, but is in many instances inappropriately restricting the government's use of information that KBR is required to gather for the government" (Glanz and Norris 2006, EV2). As additional evidence of stonewalling inspectors, KBR would release their financial data in the form of gigantic but indigestible tables rather than within the kind of software (e.g., Excel spreadsheets) that would otherwise permit auditors to perform their calculations. Members of Congress have been blunt in their characterizations KBR. Henry Waxman, the ranking minority member of the House Committee on Government Reform said the KBR's use of the proprietary label, shows how the company had tried to conceal "corporate profiteering during wartime" (Glanz and Norris 2006, EV3; see Dean 2004 for an overview of "stonewalling," a tactic deployed repeatedly by Bush and Cheney).[14]

Systematic attempts to undermine accountability are also evident: this time, however, in the form of legislation. Tucked away in a huge military authorization bill that President Bush executed in 2006 is the termination of a key federal oversight agency. The order comes in the form of an obscure provision that formally closes the Office of the Special Inspector General for Iraq Reconstruction on October 1, 2007. The clause was inserted by the Republicans serving on the House Armed Services Committee over the objections of Democratic counterparts during a closed-door conference, prompting outrage among some lawmakers, who say they were unaware that the provision appeared in the final legislation. At the time of drafting the legislation, the Special Inspector General had been narrowing his investigation of three of the companies with contracts to work in the Iraqi reconstruction: Halliburton, Parsons, and Bechtel (Glanz 2006). As Democrats swept control of the House and Senate in the midterm elections, they vowed to reverse the previous legislation so as to restore the power of the Special Inspector General for Iraq Reconstruction, thereby exposing war profiteering and financial fraud in government contracting. Senator Carl Levin (D–MI) said that he would be looking carefully at military contracting: "There have been serious allegations and evidence of misconduct among suppliers. And the taxpayers, of course, get socked on that. And the troops are not properly taken care of when that happens" (Glanz, Johnston, and Shanker 2006, EV2; see Glanz, 2007b; *New York Times* 2006).

CONCLUSION

By 2007, it had become painfully clear to mainstream Americans that the adventure in Iraq was a mistake (Bonn 2007; Sussman 2007). In addition to enormous death toll to be discussed in the next chapter, there are signs that the basic infrastructure was not being properly reconstructed. The Office of the Special Inspector General for Iraq Reconstruction determined that in a sampling of eight projects declared successes, seven were no longer operating as designed because of plumbing and electrical failures, lack of proper maintenance, apparent looting and expensive equipment that lay idle. At the Baghdad International Airport, for instance, inspectors found that while $11.8 million had been spent on new electrical generators, $8.6 million worth were no longer functioning. In its report, the agency did not pinpoint blame other than recognizing that the reconstruction program suffered from a proper rebuilding budget that should have included enough costs for spare parts, training, stronger construction and other elements that would enable projects continue to function once they have been built (Glanz 2007c).

The report of SIGR not withstanding, other experts have leveled deep criticism for the Bush administration, including the president. Somewhat surprising are comments from the neoconservatives, political pundits otherwise known for their loyalty to the Bush team (see Fukuyama 2006; Tenet 2007). Mirroring the shoddy reconstruction in Iraq, the neocon ideology seems to be dissolving in importance. Long gone are the days in early 2003 when the neocons felt on top of the world. Richard Perl, who chaired the Pentagon's Defense Policy Board Advisory Committee during the planning of Operation Iraqi Freedom, now concedes that Iraq is likely to fall as a "failed state," and then "you'll get all the mayhem that the world is capable of creating" (Rose 2006, EV1). According to Perle, the unfolding catastrophe has a central cause: the devastating dysfunction within the administration of President Bush. Perle adds, "At the end of the day, you have to hold the president responsible" (Rose

2006, EV1; see Shanker 2007a). Kenneth Adelman, a former member of the Defense Policy Board, also issues harsh blame for the failures in Iraq:

> The most dispiriting and awful moment of the whole administration was the day that Bush gave the Presidential Medal of Freedom to [former C.I.A. director] George Tenet, General Tommy Franks, and [Coalition Provisional Authority chief] Jerry [Paul] Bremer—three of the most incompetent people who've ever served in such key spots. And they get the highest civilian honor a president can bestow on anyone! That was the day I checked out of this administration. It was then I thought, There's no seriousness here, these are not serious people. If he had been serious, the president would have realized that those three are each directly responsible for the disaster of Iraq. (Rose 2006, EV6)

Adelman, is noted for his 2002 proclamation that "demolishing Hussein's military power and liberating Iraq would be a cakewalk," but now he laments that neoconservatism itself—what he defines as "the idea of a tough foreign policy on behalf of morality, the idea of using our power for moral good in the world"—is dead, at least for a generation (Rose 2006, EV3; see Jacques 2006).

While neocons sanctimoniously snipe at fellow political insiders for the misadventure in Iraq, scholars are committed to putting those events in their proper social, political, and economic contexts. Whyte concludes, "In Iraq, war crimes and offences against Iraqi oil wealth powerfully combined to establish a neoliberal colonial order. Just as the violation of basic principles of international law was a necessary precondition for the capture of the economy, the endemic corruption that we have witnessed in Iraq was a key element of the regime of occupation" (2007, 191–192). He goes on to remind us that similar forms of capitalist development unfolding in Iraq display the tendencies of early modern state formation, particularly where economic activities intersect with violence, piracy, and organized crime (Gallant 1999; Tilly 1985). Corruption under CPA rule extended the structural advantages necessary for foreign interests to infiltrate and transform the economy in their image, becoming what Gregory (2004) calls the colonial other (see Ali 2003a, 2003b).

Of course, the process of ordering Iraq (or disordering as some critics would claim) marks a colonial project occurring within a larger campaign against terror that has resorted to unprecedented military force. Deeply embedded in that form of power are significant features of culture that facilitate victimization on a mass scale (Hagan and Greer 2002; Hagan and Levi 2005; Hagan, Rymond-Richmond, and Parker 2005; Kauzlarich, Matthews, and Miller 2001).

> For the war on terror is an attempt to establish a new global narrative in which the power to narrate is vested in a particular constellation of power

and knowledge within the United States of America. . . . The colonial present is not produced through geopolitics and geoeconomics alone, through foreign and economic policy set into motion by presidents, prime ministers and chief executives, the state, the military apparatus and transnational corporations. It is also set into motion through mundane cultural forms and cultural practices that mark other people irredeemably "Other" and that license the unleashing of exemplary violence against them. (Gregory 2004, 16)

As we turn to the next chapter, primarily attending to the civilian population in Iraq, we should bear in mind the cultural lessons drawn from the colonial present in combination with states of exception (Agamben 2005). Together, we witness the formation of spaces of exception consisting of certain zones in which the "other" is subjected to lethal victimization, casually written off as collateral damage in pursuit of military victory.

CHAPTER 7

Collateral Damage

As the insurgency in Iraq escalates, so does has the U.S. military's response, perpetuating a cycle of violence that envelopes not only combatants but also civilians caught in the middle. In one of the many battles over Fallujah, there remain questions concerning the U.S. bombing of the Central Health Center on November 9, 2004. Whereas the U.S. military has dismissed accounts of the health center bombing as unsubstantiated, Dr. Samil al-Jumaili who was working at the center at the time of the incident said that American warplanes dropped three bombs on the clinic where approximately sixty patients were being treated, many of whom had serious injuries from previous U.S. aerial bombings and attacks. Dr. al-Jumaili reported that 35 patients were killed in the airstrike, including two girls and three boys under the age of 10. He said, fifteen medics, four nurses and five support staff also died after the entire health center—a protected institution under international law—collapsed on the patients. According to James Ross, Human Rights Watch, "the onus would be on the U.S. government to demonstrate that the hospital was being used for military purposes and that its response was proportionate. Even if there were snipers there it would never justify destroying the hospital" (Schuman 2004, 5–6). The Association of Humanitarian Lawyers has petitioned the Inter-American Commission on Human Rights of the Organization of American States to investigate the incident. Similarly, international law experts said that U.S. soldiers might have committed a war crime on November 11, 2004 when they sent fleeing Iraqi civilians back into Fallujah. Citing several articles of the Geneva Conventions, they said that established laws of war require military forces to protect civilians as refugees and must not return them to a combat zone. Jordan Paust, a law professor at the University of Houston and former army prosecutor said, "This is highly problematical conduct in terms of exposing people to grave danger by returning them to an area where fighting is going on." Similarly, Ross added "If that's what happened, it would be a war crime" (Janofsky 2004, A8).

INTRODUCTION

The previous chapter offered a critical view aimed at the economic infrastructure as it undergoes colonial reconstruction. Not to be neglected in a far-reaching analysis is the devastation wreaked on the Iraqi people. In the attempt to order the country, there is tremendous disorder that produces collateral damage: a military euphemism referring to the unintended wounding or killing of noncombatants. The following pages exhibit serious incidents of bombs veering off course, errant machine gun firings, false arrests and detentions, etc. As tragic as collateral damage is, regrettably there is little recourse. Although some families have received financial compensation for errors in the use of lethal force, the vast majority of victimizations often go without formal acknowledgement by the U.S. military (Keen 2006; Shiner 2007). In the absence of such recognition rests impunity, the failure to hold specific wrong-doers accountable for mistakes or deliberate acts of war crimes.

Impunity in the war in Iraq derives from denial that may transpire at the individual, organizational, or state levels (see S. Cohen 2001). The invasion and its collateral damage are consequences of several interlocking denials from the Bush administration. Against the backdrop of the myth over Iraq's weapons of mass destruction, the Pentagon claims that the U.S. military is not an occupying power, evidently so as to skirt its responsibilities. In response, U.N. Secretary General Kofi Annan, fully aware that the United States and the United Kingdom had invaded Iraq without the authorization of the Security Council, demanded that the coalition adhere to the requirements of international law. Annan's statement infuriated the U.S. envoy to the U.N. Human Rights Commission, arguing that the war was legal and that the coalition is not an occupying power but rather a liberating force (Fowler 2003). The U.S. position squarely contradicts the Hague Convention (1907) and the Fourth Geneva Convention (1949) which specify that the laws of belligerent occupation come into effect the moment a territory is occupied by adversaries. Unequivocally, international law takes effect when the attacker imposes control over an invaded area; furthermore, the entire country need not by conquered before the laws governing occupation actually apply (Fallows 2004).

"Occupation is a matter of fact—not of intention or declaration—and the United States army's own manual acknowledges 'the primacy of fact as the test of whether or not occupation exists'" (Gregory 2004, 219; Schmitt 2003). As a result, an occupying power is responsible for not only restoring public order but also preventing looting and protecting civilians. Secretary of Defense Donald Rumsfeld stunned international law experts with his blithe refusal to command U.S. troops to intervene against criminal acts (e.g., widespread looting), saying, "Freedom's untidy. Stuff happens. Free people are free to make mistakes and commit crimes and do bad things" (Fisk 2003a, 22; Whitaker 2003). Postwar assessments found that some military officers were confused over being called liberators rather than occupiers, leaving them and their soldiers uncertain about their legal authority to stop looting and imposing curfews (Lumpkin and Linzer 2003). Further reports found that in some instances U.S. soldiers encouraged looters and engaged in theft themselves (McGrory 2003; Squitieri 2003). The U.S. Army's field manual states clearly that in the aftermath of war, the army has the duty to ensure public safety. Still, months after the invasion, the International Crisis Group inspected Baghdad to find a city in disarray and chaos, concluding that the coalition's failure to instill civil order was a "reckless abdication of the occupying powers' obligation to protect the population" (2003, 1; see Paust 2003).

This chapter examines closely the range and depth of collateral damage in Iraq. It draws on the work of Kramer and Michalowski (2005), which provides a criminological interpretation of war crimes and other failures to uphold the rule of law. Developing further a conceptual perspective on the human toll, the analysis reaches beyond descriptive accounts of violations of international law (e.g., failure to protect civilians, deliberate acts of violence against noncombatants, abusing and killing detainees). To that end, the discussion incorporates recent writings of Agamben (1998) and Gregory (2004), both of whom see Foucault as a starting point toward deciphering the role that social space plays in marginalizing certain people. Collateral damage occurs within a particular zone of impunity that Agamben and Gregory refer to as the spaces of exception. Similarly, Gilroy (2003) contributes to a sharp critique of collateral damage by turning attention to imperial topographies that privilege some victims of war (e.g., U.S. soldiers) while casting a blind eye onto others, namely innocent civilians. The chapter closes with some final observations on other aspects of the human toll in Iraq, in particular the plight of millions of refugees flooding into neighboring countries.

HUMAN TOLL IN IRAQ

With the myth of weapons of mass destruction widely dispelled, the Bush administration has repositioned the war on terror as its leading motive for invading and occupying Iraq. In the face of calls for the withdrawal of U.S. military, White House spokesman Tony Snow reasserted the administration's view: "Iraq is the central front in the war on terror" (Stout 2007a, EV1). While observing a solemn Memorial Day in 2007 when nearly 3,500 had been killed while on duty in Iraq, the president expressed deep sympathy to the families affected, assuring them that Americans would not forget their terrible loss. That same day, Vice President Cheney took a bolder tone by announcing at the U.S. Military Academy at West Point: "We're fighting a war on terror because the enemy attacked us first, and hit us hard" (Stolberg 2007, EV2). Absent from the Bush team's public outpouring of grief for U.S. soldiers cut down in the war, however, is any mention of the civilians who have died, or been injured or displaced due to the rampant violence that continues long after the Pentagon announced in May 2003 that major U.S. military actions had come to a close. Those victims of collateral damage have yet to become an overarching concern for the White House as well as for much of the American public, even though the human toll in terms of casualties continues to mount (see www.iraqbodycount.net). The United Nations report lists October 2006 as the deadliest month for civilians, when 3,709 Iraqis were killed, an increase that underscores the growing cost of a deepening sectarian war. The figures have been a point of contention for the government of Prime Minister Nuri Kamal al-Maliki, which suppressed them in September, claiming the number of deaths was exaggerated. The American military has also criticized the figures as high, but it does not release statistics of its own. "We have a situation in which impunity prevails," said Gianni Magazzeni, chief of the United Nations' Human Rights Office in Baghdad, which compiled the report. "It's critically important for the government to ensure that justice is done" (Tavernise 2006, EV2; see Cloud and Gordon 2006).

As noted previously, Kramer and Michalowski (2005) issue sharp criticism for the Bush administration's unwillingness to abide by international human-itarian law (IHL, or law of armed conflict). Most notably fault is located in the following areas: the failure of the occupying power to secure public safety and protect civilian rights; indiscriminate responses to Iraqi resistance that have contributed to a greater number of civilian casualties; war crimes against civil-ians as well as the abuse and torture of Iraqi prisoners (see Parenti 2004; Welch 2006a). To provide a fuller account of the war in Iraq and more importantly its lasting impact on the civilian population, this section sets out to specify cer-tain events and developments. Because of constraints on space, the examina-tion has limits; nonetheless, it does offer a sketch of the human toll in Iraq as violence rages.

Failing to Protect Civilians

In 2005, on a simmering hot Iraqi morning, thirty-four boys who were scooping up candy thrown from an U.S. military Humvee were killed in a sudden flash of smoke and metal. All but four were younger than fifteen. The youngest victim was six. A total of twenty-nine families lost children, one lost three sons. Moments following the blast, the world narrowed for Sattar Hashim, a thirty-nine-year-old security guard whose son had rushed to see the American patrol. As Sattar frantically moved through the wreckage, he found his son unconscious, his body torn by shrapnel. Several hours later, his son died in a hospital operating room. It is estimated that more than 3,000 Iraqis were dying each monh of the war—roughly the total deaths in the attacks of September 11. Beyond the occasional news coverage on civilian deaths in the Western media, the impact of the war is felt in Iraqi neighborhoods where families **struggle** with the intense pain of loss. Suicide bombings stop nearby clocks, **a morbid** signature that freezes in time the precise moment of the blast. For the **parents** in Naariya, the clocks ceased at just after ten in the morning. More **than a year** later, many residents have been unable to reassemble their lives. **Some spouses** drift apart in the absence of their children while others switch **jobs or simply** quit working altogether. Remnants of loss persist. At the **elementary schools,** class sizes are noticeably smaller. Athletic contests for **young children no** longer take place, and hobbies such as bug collecting no **longer attract interest.** "Our life now, it's not a life, it's a kind of dream," said Qais Ataiwee Yaseen, whose two boys, ages eight and eleven, were killed that day. "Life has no taste. I even feel sick of myself." Another mourning parent, Hadi Faris, stopped working as a driver because he could not keep his mind on the road. "I kept thinking how life is cheap, how so many innocent people are killed" (Tavernise 2007, EV1–2).

As the occupying power, the United States has an obligation to provide public safety and protect civilian rights in the wake of widespread violence and looting along with home demolitions and arbitrary arrests leading to detentions (Amnesty International 2004). While the pillaging of department stores and archaeology museums were deliberately ignored by U.S. forces, its failure to secure a site containing stockpiles of weapons and tons of munitions has clearly contributed to the insurgency as attacks and bombings occur daily with no end in sight (Keen 2006). Because of the expanding insurgency, serious concern also has turned to the black market that has benefited—inadvertently—from the Pentagon. The Special Inspector General for Iraq Reconstruction has estimated that 4 percent (about 14,000) of weapons delivered to the Iraqi army and police have gone missing, most of them pistols. The weapons are easy to find for Iraqi locals, resting among others in the semihidden street markets. Proprietors show journalists samples for immediate purchase and offer to take orders: ten guns can be found in less than two hours, and a hundred or more can be located for the next day's business. In particular three kinds of American-issued weapons are now available in various shops: Glock and Walther nine-millimeter pistols, and pristine, unused Kalashnikovs from post-Soviet Eastern European countries; they are among the principal types of the 370,000 weapons purchased by the United States for Iraq's security forces. That program was criticized by a special inspector general in 2006 for failing to properly account for the arms. "Every type of gun that the Americans give comes to the market. They go from the U.S. Army to the Iraqi Army to the smugglers. I have captured many of these guns that the terrorists bought," says Brig. Hassan Nouri, chief of the political investigations bureau for the Sulaimaniya district (Chivers 2006, EV4). One arms dealer explains that almost all of the weapons come from the Iraqi army soldiers and policemen, "They are our best suppliers." Tracing American-issued weapons back to

Iraqi units that sell them has proven impossible since the United States did not register serial numbers for almost all of the small arms purchased for Iraqi security forces. The weapons were paid for with $133 million from the Iraq Relief and Reconstruction Fund (Chivers 2006, EV5).

To be sure, the failure to secure Iraq goes beyond missing weapons. There are deep societal divisions in Iraq that continue to pull the nation—perhaps the region—into civil chaos. The degree of sectarian violence, however, does not excuse the United States from its obligations as an occupying power to provide safety; moreover, it merely confirms its inability to meet its responsibilities to protect civilians against harm, whatever the source. Far from the days when neocons described the invasion, occupation, and reconstruction as a "cake-walk," Iraq's future as safe and prosperous society is in grave doubt (Rose 2006). At the end of 2006, former Secretary of State James A. Baker III issued an assessment of Iraq that has been characterized as "a devastating critique and an official certification of a failed policy," according to Richard Holbrooke, former U.S. ambassador to the United Nations (R. Cohen 2006, EV3). Civilians have indeed taken notice.

> I am facing the most difficult times of my life here in Baghdad. Since I am a Sunni, I became a target to be killed. You know that our army and police are Shia, so every checkpoint represents a serious threat to Sunnis. During the last three weeks, two of my friends were killed at check points belonging to the police. They first asked to show IDs and when they saw the Sunni family name, they killed them. (Cohen 2006, EV2)

Baker—well known as a political "realist"—recommended that the United States ease out of Iraq, leaving the chores of public safety to the Iraqi Army and police, even though they have proven to be less than neutral. Even optimistic military leaders, such as Lieutenant-General Peter W. Chiarelli, who commands American forces in Iraq, rates the Iraqi Army as "fragile" while also acknowledging that the Shia-controlled police force is using its "authority" to settle the score with rival Sunnis (Cohen 2006, EV3). At the core of the Baker's report are fundamental political and economic reforms: rapid provincial elections, fairer distribution of oil revenue, the reintegration of Baathists and constitutional reform (see Sanger and Cloud 2006). What the Iraqi Study Group fails to acknowledge, however, is that much of the sectarian violence and insurgency are products of failed efforts to colonize Iraq (see Ali 2003a, 2003b; Gilroy 2003).

Acting with Deliberate Violence

Apart from scenarios whereby civilians get stuck in the crossfire, there are other incidents in which innocent people have been direct targets of violence carried out by U.S. military personnel. Consider the killings in Haditha on

November 19, 2005, where U.S. marines killed twenty-four Iraqi civilians, including ten women and children and an elderly man in a wheelchair. The actual details of the violence and the events lead up to deaths continue to unfold amid investigations by military officials. Thus far, investigators have corroborated testimonies by townspeople have said that marines overreacted to a fatal roadside bombing.[1] Over the course of five hours, the squad reportedly dispersed and called in reinforcements. Staff Sergeant Frank D. Wuterich said that he had quickly set up a defensive perimeter around the convoy. Nearby a white car with five men inside was spotted; the marines suspected that those men were spotters for the bomb. Several marines approached the car, shouting commands in broken Arabic. Rather than following orders to halt, the men jumped out of the car and the marines shot them down. Residents watching the episode, however, issue a contradictory account of what happened.[2] Investigators uncovered photographs revealing that the positions of the corpses and pooling of their blood are inconsistent with the marines' version that the Iraqi men were shot as they fled.

Following the explosion, the marines have said they came under small-arms fire from a nearby house. A four-man "stack" of marines then broke into the house. Although no one was found in the first room, noises were heard from behind a door. A marine rolled in a grenade while another marine fired blind "clearing rounds" into the room. The technique known as "clearing by fire" or "peppering" involves sticking a weapon around and spray the room. "You've got to do whatever it takes to get home. If it takes clearing by fire where there's civilians, that's it," explained one marine (Broder 2006, EV5). Such tactics are common in areas known to provide safe refuge for insurgents, including Haditha, deep in Sunni-dominated Anbar Province, where for months in 2005 marines had been ambushed. "Saying who's a civilian or a 'muj' in Iraq, you really can't," added a marine, "That's how wishy-washy it was. This town did not want us there at all." Neal A. Puckett, a lawyer for the marines, in Haditha said they were operating within established rules when they cleared the house. In the aftermath of the "clearing rounds," however, the marines found seven civilians dead, including two women and a four-year-old boy. Two young children survived the attack by hiding under a bed; another child and a woman escaped. Upon finding a back door open, Puckett said, the marines believed to be in "hot pursuit" of an insurgent gunman, bursting into a second house and using assault rifles and grenades to clear a room. There eight civilians were fatally shot, including two women and five children ages three to fourteen (Broder 2006, EV6). Investigators later learned that the wounds of the dead Iraqis, as seen in photographs and viewed by the morgue director, were inconsistent with attacks by fragmentation grenades and indiscriminate rifle fire. The survivors of the assault said the victims were shot at close range, some while trying to protect their children or praying for their lives. The death certificates examined were chillingly succinct: "well-aimed shots to the head and chest" (Broder 2006, EV6). Moreover, had the marines violently cleared the houses using automatic weapons and fragmentation grenades, there would be ample evidence of damage and bullet marks in the walls; investigators found the walls to be in normal condition.

Following the clearing of the second house, Staff Sergeant Frank D. Wuterich, the leader of the squad realized there had been a significant number of civilian deaths, and reported that there had been "collateral damage" from the operations. Before its conclusion, marines killed four more men in a third house, one of whom was armed with an AK-47, according to Puckett's account; another unit shot a forty-five-year-old man they believed was carrying a weapon—the item was actually a cane. Soon other marines reported to the scene to evacuate the wounded and bundle up the dead.

> When they found civilians had been killed, a marine said, Sergeant Wuterich "was pretty torn up about it. He was pretty remorseful." Captain McConnell, the same marine said, refused a request later that day to have a tank fire on a house considered threatening, saying, "There could be women and children. We've had enough women and children die today." (Broder 2006, EV7)

The next day, a press release issued by the marines reported that fifteen Iraqi civilians had been killed in a bombing in Haditha and that marines had killed eight insurgents after they opened fire on squad. Despite evidence to the contrary, the statement was not corrected or retracted (Broder 2006). The killings have been described as "methodical in nature," and, as John Sifton of Human Rights Watch observed, "If the accounts as they have been alleged are true, the Haditha incident is likely the most serious war crime that has been reported in Iraq since the beginning of the war." Said Sifton. "Here we have two dozen civilians being killed—apparently intentionally. This isn't a gray area. This is a massacre" (Shanker, Schmitt, and Oppel 2006, EV7). In an unusual sign of high-level concern, the commandant of the Marine Corps, General Michael W. Hagee, flew from Washington to Iraq to deliver a series of speeches to his forces, emphasizing the importance of international laws of armed conflict, the Geneva Conventions and the American military's own rules of engagement.

In December 2006, more than a year after the killings, four enlisted men charged with unpremeditated murder. Sergeant Wuterich was charged with killing thirteen Iraqis. Sergeant De La Cruz, a lance corporal at the time, was charged with five counts of murder. Lance Corporal Sharratt, a marine rifleman, was charged with three counts of murder. Lance Corporal Tatum was charged with murder in the death of two Iraqis, negligent homicide in the deaths of four others, and assault (Von Zielbauer and Marshall 2006).[3]

Five months later, a military investigation has found that senior Marine Corps commanders in showed a routine disregard for the lives of Iraqi civilians that contributed to a "willful" failure to investigate the killings in Haditha. The report did not conclude that the senior officers covered up evidence or committed a crime; however, it found that the Marine Corps command in Iraq was far too willing to tolerate civilian casualties and dismiss Iraqi claims of abuse by marines as insurgent. The investigation puts blame on the marine leadership for fostering a perception that civilian Iraqi lives were insignificant. General Bargewell wrote in the report,

> All levels of command tended to view civilian casualties, even in significant numbers, as routine and as the natural and intended result of insurgent tactics. Statements made by the chain of command during interviews for this investigation, taken as a whole, suggest that Iraqi civilian lives are not as important as U.S. lives, their deaths are just the cost of doing business, and that the Marines need to get the job done no matter what it takes." (Von Zielbauer 2007a, EV2; 2007b, 2007c)

Regrettably, other Iraqi civilians have been victimized by U.S. military. Steven Dale Green, a former Army private, faces federal criminal charges for shooting four family members, including a child, with an AK-47 assault rifle on March 12 (2006) near Mahmudiya. The complaint specifies that Green and the four other soldiers charged in the case drank alcohol, changed into black clothes, and then raided the home of a husband and wife and their two daughters. Green is reported to have entered a room and killed the parents and the younger daughter. Then he and a second soldier raped the fourteen year old, shot her several times, and tried to burn her body. After the incident, Green was granted an honorable discharge under guidelines that required a medical finding that he was suffering from a severe personality disorder. Adding to the controversy, Army regulations prohibit commanders from discharging soldiers found to have personality disorders if the action is intended "to spare a soldier who may have committed serious acts of misconduct" from prosecution by military authorities (Cloud 2006, EV2; see Dwyer and Worth 2006). The Green case is one of several 2006 incidents in which American military personnel have come under investigation in killings of unarmed Iraqis. Although no American serviceman has been executed since 1961, new cases in Iraq have led to charges against sixteen who may face the death penalty in connection with the killing of Iraqi civilians throughout the first three years of the war, and the overall number is expected to grow as more incidents are undergoing investigation (Worth 2006a).[4] Among other factors is the role of multiple tours in Iraq. "They can become almost numb to the killing," said Charles W. Gittins, a former marine and a lawyer who has represented marines accused of murder in Iraq. "The more you're in it, the more you want to live through it.

You think more about preserving your own life than about what's the right thing to do" (Worth 2006a). In terms of prosecution, however, the definition of murder can be far more elusive in a war zone than in civilian life; some previous criminal cases, accused servicemen have claimed they acted in self-defense or carrying out mercy killings.[5]

In the heaviest penalty delivered thus far, Sergeant Michael P. Williams was sentenced to life in prison after being convicted of premeditated murder in 2005 in the killing of two Iraqi civilians in Baghdad; the sentence was later reduced to twenty-five years. Numerous obstacles undermine the prosecution's efforts to convict servicemen of crimes against civilians during wartime. Eugene R. Fidell, a specialist in military law, says, "I think there's a recognition that these are weird environments. The danger is, carried to an extreme, can mean throwing the law books out" (Worth 2006a, EV4). Recovering credible evidence in Iraq's chaos can be very difficult, and Iraqi witnesses are open to challenge. As Gittins remarks, "Jury members who have served in Iraq know that it is pretty common for Iraqis to lie to Americans. Also, the military pays the relatives of civilians who are killed—so they have an incentive to lie" (Worth 2006a, EV4). Equally important to consider is that some members of the military juries who have served in Iraq are familiar with the chaotic atmosphere surrounding any decision to use force. "The presumption of innocence is going to reign supreme," Gittens said (Worth 2006a, EV4).

Abusing and Killing Detainees

Detainees are a unique class of civilians in a war zone, and because of the nature of their confinement, they are particularly vulnerable to abuse, torture, and murder. As numerous incidents demonstrate, the degree of official responsibility for such violence runs extremely low, especially in the midst of urban warfare (Danner 2004; Harbury 2005; Hersh 2004). The legacy of Abu Ghraib holds that those particular human rights abuses would be blamed solely on a handful of reservists featured in the photographs and not on high-level military officers. Multiple examinations of the controversy reveal evidence that the Pentagon along with the White House perpetuated a culture of impunity in which ranking military leadership and key policymakers are immune from accountability and punishment (Greenberg and Dratel 2005; Welch 2006a). John Yoo, a law professor at the University of California, and a former justice department official who participated in the development of the administration's early legal response to the terrorist threat, continues to defends his work: "At the Justice Department we did not think the Geneva Conventions applied in the war against Al Qaeda because they did not sign the Geneva Conventions, and they don't follow any of the rules of warfare" (Stanley 2007, EV3). As discussed in detail in chapter 5, the Bush team put a heavy premium on intelligence gathering as one of the most important weapons against

terrorism; in doing so, it pressured military commanders to produce information about the insurgency, but was determined to remain fully uninformed as
to how it was done (see Cohen 2006; 2001). At Abu Ghraib, thousands of
detainees were guarded by a few hundred soldiers who appeared not to know
the boundaries of lawful conduct: "It was never clear to me what was allowed
and what wasn't allowed in Iraq," Ken Davis, a military policeman, recalls. "No
one ever could make anything clear to me. When the questions were asked, it
was like, Hey, I don't know" (Stanley 2007, EV3). Still, military intelligence
interrogators were calling the shots and relied on untrained troops filling in as
prison guards to soften up suspects. "This guy needs to have a bad night,"
Davis says he was told, "Use your imagination" (Stanley 2007, EV3; see
Kennedy 2007).

While much public and political attention has been directed at the horrors of Abu Ghraib (see McCoy 2006; Welch 2006a), there has been less focus
on the abuse and torture of detainees held elsewhere in Iraq.[6] Before and even
during the Abu Ghraib investigation, three former members of the Army's
elite 82nd Airborne Division say soldiers in their battalion at Camp Mercury
near Fallujah routinely beat and abused prisoners in an effort to gather intelligence on the insurgency—as well as to amuse themselves (Human Rights
Watch 2005; Schmitt 2005). As noted previously, one soldier admitted to abusing and humiliating detainees. "We would give them blows to the head, chest,
legs and stomach, and pull them down, kick dirt on them. This happened
every day" The sergeant continued, "Some days we would just get bored, so
we would have everyone sit in a corner and then make them get in a pyramid.
This was before Abu Ghraib but just like it. We did it for amusement" (Schmitt
2005, A1, A6). The sergeant explained that military intelligence personnel
instructed us to soften up detainees to make them more cooperative during
interrogations. "They wanted intel. As long as no PUC's [Persons under
Control] came up dead, it happened." He added, "We kept it to broken arms
and legs and shit." In one disclosure a sergeant said he had seen a soldier break
open a chemical light stick and beat the detainees with it. "That made them
glow in the dark, which was real funny, but it burned their eyes, and their skin
was irritated real bad" (Human Rights Watch 2005, 2). Those testimonies contradict claims by the Bush team that detainee abuses by U.S. military abroad
have been infrequent, exceptional and unrelated to policy.[7]

In 2007, Laith al-Ani was finally released after being detained for more
than two years the American-run jail, Camp Bucca in southern Iraq. During
which time, he was never charged with a crime and was questioned only once.
Ani and other former detainees characterized the sprawling complex of barracks as a bleak place where guards casually used their stun guns for infractions
as minor as speaking out of turn. Ani said detainees were exposed to long periods of extreme heat and cold.[8] Inside detainees fought among themselves and

extremist elements tried to radicalize others, but together responded to the harsh conditions with hunger strikes and occasional violent protests. U.S. detention officials acknowledged that guards used electric devices called Tasers to control detainees, but they insisted they did so infrequently and only when the guards were physically threatened. Ani said it was while being transported to Camp Bucca when he was first shocked by an electric prod, describing the device as black plastic with a yellow tip and two iron prongs: "I was talking to someone next to me and they used it" (Moss and Mekhennet 2007, EV3). He went on to say the prods were commonly used on him and other detainees as punishment. "The whole body starts to shake and hurt," Ani said. "And you lose consciousness for a couple of seconds. One time they used it on my tongue. One guard held me from the left and another on my back and another used it against my tongue and for four or five days I couldn't eat" (Moss and Mekhennet 2007, EV3).[9] Lieutenant-Colonel Keir-Kevin Curry, a detention system spokesman, said, "Every use of less than lethal force, to include use of Tasers, is formally reported by facility leadership, ensuring soldiers are in accordance with proper use. Touching a Taser to someone's tongue is not one of the approved uses" (Moss and Mekhennet 2007, EV4).

Ani also said the tension at the camp was compounded by some of the guards who did not respect the Islam faith. One day the guards searched a makeshift prayer area, Ani said, "and they started to step on the Korans, which fell down," then "a fight started," he continued. "There was a huge demonstration. The prisoners started to throw their shoes at the guards, and we started to beat them with empty plastic bottles. The guards shot at us with rubber bullets, but then prisoners were killed and others were injured" (Moss and Mekhennet 2007, EV5). In January 2005, a Pentagon statement described the incident, concluding that four detainees were killed when guards were compelled to use deadly force to quell the riot which was set off by a search for contraband. Colonel Curry said an investigation determined that a detainee leader had fabricated the Koran allegations to instigate violence (Moss and Mekhennet 2007, EV5). Ani and other former detainees said Camp Bucca was rife with frequent demonstrations to protest various grievances, prompting many detainees to participate in hunger strikes. Upon release, Ani was transferred to Camp Cropper in Baghdad where U.S. military officials gave him twenty-five dollars so he and his family could hire a taxi. During their journey back home, they had to dodge Shiite-controlled checkpoints; days later, Ani—a Sunni—narrowly escaped capture by a Shiite militia.

Pentagon reports on the mistreatment of detainees in Iraq (and Guantánamo Bay and Afghanistan) give continued cause for concern. For instance, a 2006 investigation found that U.S. special operations troops employed a set of harsh, unauthorized interrogation techniques against detainees long after approval for their use was rescinded.[10] Special operations troops, working with more latitude than other military units, are reported to have fed some detainees only bread or crackers and water if they did not cooperate with interrogators. One prisoner was fed only bread and water for seventeen days and others were locked for as many as seven days in cells so small that they could neither stand nor lie down, while interrogators blasted loud music that disrupted their sleep. In addition to the continued use of military dogs that traumatize detainees, the inquiry discovered that some detainees were stripped naked, drenched with water and then interrogated in air-conditioned rooms or in cold weather. Members of the navy Seals had used that technique in the case of one detainee who died after questioning in Mosul (Iraq) in 2004. Nonetheless, Brigadier-General Richard P. Formica of the army recommended that none of the service members be disciplined. While conceding that their conduct was wrong it was not deliberate abuse. The general faulted "inadequate policy guidance" rather than "personal failure" for the mistreatment, and cited the dangerous environment in which special operations forces carried out their duties (Schmitt 2007, EV3; see Zernike 2006).

It is precisely in the tense ecology of war, compounded with ambiguous commands laced with the pressure of loyalty, where abuse and even murder can occur. Consider the case involving Sgt. Lemuel Lemus who defended his unit after it shot and killed three Iraqi detainees after a raid northwest of Baghdad on May 9, 2006. Lemus insisted, "Proper escalation of force was used" (Worth 2006b, EV). Later his account of the incident changed for the worse. Lemus concedes that he witnessed a deliberate plot by his fellow soldiers to kill the three handcuffed Iraqis. Members of the unit then planned to cover up the incident by inflicting wounds on each another so as to give their story more weight. The squad leader threatened to kill anyone who talked to authorities. Four soldiers have since been charged with premeditated murder in the case and lawyers for two of them say the soldiers were given an order by a decorated colonel on the day in question to "kill all military-age men," a command that constitutes blunt breach of the law of war (Worth 2006b, EV1).[11] Asked why he did not try to stop the other soldiers from carrying out the killings, Lemus said simply that he feared reprisals and being labeled a coward, adding he acted because of "peer pressure, and I have to be loyal to the squad" (Worth 2006b, July 28, EV1). Lemus' initial reluctance to keep quiet about war crimes parallels a recent Pentagon study that found only 40 percent of U.S. marines and 55 percent of soldiers in Iraq say they would report a fellow service member for killing or injuring an innocent Iraqi. The survey of 1,320 soldiers and 447 marines reveals that about 10 percent said they had mistreated civilians through physical violence or damage to personal property. Well over a third of soldiers and marines believed that torture should be allowed to gain information that could save the lives of American troops, or knowledge about insurgents. In addition, the study shows the increasing rates of mental health problems for troops on extended or multiple deployments. "Soldiers with high levels of anger, who had experienced high levels of combat or who screened positive for mental health symptoms, were nearly twice as likely to mistreat noncombatants," said acting Army surgeon general, Major-General Gale S. Pollock (Reuters 2007, EV1; see www.armymedicine.army.mil).The survey data was released one month after Defense Secretary Robert M. Gates extended tours for soldiers in Iraq and Afghanistan to up to fifteen months (from twelve), under a security plan ordered by President Bush (see Frosch 2007).

The use of extraordinary renditions is explored in chapter 9, but similar forms of outsourcing abuse are evident in Iraq. In one of the newly formed joint American-Iraqi security stations in Baghdad, Captain Darren Fowler heaped praise on his Iraqi counterparts for capturing three insurgent suspects who furnished detailed information about plans to plant bombs. The Iraqi officers beamed with pride even though their tactics to extract confessions clearly violate the U.S. Army's field manual, as well as U.S. and Iraqi laws. Before handing over the detainees to the Americans, the Iraqi soldiers had inflicted a firm beating on one of the suspects. The fresh stripes on the detainee's back appeared to be the product of a whipping with electrical cables. "I prepared him for the Americans and let them take his confession," Captain Bassim Hassan said through an interpreter. "We know how to make them talk. We know their back streets. We beat them. I don't beat them that much, but enough so he feels the pain and it makes him desperate" (Rubin 2007, EV2). Well-publicized photos of American soldiers and contractors abusing detainees at Abu Ghraib linger in the minds of many Iraqis, further undermining efforts to win the hearts and minds of local people. Moreover, such techniques produced little valuable information. Coerced confessions are an unreliable way to learn about enemy operations because people being tortured will often appear to cooperate so as to stop their suffering (see McCoy 2006). Nonetheless, abuse persists as a seemingly nasty necessity in the war on terror. Captain Fowler was asked whether he was aware that the information was given only after the Iraqis had beaten the detainee: "They are not supposed to do that," he said. "What I don't see, I don't know, and I can't stop. The detainees are deathly afraid of being sent to the Iraqi justice system, because this is the kind of thing they do. But this is their culture" (Rubin 2007, EV5).

HOMO SACER AND SPACES OF EXCEPTION

Descriptive accounts of collateral damage are truly disturbing. Still, in an effort to advance a deeper understanding of the human toll in Iraq it is important to consider some theoretical critiques of power, particularly those of Agamben, Foucault, and Gregory. Together, those works help explain how innocent people in a war zone become trapped in a unique social space that increases their vulnerabilities. In his writing on the subject, Agamben (1998) proposes the idea of *homo sacer* ("sacred man") to interpret the impunity of lethal force carried out against certain groups of people. Under ancient Roman law, he observes, some persons could not be sacrificed according to ritual because they resided outside divine law; hence, their deaths were of no value to the gods. They could, however, still be killed because they were also situated beyond juridical law, meaning their lives were of no value to their contemporaries. The authority that holds the power to make such designations is the sovereign since it is he that decides the exception (Schmitt 1985). Agamben's project is interesting here because it involves a reworking of Foucault's genealogy of modern power in an attempt to add sharper resolution to biopolitics and the sovereign (see Edkins 2000).

As discussed in chapter 2, Agamben (2005) writes at length about states of exception that refer to distinct historical moments that produce suspensions of law. Correspondingly, such emergencies also create spaces of exception inside which violence is unleashed by the powerful. Moreover, it is within both the states and spaces of exception where official accountability is significantly diminished. Gregory (2004) goes on to explore the concept *homo sacer* in three important ways. First, by paying close attention to the consequences of the suspension of law, Gregory demonstrates that *homo sacer* is designated to a zone of abandonment. The exception—*ex capere*—literally means the act of taking something outside, thus reinforcing the boundary drawn at the discretion of the sovereign. Gregory insists that *homines sacri* are included as the objects of sovereign power while simultaneously excluded from being its subjects. They are the mute bearers of what Agamben (1998) calls "bare life," deprived of political power that gives certain lives value. Agamben carefully inverts of Foucault's conceptualization of space. Whereas Foucault demonstrates how spaces of disciplinary power produce a subject (e.g., the prison), Agamben insists that spaces of exception operate somewhat like a vacuum insofar as they efface—wipe out—a subject (see also Brighenti 2007, 2006).

Second, Gregory reminds us that the spaces of exception are made possible through an operative act since the sovereign decides who is either in or out a particular zone of legal or military protection. As discussed previously, those ideas invites observations on petty sovereigns since decisions and discretions are made at different stations within the chain of command; clearly, however, there is a transmission of power taking place that embodies the larger ambition of the sovereign located at the top of the hierarchy (see Butler 2004; Carrabine 2001). Much of the human toll in Iraq has been inflicted by petty sovereigns (e.g., soldiers, field commanders) who believed—rightly or wrongly—that they were acting on behalf of the sovereign or commander-in-chief. Once certain neighborhoods or homes are declared hostile, the rules of engagement produce a kill zone which leaves vulnerable civilians trapped in the crossfire. To recapitulate, it is the relays of delegations that are significant because such performances underscore Agamben's argument that "*homo sacer* is the one with respect to whom all men act as sovereign" (1998, 25). In the third segment of his thesis, Gregory notes that spaces of exception are sanctioned by forces that are at once profane and sacred. In the sphere of the profane, such zones are maintained by the juridical thereby further upholding the sovereign. Toward a higher degree of abstraction, there exists a sacred quality of power which invisibly inaugurates authority, echoing what sociologist Jack Katz (1985) calls "the defense of the eternal good" in justifying certain acts of lethal violence (e.g., "righteous slaughter").

Despite his influence, Agamben and his formulation of *homo sacer* are not uncritically accepted among legal philosophers (Fitzpatrick 2001; Norris 2003; Venn 2002). In particular, there is concern over whether archaic Roman law can apply to late modernity. Without entering that debate, however, Gregory insists there is good reason to appreciate Agamben and his meta-physics of power. Such dynamics reveal the interplay between the juridical and the sacred as manifested in the war in Iraq (and Afghanistan). More precisely, there is room once again to see how a "crusade against terror" contributes to collateral damage. The alliance between neoconservatives and evangelical Christians is validated as much by the juridical as well as the sacred: "America's 'holy war'—Taliban fighters and al-Qaeda terrorists, Afghan [and Iraqi] refugees and civilians, were all regarded as *homines sacri*" (Gregory 2004, 63; see Welch 2006a). Other commentators have weighed into the controversy over collateral damage in a manner that reflects the metaphysics of power. Noam Chomsky, in reference to civilian casualties, said that most of those men, women, and children were killed or maimed "not by design but because it did not matter," thereby suggesting an even "deeper level of moral depravity" (2002b, 150). Indeed, the absence of U.S. record-keeping of civilian deaths by the American military exhibits a seemingly bizarre war-zone mentality, suggesting that that people who are not counted simply do not count. Still, there must be some estimate for collateral damage since minimizing civilian deaths remains an important concern in modern warfare. As the invasion roared on, Rumsfeld demanded that all air strikes likely to yield more than thirty civilians deaths be submitted for approval. More than fifty plans were reviewed, and all were approved; however, actual figures of civilian deaths were never released by the Pentagon (Graham and Morgan 2003; Jackson 2003; Sloboda and Dardagan 2003).

Adding to a sense of impunity is the defense department's callous response to air strikes that miss their target and hit civilian enclaves. On April 7, 2003 four "bunker-busting" bombs weighing one ton each were dropped on Mansur, a Baghdad suburb. U.S. intelligence suspected that Saddam Hussein and his sons were meeting inside a local restaurant. The satellite-guided "smart bomb" veered off course and landed in a nearly neighborhood, destroying five homes and vaporizing their inhabitants into a "pink mist." Residents were mystified as to why the United States unloaded such powerful weapons after it declared that the bombing campaign had ceased. Soon serious doubts emerged over whether Hussein had even been at the restaurant. A Pentagon spokeswoman said she "didn't think it matters very much. I'm not losing sleep trying to figure out if he was in there" (Fisk 2003a, 21; Cambanis 2003, 1).

> One might assume that these reactions were untypical. But one might also see them as the products not only of military violence but also a political culture of denial and dismissal, which treats its civilian victims not even as 'collateral damage'—objects and obstacles who got in the way—but as irrelevancies. No regret, no remorse; just more *hominess sacri*. They simply did not matter. (Gregory 2004, 212; see Slim 2003)

Under international law, an occupying power has clearly defined legal responsibilities for public order and safety, especially with respect to safeguarding the civilian population (Hague Convention 1907; Fourth Geneva Convention 1949). Apparently, the enormous volume of collateral damage in Iraq is a consequence of the United States not taking seriously its commitment to protect noncombatants, in effect suspending its responsibilities. By doing so, sovereign power has created a space of exception in which civilian deaths fail to be officially recognized. In a similar vein, Paul Gilroy (2003) points to an imperial topography that distinguishes between the "honorable" deaths of U.S. soldiers designated as "heroes" in American culture and the mundane killing of "terrorists" and "insurgents" along with civilian fatalities. He goes on to note that a general apathy in the United States toward collateral damage in Iraq is contoured not only along lines of racism but also a colonial economy that marginalizes local people and neglects their suffering (see Roy 2001).

Conclusion

Gilroy's observations on the colonial economy and its capacity to render irrelevant certain people suggest an asymmetry in humanity that privileges "well-heeled captors, conquerors, judges, executioners, and other racial betters" (2003, 263). Indeed, for a U.S. audience there exists a potent imperial mapping which frames how some victims of warfare are memorialized while ignoring others. On May 26, 2007, AOL (America On-Line) subscribers were greeted with a story about Army Specialist Justin Rollins, twenty-two year old who had been killed in roadside bombing while on tour in Iraq. The night before his death, he sent to his family a photograph of him nuzzling a puppy from a newborn litter. To commemorate the fallen soldier, the family pushed to adopt the puppy they named Hero. Rollins' girlfriend sought help from

Congressman Paul Hodes who contacted the U.S. Central Command, which ordered the 82nd to retrieve the dog and turn it over to delivery company DHL. Soon the puppy was transported 6,000 miles to New Hampshire. "The floppy-eared pooch—mostly white, with brown spots along the right side of its muzzle and paws still too big for its 15-pound body—was a hit Friday as she sniffed around Hodes' office, pausing to piddle on the carpet" (Associated Press 2007b, 1). Whether the puppy is actually the one in the photo doesn't really matter since everyone involved agreed it was a fitting tribute to Rollins.

While Pentagon policy prohibits journalists from photographing flag-drapped caskets containing the remains of military servicemen and women, there is considerable effort to retrieve those missing in action. Moreover, such stories are given enormous media coverage. Consider the massive search for three U.S. soldiers who disappeared in May 2007 after their patrol was ambushed. More than 4,000 American ground troops supported by surveillance aircraft, attack helicopters, and spy satellites swept towns and farmland south of Baghdad. "Everybody is fully engaged, the commanders are intimately focused on this," said Major-General William B. Caldwell IV. The searchers were using "every asset we have, from national assets to tactical assets" (Semple 2007, EV2). In a similar story that generated wide media interest, 8,000 American and Iraqi troops engaged in a four-day search for two U.S. servicemen kidnapped by insurgents in June 2006 (Semple 2007, EV3).

By sharp contrast, incidents of collateral damage attract much less media attention in the United States and certainly do not mobilize the American military in ways that can even compare to the massive searches for missing soldiers. Still, the civilian population injured or killed amid the war in Iraq is not the only form of collateral damage. Human rights organizations have expressed alarm over the volume of Iraqis fleeing the country. In April 2007, António Guterres, the U.N. High Commissioner for Refugees, confirmed what had long been suspected. That is, there is a collapse of Iraq giving way to an extraordinary refugee crisis. The situation is so severe that it threatens to precipitate a breakdown of the entire region. In Syria, there are estimated to be 1.2 million Iraqi refugees: another 750,000 in Jordan, 100,000 in Egypt, 54,000 in Iran, 40,000 in Lebanon, and 10,000 in Turkey. The overall estimated number of Iraqis who had fled is set at two million by Guterres. As many as 1.9 million Iraqis are displaced inside the country; correspondingly, approximately 15 percent of Iraqis have abandoned their homes. By April 2007, the outward flight reached a rate of up to 50,000 people per month (Rosen 2007, EV1).

Whereas some neighboring countries have been hospitable toward Iraqi refugees, bleak prospects for gainful employment has lead to desperation and, in some cases, prostitution for girls barely in their teens. In Damascus, Syria these days, Iraqi refugees selling sex or working in sex clubs is difficult to overlook. In the city center, men freely talk of being approached by pimps trawling for customers outside juice shops and shawarma sandwich stalls, and of women walking up to passing men, an act unthinkable in Arab culture. As one sex club worker said "from what I've seen, 70 percent to 80 percent of the girls working this business in Damascus today are Iraqis. The rents here in Syria are too expensive for their families. If they go back to Iraq they'll be slaughtered, and this is the only work available (Zoepf 2007, EV7). An Iraqi refugee added, "During the war we lost everything. We even lost our honor" (Zoepf 2007, EV7). Some Iraqi refugees, however, have been more fortunate in other countries, for instance Sweden. In 2006, Sodertalje, a town of 60,000 people, took in twice as many Iraqi refugees as the entire United States, almost all of them Christians fleeing the religious cleansing. That year, an estimated 9,000 Iraqis made it to Sweden, about half of the 22,000 who sought asylum in the whole industrialized world. In 2007 when the United States promised to accept 7,000 Iraqis, around 20,000 are expected to seek asylum in Sweden (Ekman 2007).

To conclude, this chapter set out to draw attention to the human toll in the Iraq war. So as to conceptualize further the problem of collateral damage, the discussion included a geopolitical perspective on the spaces of exception and how the injuries and deaths of certain people fail to register a greater concern, especially in the United States. In the next chapter, we take a critical look at the lasting legacies of the war in Iraq and the campaign against terror, particularly along lines of governmentality and the management of populations. As we shall see, those state activities in a post–9/11 world also contribute to a culture of impunity that diminishes government accountability.

PART FOUR

Lasting Legacies

CHAPTER 8

Governing through Terror

In 2007, the National Intelligence Council (NIC) issued a worrisome report that the United States will face "a persistent and evolving terrorist threat" over the next three years, as Al-Qaeda continues to plan attacks comparable in scale to those of September 11, 2001.[1] In its forecast, the panel of government experts assess

> that al-Qa'ida's Homeland plotting is likely to continue to focus on promi-nent political, economic, and infrastructure targets with the goal of producing mass casualties, visually dramatic destruction, significant economic after-shocks, and/or fear among the U.S. population. The group is proficient with conventional small arms and improvised explosive devices, and is innovative in creating new capabilities and overcoming security obstacles. (NIC 2007, 6)

The NIC concludes that while the worldwide campaign against terrorism has "constrained" the ability of Al-Qaeda to attack the American homeland again, it has not reduced the group's desire to do so. "Al-Qaeda is strong today," President Bush conceded in a brief White House appearance, "but they're not nearly as strong as they were prior to September the 11th, 2001, and the reason is, is because we've been working with the world to keep the pressure on"(Stout 2007b, EV6). Despite these assurances, the report reignited the debate over the status of national security and whether the war in Iraq has put the United States in more peril by stirring up terrorism and anti-American sentiment. Congressman Ike Skelton who heads the House Armed Services Committee argued, "We must responsibly redeploy our troops out of Iraq. This will allow us to concentrate our efforts on Afghanistan and the Al-Qaeda terrorists who attacked us on 9/11." But Republican minority leader John Boehner responded that the new intelligence estimate confirms that the administration's policies have weakened terrorist capa-bilities, adding, "Retreat is not a new way forward when the safety and security of future generations of Americans are at stake" (Stout 2007b, EV5).

Introduction

In his revealing critique of the war on crime, Jonathan Simon (2007) delves into the political crosscurrents over the past several decades in search of

clues on how a pervasive commitment to fight crime has significantly transformed American society. Rather than providing greater security, however,
new forms of governance have stoked fear of crime that, in turn, generates a
demand for tough on crime initiatives. The crackdown on crime further pulls the
United States from its welfarist foundation in dealing with social inequality
toward what Simon calls a "penal state," inviting more—not less—government as
well as a more authoritarian executive, a passive legislature, and defensive judiciary. The campaign against terror is not a departure from the war on crime;
rather, it marks a continuation and in many instances an escalation of autocratic politics. Similarly, the war on terror also draws on a form of populism
that can also be described as authoritarian. To be clear, governing through
crime and terror is not the same as actually governing—or even
solving—those social problems. The distinction rests in the manner by which
the state expresses its power in general and its particular ambition to manage
the population within its territory; along the way, government officials offer
scant acknowledgement to the underlying sources of crime and political
violence.

Governing through crime—and terror—also refers to a process by which
new strategies of governance impose greater restrictions on citizens, permitting the state to indulge in more intrusive forms of surveillance. Likewise, the
state resorts to profiling schemes aimed at certain minority groups whether
they are young African-American and Latino men blamed for urban crime or
their Middle-Eastern and South Asian counterparts suspected of terrorism.
Such profiling rarely sparks controversies among the mainstream Americans
because they, too, support tough measures aimed at people who appear to be
different and "dangerous" from the rest of "us." Indeed, an anxious public is
primed to accept new authoritarian strategies of governance as long as they
appear to be directed at "other" people.

Of course, sociologists and criminologists have taken notice of those
recent shifts in governance, especially as they stem from changes in the political landscape. It is in that social context where elected leaders opt for solu-
tions to crime and terrorism which fold neatly into the neo-liberal platform
(Crawford 2002; Rose 2000). As a result, the state continues to distance itself
from providing citizens essential forms of social and economic security, calling
on their constituents to take greater responsibility for their own well-being.
"The command to 'think security' instead of full employment, public education or the good society illustrates the depoliticizing potential of crime prevention and community safety (de Lint and Virta 2004, 466; see McLaughlin,
Muncie and Hughes 2001). Much of the critical discussion of how the state
manages its population centers on the concept of governmentality, or what
Foucault (1991) describes as the art of government and the conduct of conduct: "a form of activity aiming to shape, guide or affect the conduct of some

person or persons" (Gordon 1991, 2).[2] Just as neoliberal governance blurs the line separating the state and civil society, it also introduces discourse influencing the ways people talk and think about crime and terrorism as well as what they believe to be appropriate responses by the state. This chapter provides a conceptual overview of governing through terror by extracting some of Foucault's insight on governmentality as well as related writings pertaining to crime control.[3] Similarly, the discussion segues into the contemporary conversation over the "new" terrorism which is associated with the threat of radical Islamic fundamentalism (e.g., Al-Qaeda). As we shall see, the emerging discourse on terrorism in a post-9/11 world not only contributes to public anxiety but also serves to justify new strategies of governance, including more surveillance and a greater reliance on profiling and detention.

Whereas the state is properly understood as the central site of power in late modern society, it continues to abdicate some of its authority to external partners in the war on terror, such as outsourcing security to private firms. Those developments throw crucial light on the nature of governing through terror in a neoliberal arena whereby the state panders to a billion-dollar security industry. As Lucia Zedner notes, we are witnessing the effects of liquid security. That phenomenon marks a shift from "solid-state technology of the criminal justice state to the more fluid, transient and dispersed operations of the private security industry" (2006, 267). Regrettably, since liquid security is driven by market forces rather than a wider agenda for dispensing justice, it is subject to high employee turnover and corruption, becoming a key source of impunity from which corporate violence and abuse go unchecked by the state (see Bauman 2000; Jones and Newburn 1998; O'Malley 1999). The chapter delivers concluding thoughts on how the rational components of governmentality and neoliberalism merge with the emotive forces contained in authoritarian populism, together fortifying a post-9/11 culture committed to governing through terror while also undermining democracy in the process.

GOVERNMENTALITY: THE SECOND FOUCAULT EFFECT

As discussed in previous chapters, Foucault's *Discipline and Punish* (1977) has made a significant impact on criminology, prompting scholars to reconsider the nature of power in social control institutions. In his later work, Foucault (1979, 1991) went to great lengths to improve his conceptualization of power by elaborating on the notion of governmentality: the governance of others (and one's self).[4] The influence that his writings on governmentality have on the social sciences is evident (Burchell, Gordon, and Miller 1991; Rose and Miller 1992) and more recently in the realm of crime control (O'Malley 1996; Stenson 1993). It is this body of literature that helps us appreciate the second "Foucault effect" within theoretical criminology (Feeley and

Simon 1992; Garland 1996). From that aspect of Foucauldian thought, criminologists are encouraged to look critically at how crime is problematized and controlled, especially as modern society moves away from its welfarist paradigm and toward neo-liberal politics.[5] The governmentality perspective is valuable because, as Garland observes,

> It avoids reductionist or totalizing analyses, encouraging instead an open-ended, positive account of practices of governance in specific fields. It aims to anatomize contemporary practices, revealing the ways of thinking (rationalities) and specific ways of acting (technologies), as well as upon specific ways of 'subjectifying' individuals and governing populations. It also problematizes these practices by subjecting them to a "genealogical" analysis—a tracing of their historical lineages that aims to undermine their 'naturalness' and open up space for alternative possibilities. (Garland 1997a, 174)[6]

Rather than being "docile bodies" confined to a penitentiary regime, Foucault (1982) modified his view of individuals: recognizing them for their agency as active subjects which in turn become entities through which power is exercised. In that sense, government power tends to be more "subjectifying" than "objectifying" whereby individuals with their own choices and actions are aligned with those of the governing authorities. Still, the trajectory of that form of power is diffused into an array of governing sites (e.g., churches, professions, criminal justice systems), all of which are committed to influencing individual conduct; by doing so, there is less distinction between the public (state) and private (civil) spheres of society. To be clear, however, it is the state that serves as the nodal point from which all governance stems even though there is relative autonomy in how various government projects unfold. Within the locales of governance exists unique ways of thinking (rationales) and doing things (technologies). Narrowing his ideas of governmentality, Foucault (1991) attends to the historical trend in which state authorities see it as their responsibility to govern individuals and populations in a manner that contributes to overall prosperity and security. Along the way, governance gains momentum by discovering new social entities (e.g., certain populations) and generating new knowledge about them (e.g., their perceived dangerousness). As a modern form of power, there is an attempt to formulate administrative governance so as to distance itself from earlier reliance on the sovereign; as a result, governmentality exerts discipline and regulation over targeted persons and groups (for a critique of Foucault and governmentality, see DuPont and Pearce 2001; Kerr 1999).

Expanding on Foucault's depiction of governmentality, intellectuals have seized an opportunity to analyze crime control. For instance, Danzelot (1979) sheds light on the emergence of expert authority that occupies a social space between the state and the individual. Those authorities—psychologists, social workers, clinicians—offer specialized knowledge about how to manage certain populations (e.g., juvenile delinquents) while simultaneously linking their programs to the ambitions of the state (e.g., public safety). Again, the role of expert authority within a thick matrix of governance demonstrates how power is diffused from the nodal point of the state while upholding liberal values of freedom. Although there seems to be degrees of coercion (e.g., detention of juveniles), it is through expert power that the cooperation of subjects is cultivated (e.g., getting families to accept responsibility for their troubled youths). Because the management of populations is given special consideration, there is an emerging dependence on categorization, thereby formulating risk-based projections according to statistics and elaborate prediction scales (Ewald 1991; Hacking 1990). That actuarial reasoning serves to deindividualize the person by casting them as part of a larger social unit that specialists have determined to share common characteristics and behavioral patterns (Simon 1988). Therefore, risk-management moves to the forefront of governmentality, which is aimed at controlling populations rather than delivering individualized justice. Through the authority granted to experts by the state, profiles are given greater consideration than single case studies (Castle 1991; Feeley and Simon 1992). Adding precision to the idea that power moves beyond the state, Rose and Miller (1992) attend to networks and alliances that permit government to operate at a distance, translating its authority from one locale to another. Similarly, centers of calculation served to regularize knowledge (e.g., standardized statistical data) that facilitates communication toward a common goal. Although expert and professional groups acting within a zone of autonomy have a strong influence in problematizing certain aspects of social life (e.g., crime), they are not detached from the wider political objectives of the state. In the end, they contribute to a shift toward neoliberal regimes embodied in market economies and privatization schemes (Garland 1997a; Harcourt 2007).

The second "Foucault effect" also is evident in work of Jonathan Simon (1997, 2007) as he explores the dynamics by which the state governs through crime. Indeed, modern social order contains a highly developed division of labor which diffuses legal relationships, creating an array of civil and administrative laws. Simon credits Emile Durkheim ([1883] 1933) who reminds us of the significance of the division of labor in the realm of legal and criminal justice affairs because it allows the state to regulate individuals without resorting to visible coercion. It is not, however, a crisis of crime and punishment, Simon contends, but a crisis of governance that explains why crime has emerged as the preferred context for governance. By governance, he refers not only the actions of the state but all efforts intended to guide the conduct of others (and ourselves). Foucault (1982) describes that exercise of power as less a confrontation between adversaries; rather, to govern involves structuring the possible field of action of others (see Rose 1990). In its efforts to control crime, the state has adopted a form of governmentality that focuses on certain populations, commonly portrayed as "dangerous classes" (e.g., urban minority groups). Those social entities are the subjects of crime control strategies that rely on methods of assessing aggregate risks, then justifying interventions so as to reduce threats to public security or at least to help citizens feel safe (e.g., community policing). The discourse of neoliberalism is emphatically contoured along notions of insecurity, a condition of modern society that has become problematized. In his critique of governmentality, Simon observes, "Crime, of course, is a primary form of insecurity for these regimes, but one can govern crime without governing through crime. Governing through security focuses on the potential for harm rather than its source or explanations" (1997, 178). Governing through crime is a form of governance that undermines progressive democracies, Simon adds. Moreover, the theme of insecurity embedded in American public discourse has reached new heights since September 11, permitting the state to exercise new powers inaugurated by legislation (e.g., USA Patriot Act) as well as executive/military orders (e.g., unlawful enemy combatant designation). Before we address those developments, it is useful to map out a few more conceptual considerations on governmentality as they pertain to what has become known as the "new" terrorism.

RISK AND THE "NEW" TERRORISM

Faced with the always tricky task of defining terrorism, such acts are commonly understood to be a "use of violence and intimidation to disrupt or coerce a government and/or an identifiable community" (Mythen and Walklate 2006, 381; see Jenkins 2003). While political violence has occurred for centuries, the attacks on the World Trade Center and the Pentagon in 2001 are characterized as being particularly ominous, suggesting that a "new" terrorism has emerged. That new form of political violence is strongly associated with extreme Islamic fundamentalist groups such as Al-Qaeda which has carried out strikes across the globe (Clarke 2004; Morgan 2004). As a more powerful and shadowy threat to national security, the new terrorism is absorbed into popular discourse in ways that intensify anxiety and fear, producing a mindset that we live in risky times (Borradori 2003). Indeed, the recent interplay between risk and political violence has prompted sociologists to reflect on how the new terrorism is shaping our perception of late modernity because it erodes "the myth that the sovereign state is capable of providing security, law and order, and crime control within its territorial boundaries" (Garland 1996, 448). Ulrich Beck (2002a, 2002b) and Richard Ericson (2007) offer deep analyses of the new terrorism situated within the risk-society framework (see chapter 2). That perspective shows how the new terrorism produces deterritorialized dangers that cut easily across state borders; consequently, national security is jeopardized, creating worries for those responsible for antiterrorism strategies as well as the general public. Beck (1992) proposes that the risk society is a postneeds society insofar as anxious individuals are driven less by the pursuit of possessions and more toward protections against an array of threats to personal security, including terrorism. Whereas the logic of the class society is based on creating winners and losers, the risk society is universal since ultimately everyone loses. That component of late modernity marks a shift away from differential class-consciousness toward a global risk-consciousness (Mythen 2004; Mythen and Walklate 2006).

The overall thrust of risk-society theory as it encompasses the management of danger (e.g., the "new" terrorism) is not inconsistent with the theoretical contributions of Foucault, as Ericson (2007) clearly exhibits. Similarly, Mythen and Walklate (2006) share Foucault's view of modern power as being channeled through a matrix of governance, recognizing that governmentality is both a set of organized practices as well as a system for guiding rationale (see Turner 1997). More to the point of risk-society theory, Foucauldians characterize risk as being operationalized as a mode of regulation through which populations are charted, classified, and sorted (Lupton 1999; Rose 2000). Mythen and Walklate's analysis of new terrorism delves into how particular state responses are shaped by discursive constructions of the terrorist "other," which, in turn, invites close inspection and surveillance of certain groups in society.

> It is clear that neo-liberal agencies of crime control are employing risk-based techniques to assess the level of terrorist threat and to make future projections of danger. In both the United States and the United Kingdom, security services have utilized predictive databases and intelligence gathering to inform safety assessments. The airing of colour-coded security symbols serves as a neat example of the filtering through of risk-management strategies to the general public. In addition, there appears to be something of a return to regulatory mechanisms of control through which 'risky' classes are surveyed. As a matter of course, intelligence agencies can be expected to collect data and information about terrorist groups. (Mythen and Walklate 2006, 389; see Moran 2006)

As Hudson (2003) and Stenson (2003) also point out, schemes to classify suspected terrorists are situated within a wider net from which potential offenders are identified by risk values rather than depicting them as rational social actors. Still, discourse on the new terrorism is shaped by a network of participants working inside and outside state agencies: security and terrorism experts, private military firms, the media, and politicians on the campaign trail all of whom contribute to growing anxiety and a general demand for government to do something to ensure public safety. A dominant response to the putative threat, therefore, involves the tactic of "othering," which targets some people perceived as different from the rest of "us." Indeed, the prevailing description of the new terrorism is closely aligned to Islamic fundamentalists who the authorities believe are of Middle-Eastern or South-Asian ethnicity.

In 2002, the Department of Justice expanded its use of profiling in the war on terror by introducing a special registration program. The directive, intended to produce vital information about terrorist activity, required all nonimmigrant male visitors who are over the age of sixteen and entered the United States before September 30, 2002. Special registration applied to those males from countries which, according to the U.S. government, have links to the new terrorism, including twelve North African and Middle Eastern countries plus North Korea, affecting more than 82,000 students, tourists, businessmen, and relatives. Special registration procedures required those persons to complete a personal information form, and be fingerprinted, photographed, and interviewed by the FBI. Justice department spokesman Jorge Martinez claimed that such information was necessary intelligence for the war against terrorism: "These people are considered a high risk. The goal of the system is to know who is coming in and out, and that they are in fact doing what they said they would do" (Gourevitch 2003, EV2). The logic of special registration as a form of terrorist profiling was seriously questioned by legal scholars who wondered why a bona fide terrorist would risk detection and detention by appearing before the special registration officials, especially since the exhaustive procedure involves fingerprinting, photographing, and interrogation by FBI agents. David Cole added, "If intelligence officials are right that Al-Qaeda sleepers generally lead quiet, unremarkable lives in conformity with legal requirements, the INS would have no way of knowing even if an Al-Qaeda member were to walk in" (2003, 5).

It is through the prism of governmentality—the management of populations—that we see the social construction of the "other" in ways that equate certain ethnic attributes to dangerousness (Welch 2007b). As discussed previously, such labeling extends beyond Muslims and Arabs residing in the United States and Europe to Iraqi civilians who have been subjected to false arrest, detention, abuse, and even murder (see chapter 7). Although it is true that the campaign against the new terrorism is driven by a vector of sovereign power emanating from the White House, there continues to be a diffusion of authority found in such controversial tactics as extraordinary renditions whereby torture is outsourced to a third party.

OUTSOURCING AND FRAGMENTED AUTHORITY

Complimenting the governmentality literature are contributions from scholars focusing on security and policing; overall, those writings pay close attention to the transformation of state power in the context of neoliberalism. While it is widely agreed that the capacity and influence of the state is not disappearing, there is "a discernible erosion of authority of the political form that has dominated the modern age—the sovereign state" (Loader and Walker 2001, 10; 2004; see Hirst and Thompson 1996). Precisely how power is being diffused is subject to debate: some suggest the state is being "hollowed out" (Rhodes 1997) or "networked" (Amoore and De Goede 2005; Castells 1997; see also Held 1995). In the realm of policing and the maintenance of order, there is continued fragmentation of authority by which state power is relinquished "outwards" to expanding commercial markets in policing and security; "downwards" to private firms and municipal administrators; and "upwards" to new projects involving international police cooperation (Loader and Walker 2001). The decoupling of police and state raises questions about the changing architecture of liberal democratic societies and among them are concerns over the waning monopoly of legitimate coercion (Walker 1999). Max Weber (1948) proposed that the monopoly over the legitimate use of lethal force was a defining feature of the modern state. Departing from that traditional interpretation, a view that the state has become the sole regulator of such violence but no longer maintains a monopoly over it has emerged (Castells 1997; see Morgan and Newburn 1997). From that perspective, it is suggested that the state ultimately has responsibility over the steering of the police ship while rowing is at times designated—or even outsourced—to a plurality of "deputized" authorities in an expanding market for police and security (Osborne and Gaebler 1992).

Given the degree of uncertainty in a risk society, there is a growing market for the management and delivery of security, especially in the private sector where global conditions present unique opportunities. "Insecurity is then cast with uncertainty as an object that may be intermediated through experts and their tools of intervention to 'fix' the problem," note de Lint and Virta, adding, "Security, like psychiatry and criminology in this way produces the pathology it alone may cure. (2004, 471). Within that arena, Newburn (2007) explores recent developments in the outward fragmentation of authority (see Crawford 2003; Jones and Newburn 1998). Preferring the term sideways rather than outward, Newburn demonstrates how that particular trajectory of fragmentation follows economic and commercial cues (see Zedner 2006). The privatized international security industry has attracted scholarly interest because of increased reliance on nonstate military outfits. Whereas the history of mercenary work reads like a tawdry tale of guns for hire, contemporary contracts hiring private military companies are widely seen as a legitimate—even respectable—activity in the sphere of globalization and late modern warfare. Certainly, the state is not abdicating complete authority to private military firms; rather it works in direct partnership with so-called corporate warriors (Avant 2005, 2004; Singer 2003; Whyte 2003).[7]

The role of privatized security in the U.S. occupation of Iraq is revealing. It is the largest deployment of private military companies in the history of warfare, including more than sixty firms contracting over 20,000 private personnel. While Halliburton has become one of the biggest beneficiaries of the war in Iraq with an estimated $6 billion worth of contracts, there are other privatized security outfits, most notably Blackwater, DynCorp, and Erinys (see Lipton 2006). Among the most controversial aspects of such sideways fragmentation of authority pertains to combat in which private companies have been known to carry out lethal violence (Singer 2005; see O'Reilly 2005; O'Reilly and Ellison 2006).

The Trouble with Blackwater

Consider the incidents in 2007 involving Blackwater, a private security firm under contract with the state department. In May of that year, its employees opened fire on the streets of Baghdad twice in two days, including a scene which provoked a standoff between the security contractors and Iraqi forces. In one of those incidents, a Blackwater guard shot and killed an Iraqi driver near the Interior Ministry,[8] and in another a Blackwater-protected convoy was ambushed in downtown Baghdad, triggering a fierce battle in which the security contractors, U.S. and Iraqi troops and AH-64 Apache attack helicopters fired into a congested area of civilians (Fainaru and al-Izzi 2007).[9]

> Blackwater's security consulting division holds at least $109 million worth of State Department contracts in Iraq, and its employees operate in a perilous environment that sometimes requires the use of deadly force. But last week's incidents underscored how deeply these hired guns have been drawn into the war, their murky legal status and the grave consequences that can ensue when they take aggressive action. Matthew Degn, a senior American civilian adviser to the Interior Ministry's intelligence directorate, described the ministry as "a powder keg" after the Iraqi driver was shot Thursday, with anger at Blackwater spilling over to other Americans working in the building. (Fainaru and al-Izzi 2007, A1)

The Blackwater guards refused to provide their names or details of the incident to Iraqi authorities. What ensued was a tense standoff between the Blackwater guards and interior ministry forces—both sides armed with assault rifles—until a U.S. soldiers intervened. The Interior Ministry, the regulatory body that oversees security companies for the Iraqi government, received numerous other complaints of shooting incidents involving Blackwater (Fainaru and al-Izzi 2007).

A few months later, Blackwater again was involved in another, even more lethal, incident. On September 16th, a bomb exploded a few hundred yards away from a meeting of diplomats with the United States Agency for International Development. The explosion caused no injuries to the Americans, but prompted the evacuation of US AID members, a maneuver that some security specialists considered unwise. "It raises the first question of why didn't they just stay in place, since they are safe in the compound. Usually the concept would be, if an I.E.D. [improvised explosive device] detonates in the street, you would wait 15 to 30 minutes, until things calmed down," a U.S. official said (Glanz and Tavernise 2007, EV1). When the Blackwater convoy carrying the diplomats moved toward the Green Zone, it passed through Nisour Square in western Baghdad where it entered congested traffic. Some of the Blackwater personnel got out of their vehicles and took positions on the street: then at least one guard began to fire in the direction of a car, killing its driver. Soon more shots were fired, killing a woman holding an infant sitting in the passenger seat. After the family was shot, a type of grenade or flare was fired into the car which set it ablaze. Numerous civilians were also killed as the shooting continued. Iraqi officials have given several death counts, ranging from eight to twenty, with perhaps several dozen wounded. Blackwater guards told investigators that they believed that they were being fired on although a preliminary Iraqi investigation concluded that there was no enemy fire (Glanz and Tavernise 2007).

The response from the Iraqi government was swift, announcing that it was pulling the license of Blackwater. The Interior Ministry said it would prosecute any foreign contractors found to have used excessive force in the September 16 shooting. The incident compounded further civilian resentment of private security firms because they operate with little or no supervision and engage in aggressive, high-speed motorcades (Mroue 2007). To the surprise of many Iraqi officials, the U.S. state department investigators offered Blackwater guards immunity during its initial inquiry: a potentially serious investigative misstep that could complicate efforts to prosecute the company's employees involved in the episode.[10] Most of the guards who took part in shooting were issue what officials described as limited-use immunity, meaning that they were assured that they would not be prosecuted for anything they revealed in their interviews as long as their statements were true. As noted previously, under CPA Order 17, Blackwater employees and other civilian contractors cannot be tried in military courts, and it is unclear what American criminal laws might cover criminal acts committed in a war zone. In the wake of the September 16 shootings, however, the U.S. House of Representative passed a bill that would make such contractors liable under a law known as the Military Extraterritorial Jurisdiction Act: the Senate is considering a similar measure (Johnston 2007; see Broder and Risen 2007a).

Discussion over the killing of civilians widened as legal experts speculated whether contractors could be considered unlawful combatants under international treaty agreements. Under the Geneva Conventions, the term lawful combatant extends to nonmilitary personnel who operate under their military's chain of command. Although others may bear arms in a war zone and even use them to defend themselves, they are not authorized to use offensive force. Justice department officials doubt that the contractors could be considered unlawful combatants; still some in the state and defense departments believe the contractors in Iraq could be vulnerable to claims that their actions make them unlawful combatants. "For a guard who is only allowed to use defensive force, killing civilians violates the law of war," said Michael N. Schmitt, a professor of international law at the Naval War College and a former Air Force lawyer, adding, "It is a war crime to kill civilians unlawfully in an armed conflict" (Barnes 2007, EV2). Scott Silliman, a retired air force lawyer and professor at Duke University, emphasized the rules governing the use of force: "The only force they can use is defensive force. But we may be seeing some instances where contractors are using offensive force, which in my judgment would be unlawful" (Barnes 2007, EV2). Concern of legal liability has been met by significant political changes in the way security firms are supervised: as of October 2007, all state department security convoys in Iraq now fall under military control. Secretary of State Rice and Secretary of Defense Gates agreed to the measure following weeks of tension between their departments over coordination of thousands of gun-carrying contractors operating in occupied Iraq. Gates appears to have won the bureaucratic struggle (Broder and Johnston 2007).

While for years military and security firms have drawn intense negative attention in Iraq, the shooting incident on September 16 (2007) has instigated a fresh round of criticism, raising deeper questions over the privatized use of force (see Welch 2009). Consider again the case of Backwater: founded in 1997 by Erik Prince, a former member of the navy Seals. The privately owned firm has a total of about 550 full-time employees; however, most of its nearly 1,000 personnel in Iraq are independent contractors rather than actual employees of the company. In looking closer at Blackwater's performance in Iraq, its personnel has a shooting rate twice that of other security firms providing similar services (i.e., DynCorp International and Triple Canopy) (Broder and Risen 2007b, EV3). Observers note that company has gained a reputation as one that flaunts a quick-draw image, thereby enticing its guards to take excessively violent actions. Some suggest that its aggressive posture in guarding diplomats reflects the wishes of its principle client, the State Department's Bureau of Diplomatic Security (Broder and Risen 2007b, EV3). In addition to shootings on September 16, Iraqi officials report that Blackwater employees also are under investigation for six other episodes that have left ten Iraqis dead and fifteen wounded. In the United States, many political leaders view Blackwater's behavior as counterproductive to American efforts to gain support for its military efforts in Iraq. "They're repeat offenders, and yet they continue to prosper in Iraq. It's really affecting attitudes toward the United States when you have these cowboy guys out there.

These guys represent the U.S. to them and there are no rules of the game for them" said Illinois Democrat Jan Schakowsky (Broder and Risen 2007b, EV5). Even against a growing chorus of criticism, Blackwater still enjoys an unusually close relationship with the Bush administration, receiving government contracts worth more than $1 billion dollars since 2002.

> The company's close ties to the Bush administration have raised questions about the political clout of Mr. Prince, Blackwater's founder and owner. He is the scion of a wealthy Michigan family that is active in Republican politics. He and the family have given more than $325,000 in political donations over the past 10 years, the vast majority to Republican candidates and party committees, according to federal campaign finance reports. Mr. Prince has helped cement his ties to the government by hiring prominent officials. J. Cofer Black, the former counterterrorism chief at the C.I.A. and State Department, is a vice chairman at Blackwater. Mr. Black is also now a senior adviser on counterterrorism and national security issues to the Republican presidential campaign of Mitt Romney. Joseph E. Schmitz, the former inspector general at the Pentagon, now is chief operating officer and general counsel for Blackwater's parent company, the Prince Group. Officials at other firms in the contracting industry said that Mr. Prince sometimes met with government contracting officers, which they say is an unusual step for the chief executive of a corporation. (Broder and Risen 2007b, EV5; see Scahill 2007)

Although there does exist several U.S. statues governing actions overseas and in wartime that could be used by prosecutors, as of yet no Blackwater employees or any other contractors have been charged with crimes related to shootings in Iraq. Moreover, Congress enacted a measure in 2006 calling for the Pentagon to bring contractors in Iraq under the jurisdiction of American military law; however, the defense department has failed to put into effect the rules needed to do so. The September 16 shootings have so angered Iraqis that their government is proposing to overturn immunity protections contained in Order 17, thereby subjecting Western private security companies to Iraqi law. The proposal requires the approval of the Iraqi Parliament.

While private security contracts have quadrupled in four years, reaching $4 billion per year, the U.S. government has not kept pace with sufficient number of monitors needed to supervise the contracts. Auditors continue to report vast cost overruns, poor contract performance, and violence that goes unpunished. "They simply didn't have enough eyes and ears watching what was going on," said Peter W. Singer, an expert on security contactors at the Brookings Institution, adding, "Secondly, they seemed to show no interest in using the sanctions they had" (Broder and Rohde 2007, EV2). Moreover, there is evidence that political cronyism has corrupted the mechanisms of oversight.

As state department inspector general, Howard J. Krongard stood accused of impeding a justice department investigation of Blackwater for its involvement in the September 16 shooting. Two months into a criminal probe, Krongard was finally forced to disqualify himself from inquiries into the company when he disclosed during a congressional hearing that his brother, Alvin, had joined Blackwater's advisory board. At the congressional hearing on November 14, Krongard initially stated under oath that his brother had no affiliation with Blackwater; later that day, he called his brother then returned to the committee to announce that he had been mistaken (*New York Times* 2007).

Controversy surrounding Blackwater continues to deepen. It has now been reported that one the company's helicopter dropped CS gas, a riot-control substance (similar to tear gas), onto an area where Iraqi civilians were gathered and at least ten American soldiers had been operating a checkpoint. On the ground, an armored Blackwater vehicle also released the gas, temporarily blinding drivers, passers-by. The incident, which occurred in May 2005, raised legal issues concerning the use of such gas against civilians in a war zone. Only the U.S. military has the authority to detonate CS gas and solely under the strictest conditions approved by top military commanders. Captain Kincy Clark of the Army, the senior officer at the scene, wrote that day, "This was decidedly uncool and very, very dangerous. It's not a good thing to cause soldiers who are standing guard against car bombs, snipers and suicide bombers to cover their faces, choke, cough and otherwise degrade our awareness"(Risen 2008, EV2). None of the U.S. soldiers exposed to the chemical required medical attention but it is not clear whether any Iraqis did. Anne Tyrrell, a spokeswoman for Blackwater, said the CS gas had been released by mistake:"It seems a CS gas canister was mistaken for a smoke canister and released near an intersection and checkpoint"(Risen 2008, EV2). Blackwater claims it was permitted to carry CS gas under its contract at the time with the state department. According to government officials, the contract did not specifically authorize Blackwater personnel to carry or use CS; however, it did not prohibit its use either. The U.S. military tightly controls use of riot control agents in war zones because they are banned as means of warfare by an international convention on chemical weapons endorsed by the U.S. government. Nevertheless, a 1975 presidential order allows their use by the military in war zones under limited defensive circumstances and only with the approval of the president or a senior officer designated by the president. President Bush, in 2003, approved the use of riot control agents by the military in Iraq under the 1975 order, but only to control rioting prisoners or prevent the use of human shields (Risen 2008).

The Ethics of Governance and State-Corporate Crime

As those developments strongly suggest, fragmented authority raises ethical and sociological questions over effective systems for governance (Krahmann

2003; Newburn 2007; Rose 1996). Such dilemmas, however, are nothing new to policy and scholars who argue that we are facing a form of "nodal governance" whereby the traditional state-centered model is giving way to an emerging network of control that has no central point (Shearing 2005; Shearing and Wood 2000). For the purposes of this analysis, those developments contribute to a culture of impunity which encourages illegal activities best described as state-corporate crime. By way of definition, state-corporate crime is a criminal act that occurs when "one or more institutions of political governance pursue a goal in direct cooperation with one or more institutions of economic production and distribution" (Kramer, Michalowski, Kauzlarich 2002, 263). State-corporate crime is propelled not only by commercial interests but is sustained by a set of powerful political dynamics (i.e., counter-law) operating to resist traditional criminalization processes that would otherwise deter by threat of punishment (see Quinney 1977; Whyte 2003). Fractured authority coupled with state-corporate crime are tandem phenomena that can be found in ways the war in Iraq and the battle against new terrorism are being administered, leading to the abuse and torture of detainees. Whereas it can be reasonably speculated that the majority of incidents involving mistreatment occur at the hands of state actors, there is evidence that employees of private intelligence firms also have been involved those crimes (Harbury 2005; Hersh 2004; see Tyler, Callahan, and Frost 2007).

Regrettably, the details of private military and intelligence firms are shrouded in such mystery that policymakers and the public are left in positions of dangerous ignorance; in fact, unlike government agencies, those companies are not subject to Freedom of Information Requests (Singer 2005). In terms of accountability, employees of private firms slip through the cracks of the legal infrastructure designed to distinguish between military personnel from civilians. Contractors are not quite civilians, in light of the fact that they often carry and use weapons, interrogate prisoners, load bombs, and fulfill other critical battle field roles. One military law analyst noted, "Legally speaking [military contractors] fall into the same grey zone as the unlawful combatants detained at Guantánamo Bay" (Singer 2005, 121). Prosecuting those employees for crimes can be difficult because they are not accountable under the Uniformed Code of Military Justice nor are they even defined by international law, thus having a status that is murky at best. Moreover, there seems to be a lack of political will for such prosecution. Although dozens of U.S. soldiers have been charged for an array of crimes and infractions (see Chapter 7), not one private military contractor has been prosecuted or punished for a crime in Iraq.

The failure to properly control the behavior of PMFs [private military firms] took on great consequence at the Abu Ghraib prisoner-abuse case.

According to reports, all of the translators and up to half of the interrogators involved were private contractors working for two firms, Titan and CACI [Consolidated Analysis Centers, Inc.]. The U.S. Army found that contractors were involved in 36 percent of the proven incidents and identified 6 employees as individually culpable. More than a year after the incidents, however, not one of these individuals has been indicted, prosecuted, or punished even though the U.S. Army has found the time to try the enlisted soldiers involved. Nor has there been any attempt to assess the corporate responsibility for the misdeeds. Indeed, the only formal inquiry into PMF wrongdoing on the corporate level was conducted by CACI itself. CACI investigated CACI and, unsurprisingly, found that CACI had done nothing wrong. (Singer 2005, 122)

As the invasion and occupation of Iraq opened the floodgates for an immediate financial market for private firms, their rush to profits forced them to cut corners in the screening of employees. Investigations of the Abu Ghraib prisoner abuse scandal revealed that approximately 35 percent of the contract interrogators hired by the firm CACI lacked formal military training as interrogators (Singer 2005; see Stover, Megally, and Mufti 2005).

While the concept of fragmented authority certainly applies to the U.S. practice of extraordinary renditions in which detainees are transferred to another nation (e.g., Egypt, Morocco, Syria, and Jordan) as a means of outsourcing interrogation and torture, there exists an apparent commercial link that goes beyond that particular state-to-state arrangement. The fundamental nature of rendering means that terrorist suspects are actually transported from one nation to another, making several stops in other nations along the way. Since American military aircraft are not always welcomed to land in many sovereign states, the CIA contracts the services of private charters that are able to shuttle from one location to another without creating suspicion of wrongdoing. In 2005, the *New York Times* reported that the CIA relies on a fleet of twenty-six private jets owned and/or operated by Aero Contractors Ltd, Pegasus Technologies, Tepper Aviation, and Premier Executive Transport Services. Each of those companies comply with aviation regulations that require that all aircraft have visible tail numbers so that their ownership can be easily checked by entering the number into the Federal Aviation Administration's online registry. Here is the catch. Those private contractors are merely a pseudo-form of fragmented authority; in fact, their precise ownership cannot be verified, lending to suspicion that the aircraft are owned by the U.S. government.

On closer examination, however, it becomes clear that those companies appear to have no premises, only post office boxes or addresses in care of lawyers' offices. Their officers and directors, listed in state corporate databases, seem to have been invented. A search of public records for ordinary identifying information about the officers—addresses, phone numbers, house purchases, and so on—comes up with only post office boxes in Virginia, Maryland and Washington, D.C. (Shane, Grey, and Williams 2005, A1)

Rather than purchase aircraft outright, the CIA creates shell companies whose names appear unremarkable in casual checks of FAA registrations. Closer scrutiny, however, reveals that Aero Contractors Ltd. has significant ancestor in Air America: a notorious transport operation officially shut down in 1976 when the Church Committee delivered a mixed report on the value of the CIA's use of proprietary companies (see Cobain 2007; McCoy 2006).

As this section demonstrates, fragmented authority—even in its pseudo-form—contributes to a culture of impunity since persons directly or indirectly involved in criminal activity or other human rights abuses evade accountability and punishment. Here we focused mostly on the sideways trajectory of fragmentation to illuminate the mutually reinforcing nature of power and profit that together integrate techniques of governance with lucrative industries capitalizing on the war in Iraq and war on terror. That changing nature of governmentalization is seen in the establishment of the "authority of authority" whereby alliances between different legitimacies are conferred by law and expertise (Rose and Valverde, 1998; see Amoore and De Goede 2005; Larner and Walters 2004).

Authoritarian Populism and the War on Terror

Foucault's understanding of governmentality reached both narrow and wide, prompting us to consider other features of the "conduct of conduct" (Gordon 1991). Expanding the notion of governmentality there are attempts to transcend the rational and technical dimensions of managing populations, looking further at its expressive and emotionally driven forces (Garland 1990). Ostensibly, criminal justice discourse is rife with symbolism, conveying a collective emotion that often overshadows instrumental calculation. Without striving to construct a "grand theory," there remain important linkages between the strictly rational component of governance and the broader emotional vector; by doing so, crucial attention is directed at culture. The war on terror stems from a broader expressive punitiveness which facilitates the scapegoating of persons perceived—accurately or not—as being involved in terrorism (Welch 2006a). Such scapegoating should not be detached from the political forces underlying populism (Pratt 2007; Pratt, Brown, Hallsworth, Brown, and Morrison 2005). Expressive populism is not empty symbolism that decorates political rhetoric; rather, it is a potent factor that guides discourse toward practice. "Indeed, it seems plausible to suggest that populist and 'governmentalized' politics are actually twinned, antithetical phenomena—the first provoking the second as a kind

of backlash against the rule of experts and the dominance of professional elites"
(Garland 1997a, 203–204, 1996; Bottoms 1995).

Whereas earlier chapters concentrated on the role of executive (and military) power in paving the path for the war on terror, there is room also to consider populist politics and what Heinz Steinert (2003) calls the indispensable
metaphor of war. The human and social experience is influenced by metaphors
that enable us to summarize the world in general and key events in particular
(Lakoff and Johnson 1980). The war on terror has joined the roster of other
"wars" against drugs and crime, thereby providing determination to solve the
current "crisis" or "emergency" that threatens public safety and national security.
Moreover, in counterterrorism the metaphor of war often is taken literally since
it gravitates toward militarism: the Bush administration depicts the attacks on
the World Trade Center and the Pentagon as acts of war that, in turn, have served
as a justification to invade Afghanistan and Iraq. However, it also serves as a populist political tactic intended to garner public support for both antiterrorism
strategies and the continued occupation of Iraq, evoking strong emotions to
support the troops. War on terror rhetoric is geared toward the mainstream public; it claims that all Americans have something at stake (e.g., personal safety) and
that there is need to make sacrifices (e.g., restrictions on civil liberties, deaths of
U.S. soldiers). Similarly, political dissent and antiwar protests are portrayed by
political conservatives as subversive efforts to undermine national unity required
to win the war on terror. In the aftermath of 9/11, Attorney General John
Ashcroft repeatedly called for Americans to support the government's task of
tracking down terrorists, adding that any criticism of its tactics would only aid
the enemy (Welch 2006a). Revealing a renewed sense of authoritarianism,
White House Press Secretary Ari Fleischer warned that Americans "need to
watch what they say" (Huff 2001, 112).[11] That particular form of populism contains elements of authoritarianism which demand obedience and adherence to
rigid rules of personal and social conduct. Fear of terrorism also facilitates much
of the emotional language emanating from political figures who intend to tap
into a larger zone of anxiety situated in a risk society as well as narrower worries of being personally victimized by a terrorist strike. Periodic elevations on
the color-coded warning board reminded citizens that they live within a permanent crisis. Their sense of uneasiness gives way to a dominating dynamic
whereby they feel powerless against the threat of terrorism; consequently
becoming dependent on the state and its leadership. Especially since 9/11, the
Bush administration has frequently resorted to emotional rhetoric knowing that
that when people are worried and fearful they are less receptive to rational
language (see Brooks 2003b; Didion 2003).

Adding to authoritarian populism are messages and images projected by
the mass media. Themes of fear and terrorism are found in the form of standard newscasts as well as in dramatic and sensationalist movies, such as World

Trade Center, United 93, and Homeland Security. Although there remain clear economic imperatives underpinning the mass media in terms of the financial rewards of selling news and entertainment, the emotional content of those narratives play into authoritarian populism.

> In both, professional politics and the broader public sphere, we find a (necessary) reliance on entertainment, and, beyond that, on sensation. Broadcasts and announcements that have to compete with several dozen others need to be loud and shrill to catch attention and they need to have a well-crafted dramaturgical grip. They cannot quietly refer to self-interested attention and support. Rather, they have to aggressively 'sell' on mass and to appeal to our basest or noblest (both work equally well) instincts to do so. They appeal to high morality or to hatred and lust, but not to simple self-interest. And they must feed us some exciting development: an increase in the problem, a last-minute decision, cycles of repetition, a point of crisis. (Steinert 2003, 272)

Steinert further notes that the populist feature of such broadcasting aimed at integrating the audience into what they view on television; the objective is not to inform us but rather to "take us in" (2003, 272). Of course, such media experience transcends the obvious examples of television programs designed to incorporate "real" people into the story (e.g., "Big Brother"), it is also evident in the way politicians deploy the media to issue carefully crafted emotional language so as to draw support for the war on terror (see Bonn 2007). On September 20, 2001, Bush addressed the public in ways that seem to heighten a sense of national vulnerability: "Americans should not expect one battle, but a lengthy campaign, unlike any other we have ever seen . . . I ask you to live your lives, and hug your children. I know many citizens have fears tonight . . . Be calm and resolute, even in the face of a continuing threat" (Brooks 2003b, 21).[12] In the months after his election, President Bush was mocked for his poor work ethic in the White House and frequent vacations. After 9/11, the jokes stopped as the nation looked to him as a strong leader in the face of a national crisis. In short order, Bush—who side-stepped serving in the Vietnam War—was transformed into a powerful commander-in-chief. "The combination of terrorist attack and urban disaster bequeathed to him the ultimate 'populist moment' " (Steinert 2003, 274). With the war in Iraq dragging along with little end in sight, Bush's prominence has faded significantly (Sussman 2007; Urbina, 2007). Nevertheless, 9/11 still stands as populist opportunity capable of enlisting vast segments of the American public for a common goal of national security. Regrettably, controversies over domestic and foreign affairs (e.g., the USA Patriot Act, Guantánamo Bay) are likely to persist in large part because of the way the White House initially seized that historical moment by injecting its brand of authoritarianism.

CONCLUSION

In his sharply perceptive book, *Culture, Crisis and America's War on Terror*, Stuart Croft (2006) offers insights into how the United States reacted to the events of 9/11. As the title suggest, there is much to learn about American culture after September 11 by attending to particular forms of discourse guiding the rational and emotive responses to its first major terrorist strike. In formulating policies aimed countering terrorism, officials built on "a narrative that could be shared amongst those who felt threatened; and that had to be America's government and, importantly, American society as a whole" (Croft 2006, 2). Whereas the policies would be devised at the very top of government, plans would involve other social institutions, including the media, thereby producing an identifiable impact on culture. Croft goes on to note that the logic of responding to terrorism had to match an emotional register; consequently, there quickly emerged a foundational image that would serve to memorialize the events and victims of 9/11. Popular culture was flooded with imagery and symbols embedded in news stories and television programs as well as related books and magazine, all which memorialized that tragic day in U.S. history. It has been observed how the newly constructed war on terror integrated the instrumental and expressive dimensions of governance. "Within the confines of this rhetorically constructed reality, or discourse, the 'war on terror' appears as a rational and reasonable response; more importantly to many people it feels like the right thing do" (Jackson 2005, 2; see Calhoun, Price, and Timmer 2002). Croft insists that the new narrative, though, could not be completely new. Drawing on past narratives, one can trace a genealogy of the war on terror to previous wars, including those against crime and drugs while at the same time touching on previous military episodes. On the anniversary of the attack on Pearl Harbor, Bush in 2002 announced during his run-up to the war in Iraq, "Facing clear evidence of peril, we cannot wait for the final proof, the smoking gun that could come in the form of a mushroom cloud" (Herbert 2004, A17).

As this chapter demonstrates, governance in post-9/11 America is shaped significantly by the war metaphor. Such symbolism is potent given the enormity of September 11 and the fear and anxiety left in its wake. In order to add weight to governance in this "new age," political leaders have opted to govern not only through crime but also through terror. As Simon points out, such measures of social and crime control should be met with caution since they have "made us more vulnerable to the strategies of those who would use terrorism as an excuse to impose new strategies of governance. The high risks of relying on an essentially penal strategy to achieve global forms of security are already becoming visible in Iraq and elsewhere" (2007, 261; see Gearty 2002). Apart from the devastation in Iraq (and Afghanistan), there are other problems plaguing counter-terrorism caused by the uncritical acceptance of the "war" on crime model. Simon reminds us that traditional criminal justice strategies assume that dangerous acts are committed by dangerous people; moreover, it is believed by some policy experts that such a menace can be identified in a person's character as exhibited in their unlawful conduct, however minor. In what has become known as the "broken windows" perspective, it is believed that major crimes can be prevented by cracking down on minor crimes (Kelling and Wilson 1982). The practice of cracking down is often aimed at a particular segment of the population viewed as potentially unruly, such as young urban African-American and Latino males. As a result, through profiling—premised on the idea of reliable statistics hinting at their inherent dangerousness—they have become the targets of war on crime. It comes as no surprise that way of thinking terrorism has generated similar profiling and detention tactics against Middle Eastern and South Asian males (Human Rights Watch 2002). Neither form of profiling has contributed much to public safety or national security, even though prisons and detention centers have been filled with those charged with minor criminal offenses and dubious accusations of supporting terrorism (Amnesty International 2003; Welch 2007b).

In a similar vein, the war on crime as applied to counter-terrorism contributes to a "hunkering down" mentality, thereby fortressing society with hard-line measures that impose greater restrictions on civil liberties. The USA Patriot Act grants new powers for the government to engage in a host of intrusive surveillance tactics, including "sneak and peek" searches (Chang 2002). Specifically, section 213 of the Patriot Act authorizes federal agents to perform covert investigations of a person's home or office without notice of the execution of the search warrant until the completion of the search. Such searches violate the common-law principle that law enforcement agents must "knock and announce" their arrival prior to conducting a search, as stipulated by the Fourth Amendment's reasonable requirement (*Wilson v. Arkansas* 1995). Section 213 also contravenes Rule 41(d) of the Federal Rules of Criminal Procedure that requires the officer removing property to furnish (or leave) a copy of the warrant and a receipt for the property taken. The provision is not subject to expiration; moreover, is not limited to terrorism investigations but applies to all criminal investigations (see *New York Times* 2004b, 2004c).[13] Also in the name of the national security, the Patriot Act adds new restrictions on peaceful demonstrations—especially antiwar rallies. Section 802 of the Patriot Act creates a federal crime of "domestic terrorism" that widely extends to "acts dangerous to human life that are a violation of the criminal laws" if they "appear to be intended . . . to influence the policy of a government by intimidation or coercion," and if they "occur primarily within the territorial jurisdiction of the United States." Like many features of the Patriot Act, that section is vague and sweeping in scope; hence, it enables federal law enforcement agencies to place under surveillance and investigate political activists and organizations that protest government policies. In effect, the act allows the government to criminalize legitimate political dissent.[14]

In closing his discussion on how the war on terror contributes to an ecology of fear, Simon (2007) notes that, unlike standardized crime rates that have some degree of reliability, the threat of terror cannot be easily measure or tracked over time, making it possible for government to deploy the possibility of terror as a political tactic. As the recent historical record clearly shows, since 9/11 the U.S. government has manipulated anxiety over terror so as to pave the way for numerous abuses of power, including and not limited to profiling, false detention, mistreatment of prisoners, torture, and the wars in Iraq and Afghanistan. Those activities and events are the lasting legacies of governing through terror. In the next final chapter, various features of the culture of impunity are explored in an effort to throw light on the problem—and prospects—of holding accountable government officials whose counterterrorism policies and practices violate domestic and international laws.

CHAPTER 9

States of Impunity

PRESIDENT BUSH IN 2007 approved plans to allow the CIA to resume its use of harsh interrogation methods for questioning terrorism suspects in secret prisons overseas. The new authorization permits that agency to move forward with a program that had been in limbo since the Supreme Court ruled that all prisoners in American captivity be treated in accordance with Geneva Convention prohibitions against humiliating and degrading treatment. A new executive order signed by the President does not authorize the compete set of extreme interrogation methods used by the CIA since the program was initiated in 2002; however, the rules would still allow some techniques considered harsher than those employed in interrogations by military personnel operating in Guantánamo Bay. Whereas the justice department has endorsed the new list of techniques, arguing that the interrogation program does not violate the Geneva Conventions, human rights experts condemned the executive order for its capacity to systematize a program of indefinite, incommunicado detention and tactics that violate international law. To counter criticism, the agency's director, General Michael V. Hayden, defended the program as being "irreplace-able," though he said extraordinary techniques had been used on fewer than half of about a hundred terrorism suspects. Hayden said the White House order authorizes the CIA to "focus on our vital work, confident that our mission and authorities are clearly defined" (Mazzetti 2007a, EV2). Officials said the agency had suspended its use of harsh interrogation procedures while the new rules were being debated in Congress, even as the White House argued that the agency should be granted extra latitude to carry out effective interrogations of terrorism suspects. Specific interrogation methods now approved for CIA use remain classified. The executive order applies only to detainees in CIA hands, not to those in military custody. It also bars the International Committee of the Red Cross from visiting detainees in agency hands, a prohibition the CIA has observed in the past (see Shane and Mazzetti 2007a; Weiner 2007).

INTRODUCTION

Adding clarity to America's controversial responses to terror since September 11, this study reveals recently committed crimes of power, including: unjust and illegal actions by the U.S. government encompassing detention without a fair trial, prisoner abuse and torture, as well as launching an unlawful war in Iraq. With all the evidence of wrongdoing staring us in the face, there remains a troubling question. Why haven't the architects and high-level officials who designed and delivered those orders been brought to justice? The easy answer is that those responsible for planning those human rights violations reside behind the protective wall of immunity surrounded by a wider public culture that either supports those policies and practices, or merely is willing to turn a blind eye. The not so easy reply involves a deeper sociological examination at what can be described as states of impunity. In his influential work, *States of Denial: Knowing About Atrocities and Suffering*, Stanley Cohen explores numerous defense mechanisms used by individuals, groups, and entire societies to shield themselves against a full realization of grave human rights violations. On a parallel plane, this chapter sets out to illuminate barriers—especially those pertaining to culture—that block and restrict efforts to punish and hold accountable major participants in state crime.

Penologists are intrigued by the interplay between culture and penality, attending to two viewpoints: an analytical dimension of social relations—"the cultural"—as well as a collective entity—hence, "a culture" (Garland 2006; Sewell 2005, 1999; Smith 2003). In the first sense of the term, the cultural is depicted as a causal force shaping punishment, drawing on a wider array of influences: ideas, symbols, values and meanings. Together, those sentiments play a role in determining the image of punishment, such as public hangings; or conversely abolishing the spectacle as it becomes viewed as uncivilized (Gatrell 1994). The second usage of the term, culture refers not to different aspects of the whole but as a complete entity. Culture, therefore, signifies a larger universe of meaning, for instance an American culture that is assumed to embody a unique form of social life and way of doing things. Indeed, along those lines of reasoning it is generally accepted that punishment is embedded in the cultural aspects of the national environment that creates it (Melossi 2001; Savelsberg 2002). Nonetheless, Garland (2006) carefully points out that there are pitfalls in artificially separating the "cultural" from its "culture"; as a corrective, he suggests that cultural analysis integrate both perspectives. Departing somewhat from a sociology that focuses on motives driving the need or desire to deliver retribution, this chapter inverts that dynamic to explain how punishment for wrongdoing is inhibited or bypassed altogether. Behind the states of impunity are significant cultural forces contributing to a larger problem described as American exceptionalism. It is apparent that many American politicians—and citizens—share a state of mind that international bodies espousing the rule of law do not apply to the U.S. government (Ignatieff 2003). Compounding matters, there remain important structural shifts in state power occurring since 9/11 that further its detachment from prosecution and subsequent penalties.

In this final round of discussion, we take a critical look at the states of impunity by bringing into relief the significance of a reconfigured executive power that not contributes to the perpetration of state crime but in doing so also resists accountability. Ostensibly such sovereign impunity poses a serious threat to human rights and democratic institutions, at home as well as abroad. Furthermore, the extension of immunity to economic players in the rebuilding of Iraq demonstrates how pervasive states of impunity have become. With an eye on culture, there is good reason to conclude that we are witnessing is a distinctly American way of evading responsibility. So as to integrate culture with the cultural, the chapter recounts various denials used to thwart accusations of wrongdoing; to be sure, there has emerged potent discourses opposing a wider acknowledgment of human rights abuses in the war on terror. In conclusion, we are left with a sober view that crimes of power present a formidable challenge to the rule of law in a post–9/11 world. Rather than concede to the prevailing form of state power and the culture that encircles it, however, several suggestions for resistance are introduced along with a cautious degree of optimism for a future that genuinely endorses human rights.

SOVEREIGN IMPUNITY IN A POST–9/11 WORLD

To understand fully state crimes in a post–9/11 world, it is crucial to take into account a reconfiguration of power that has contributed to detention without a fair trial, torture and abuse of prisoners, as well as the unlawful invasion of Iraq. As discussed previously, executive power has become increasingly recentralized, distancing itself from other branches of government. Indeed, without much interference from legislators or the courts, the executive has used the attacks of September 11 as a pretext to suspend law, claiming a national emergency. Determining precisely what those sociolegal shifts signify in American society continues to be a subject of scholarly conversation. From the standpoint of a risk society, Ericson (2007) draws connections between recent legal transformations and a neoliberal political culture preoccupied with uncertainty whereby a precautionary logic leads to extreme security maneuvers. Consequently, the executive has altered criminal law and established more civil and administrative antiterrorism measures which diminish due process and safeguards against arbitrary prosecution. Ericson concludes that since 9/11, criminal law is becoming unraveled from its previous incarnation as a tightly woven set of rules that affords specific rights to those charged with crimes.

The tendency for the state to undo criminal law is a phenomenon that Foucault (1977) characterizes as counter-law. Nonetheless, Ericson's use of the term is intended to make a particular theoretical point. That is, counter-law emerges within a risk-society so as to facilitate the state's ambition to harness uncertainty against a broader neoliberal anxiety over insecurity in late modern society. By doing so, controversial strategies are adopted which undermine the rule of law. Agamben (2005) similarly observes that we are witnessing the rise of a state of exception whereby law is suspended in the wake of a national emergency. Under those circumstances, normal legal principles and procedures are replaced by executive orders that determine the process for apprehending, detaining, and charging terror suspects. To that end, the executive contends that to defend the state against threats to national security, the existing legal order must be revamped in order to protect the social order. Ericson and Agamben agree that states of exception do not produce merely temporary suspensions of the legal order; rather, it gives way to a new paradigm of government.

Contributing further to a critical view of the new configuration of power, Butler (2004) enters the debate by reworking Foucault's (1991) conceptions of sovereignty and governmentality. Whereas sovereignty provides a guarantor for the representational claims for state power, governmentality becomes a mode of power inaugurated with the responsibility to control a population by way of policies implemented through a matrix of agencies that gain their authority under state power. Still, Foucault insists that sovereignty and governmentality coexist. Using as an illustration the detention center at Guantanamo Bay, Butler argues that state power in relation to governmentality and sovereignty has been overhauled since September 11. Indeed, the suspension of law has become a tactic of governmentality while simultaneously creating space for the resurgence of sovereignty. In concert, governmentality and sovereignty transform the state into a set of administrative powers; as a result, the executive enjoys greater—and virtually unchecked—power. In addition, the executive authorizes petty sovereigns (e.g., the CIA, special operations) to administer the war on terror, exercising power that they do not completely control. Citing executive privilege, the executive and its petty sovereigns maneuver without oversight from other government bodies (e.g., legislative and judicial branches), therefore possessing the discretion to render unilateral decisions. Butler argues that those transformations of power are so deprived of legitimate law that they constitute "a 'rogue' power par excellence" (2004, 56: see Suskind 2006).

As noted in chapter 2, there is good reason to conclude that in response to the attacks on September 11, a significant sociolegal phenomenon has emerged in the form of sovereign impunity. Blending Ericson's version of counter-law, Agamben's state of exception and Butler's sovereign governmentality, the concept draws attention to the consequences of a new configuration of power. Indeed, what makes reconfigured power all the more threatening to democratic institutions and human rights is its immunity; indeed, in the absence of meaningful oversight, crimes of power are likely to persist. As prisoner abuse and torture, for instance, tend to occur behind a shroud of secrecy, sovereign impunity does not simply serve to evade scrutiny; rather, it allows officials to go on the offensive, boldly claiming executive privilege in refusing to cooperate with any legal or criminal investigation. Because of its inherent lack accountability, sovereign impunity is a prime source for state crimes in the war on terror, immunizing state actors and their operatives from prosecution while removing roads for victims seeking justice and compensation. Such state crimes are likely to continue given a wider political culture that reframes such actions as necessary tools—or "lesser evils"—to safeguard national security (Ignatieff 2004; see Dershowitz 2002). Certainly, there are laws in the United States that forbid torture and the mistreatment of prisoners.[1] Still, even though some low-level soldiers have been prosecuted for such crimes as in the case of Abu Ghraib, it is unlikely that a member of the CIA or special operations would be similarly prosecuted. The political will to do so simply does not exist. Therefore, government officials who order or participate in such crimes of power generally do so without much compunction or fear of being forced to stand trial for war crimes. As governing through terror becomes a frequently traveled path, the zone of impunity is likely to expand particularly since immunity is also extended to corporate actors working under the tent of state operations. As put forth in the next segment, there is evidence of a widening political economy of impunity.

A Political Economy of Immunity

Not only is the idea of sovereign impunity an important sociolegal development, it also carries weight within a broader political economy affecting global affairs. Consider the emergence of the International Criminal Court (ICC), an institution that continues to face enormous political and economic pressure from U.S. officials intent on undermining the court's authority. Following decades of careful planning, the ICC was established in 1998 when delegates of more than 140 nations agreed on the terms of the Rome Statute, which granted the court jurisdiction to prosecute crimes of genocide, crimes against humanity, war crimes, and crimes of aggression. In its preamble, the Rome Statute emphasizes that the international community should not allow such atrocities to go unpunished. Despite recent progress, however, the formation of the ICC has a complex history and a complicated structure. For instance, the ratification process varies with each state's domestic legal system: in the United States, adoption requires Senate approval. Although the U.S. was initially supportive of the Rome Statute, it later back pedaled citing procedural and organization problems surrounding the court (Schabas 2004; Scheffer 1999; Sewall and Kaysen 2000).[2]

After signing the treaty in 2000, President Clinton retreated and even recommended that the Senate not ratify the treaty. President Bush went further to obstruct the court's authority by signing into law H.R. 2500 (Departments of Commerce, Justice, State, the Judiciary, and Related Agencies Act, 2001) which contains a provision that strips funds for any cooperation or assistance to the ICC. In 2002, the Bush administration delivered a letter to the UN declaring to "unsign" the Rome Statute (Bolton 2002). So as to ensure its immunity from the ICC's jurisdiction, the United States threatened to cease all relief aid to Bosnia and Herzegovina as well as to East Timor. In their summary of the U.S. campaign against the ICC, Mullins, Kauzlarich, and Rothe (2004, 295) write,

> The result of the pressure put on the U.N. and the international community resulted with a controversial U.N. resolution. On 12 July 2002, the Security Council voted on resolution 1422 granting peacekeepers from non-State Parties a one-year immunity from prosecution by the ICC. Resolution 1422 has been viewed as an attempt by the U.S. to undertake a multifaceted approach in its efforts to prevent the functioning of the ICC as it was intended (U.S. Ambassador John Negroponte 7-12-02). Resolution 1422 was followed by the ASMPA, passed 2 August 2002, which restricts: (1) U.S. cooperation in any manner with the ICC, (2) participation in U.N. peacekeeping, and (3) the provision of military assistance to most countries which ratify the Rome Statute. It also gives the President complete power to take any action necessary to release any U.S. or allied person held by the ICC (American Servicepersons Protection Act; ICC ASP Special Edition 8/2002, HR 4775).

White House officials also set out to rewrite significant passages of the Rome Statute such as article 98, thereby rendering the court impotent in attaining jurisdictional authority over U.S. nationals, military personnel and peacekeepers abroad. The United States declared that it would consider revoking military aid and assistance to any State that refused to approve the revised version of article 98 (Rothe and Mullins 2006a, 2006b).[3] Adding to the growing dialogue on American exceptionalism, an observer writes, "The extraordinary vendetta conducted—largely but not exclusively by John Bolton—against the International Criminal Court brought out not only the Bush administration's paranoia about how a malevolent UN and Court could indict innocent American soldiers and officers, but how punitive the United States could become against states (allies or not) unwilling to meet U.S. demands" (Hoffman 2005, 229). It is clear that the hardball tactics deployed by the United States against weaker nations demonstrate a political economy of immunity that significantly restricts the reach of the court, producing a shield of impunity for perpetrators of state crimes (see Cuellar 2003; Koh 2005).[4]

Although sovereign impunity refers to the immunization of state actors against prosecution for war crimes, there is growing concern over the state's willingness to abdicate some of its responsibilities to private military and security firms as well as intelligence and interrogation contractors (Avant 2005,

2004; Singer 2005, 2003). Furthering the notion of a political economy of impunity, security services are outsourced to players in the market place. By doing so the state not only transfers authority to the private sector but also extends immunity against charges of wrongdoing (Newburn 2007; Zedner 2006). Critical attention goes beyond crimes involving corporate theft and fraud to serious human rights abuses, including the wounding and killing civilians and abusing and torturing detainees.

To be clear, a political economy of impunity has emerged in the aftermath of the invasion of Iraq when the U.S. government began setting up its financial projects with its private partners. Chapter 6 reviews in detail evidence showing that the reconstruction of Iraq occurs within a lassez-faire ideology (i.e., neoliberalism) that promotes the pursuit of profits while minimizing state-sponsored regulation of the market place, a formula that has contributed to rampant corruption (Kramer and Michalowski 2005; Whyte 2007). Vanishing official accountability has paved the way for legal immunity covering all U.S. personnel for activities related to the reconstruction of the Iraqi economy. Bush's authorization of Executive Order 13303 shields any U.S. national from prosecution (or other judicial proceedings) from any wrongdoing with respect to the Defense Fund for Iraq and all Iraqi proceeds, including corruption, theft, and embezzlement involving Iraqi oil. Furthermore, the umbrella of impunity covering the private sector is upheld by Order 17 referring to members of the coalition military forces, foreign missions, and contractors operating in Iraq (Kelly 2004). Whereas some "token enforcements" against persons charged with fraud have occurred (Willis 2005), there remains a deeper political economy of impunity that merely fuels illegal and unethical financial schemes in the reconstruction of Iraq (Christadoulou 2006; Christian Aid 2003; Green and Ward 2004). Moreover, on a much larger scale, there is evidence of serious breaches of international humanitarian law pertaining to the illegal transformation of the Iraqi economy since the Fourth Geneva Convention (1949) prohibits an occupying power from redeveloping the economy in its own vision (see Greider 2003; Klein 2007; Krugman 2004). Despite compelling evidence of economic war crimes, including violations of UNSCR 1483, it is unrealistic to expect prosecutions of any high-level officials in the CPA and U.S. government (see Hogan, Long, Stretesky, and Lynch 2006; Long, Hogan, Stretesky, and Lynch 2007; Shanker and Myers 2008).

The political economy of impunity in occupied Iraq also is worrisome, considering other forms of criminal conduct, particularly the victimization of civilians and detainees at the hands of corporate employees. The previous chapter offers details of private security firms engaging in lethal violence on the streets of Iraq's cities, including the 2007 incidents involving Blackwater, a company contracted by U.S. state department (Fainaru and al-Izzi 2007). In addition, evidence of detainees being abused and tortured by staff members of private intelligence firms is well established (Harbury 2005; Hersh 2004). While secrecy continues to conceal much of the mistreatment of detainees by U.S. servicemen, efforts to investigate private firms for war crimes is even more difficult because of the limits of legality. As noted, in contrast to their government counterparts, private companies are not subject to Freedom of Information Requests (Singer 2005). Moreover, prosecuting contractors for injuring or killing civilians or detainees is also difficult; because of the terms of their work agreement, they are neither military personnel nor civilians. Therefore, unlawful violence committed by contractors constitutes a form of state-corporate crime immune to prosecution because their commercial imperatives are linked to strong political interests; in tandem, they weaken the criminalization processes that would otherwise induce as a deterrent (Quinney 1977). Those crimes also are hard to control because they take place inside an orbit beyond the state or even the conventional business world (Kramer, Michalowski, Kauzlarich 2002, 263; Friedrichs 1996). Those observations notwithstanding there are other significant forces at play that contribute to a culture of impunity, including various forms of denial that undermine attempts to implicate persons involved in crimes of power.

DENIAL AND DISCOURSE

To deepen our understanding of a culture of impunity, we turn to some social psychological dimensions of denial. On that subject Cohen's (2001) work remains at the forefront of an emerging sociology of denial, prompting subsequent examinations of denial in a post–9/11 world (Downes, Rock, Chinkin, and Gearty 2007; Welch 2007c; 2006a, 2003). It was during his research on torture in Israel that Cohen (1995) realized that the phenomenon of denial is exceedingly complex. In response to his findings that the torture of Palestinian detainees had become routine, Israeli officials as well as the mainstream public issued an array oppositions: "outright denial (it doesn't happen); discrediting (the organization was biased, manipulated or gullible); renaming (yes, something does happen, but it is not torture); and justification (anyway 'it' was morally justified)" (2001, xi). Cohen's analysis does not end there; he goes on to develop further what he refers to as the elementary forms of denial, throwing crucial light on its various dimensions. As we delve into the nature of disavowal it becomes apparent that it is tightly stitched around discourse: the ways people talk and its influence on how they act or don't act. Statements of denial, as observed by Cohen, are assertions that something did not happen. Such declarations have three possibilities, two of which are rather straightforward. First, it is true that something did not happen. Second, it is possible that something did happen and those who deny it are simply lying so as to cover up the incident and deceive a larger audience.

The third possibility is more intricate insofar as denial may neither be a matter of simply telling the truth or deliberately providing false information. Somewhere in between there seems to be a state of mind in which one simultaneously knows and does not know. There rests an important paradox. Employing the term denial to characterize a person's statement "I didn't know" implies that the person in question actually knows something about what happened. That state of mind may also very well exist at the collective level, for instance, among villagers living near a concentration camp. In that context, denial in the form of "turning a blind eye" or "looking the other way" is instrumental, serving as a defense mechanism for coping with the realization that what is happening is simply too painful to ponder. Mass denial often becomes a cultural habit as members of dominant groups create psychological and emotional distance separating themselves from those subjected to repression, discrimination, and racism. Denial therefore is multilayered, including "cognition (not acknowledging the facts); emotion (not feeling, not being disturbed); morality (not recognizing wrongness or responsibility) and action (not taking steps in response to knowledge) (Cohen 2001, 9). Whereas denial may occur at the individual level, it is at the official and cultural tiers that we find it significant to impunity. As denial becomes collective and highly organized, barriers to finding out what actually happened become increasingly fortified, especially as government leaders go to great lengths to stonewall and cover up human rights abuses while deploying a sharply crafted spin (see Welch 2006a). Adding to an absence of accountability for upper military and political figures implicated in crimes of power is the American public unwillingness to demand more forthright details on prisoner abuse (e.g., Abu Ghraib, Guantanamo Bay), torture, and extraordinary renditions, as well as the doctored evidence linking Saddam Hussein to weapons of mass destruction—the principle rationale for the U.S. invasion of Iraq.

Another key component of the elementary forms of denial is what Cohen identifies as the atrocity triangle comprised of victims (to whom things are done), perpetrators (who do these things), and observers (who witness or have knowledge about what is happening). In the realm of victimization, one can distinguish between things that "happen" to certain people and things that are deliberately done to them. The former is often framed as "accidents," however tragic (e.g., being hit by an errant missile), while the latter is best described as conscious "acts" of harm (e.g., being raped and murdered by a soldier). In either scenario, there is a perpetrator whose conduct is usually defined by government officials as either unfortunate in case of "accidents" or as unusual—"bad apples"—in the case of deliberate "acts" of violence. Such discourse facilitates denial by providing a quick explanation of events without having to look closer into circumstances surrounding violence, thereby deflecting criticism. In the end, bystanders (e.g., fellow soldiers and citizens) are more or less satisfied with the official characterization of events, allowing them to move on and think about other matters. Still, the role of bystanders in the larger frame of denial is crucial to comprehending impunity. Cohen offers a wider typology of bystanders to include: (1) immediate, literal, physical or internal (firsthand witnesses or those nearby); (2) external or metaphorical (consumers of secondary sources about an atrocity as transmitted by the media or humanitarian groups); (3) bystander states (other governments or international organizations).

Even something as secret as torture has immediate bystanders who witness or have specific knowledge about infliction of pain on a detainee; indeed, interrogators frequently receive instructions from those higher up in the military or intelligence service and usually soldiers serving as guards in prisons have a pretty good idea what is going on around them (Rose 2004). At Abu Ghraib, for instance, photographs of tortured and humiliated detainees were used as computer screensavers on military laptops long before those images were released to the public (Hersh 2004). It is suggested that many immediate bystanders remain passive because responsibility is diffused; that is, with so many people watching, surely someone else will take action. In other situations, witnesses may be unlikely to act because they are unable to identify with the victim (e.g., because of ethnic differences) or are unable to conceive of effective intervention (e.g., because of the pressure to keep quiet within military units) (Cohen 2001, 16). While it is true that some servicemen did intervene to report incidents of prisoner abuse, such complaints were stalled by superior officers until the information was directed to other political actors in Congress, as was the case of Captain Fishback at Camp Mercury in Iraq (Schmitt 2005). For external bystanders who receive knowledge through the media about, for example, prisoner abuse, responsibility also is diffused due similar dynamics. There may exist a sense that the Pentagon is either too powerful to challenge directly or that its leaders are taking appropriate action to deal with the "bad apple" perpetrators. Indeed, virtually all of the military panels commissioned to study the Abu Ghraib scandal concluded that the abuse was confined to a small unit of guards and, by no means, was a systemic problem (Harbury 2005; McCoy 2006). Similarly, bystander states contribute to impunity when they do not confront other governments for human rights violations. Whereas condemnation of the U.S. military for its role in prisoner abuse at Abu Ghraib and for its operations at Guantanamo Bay is shared by nations across the globe, there is less fanfare in admonishing the United States for its use of extraordinary renditions and secret prisons which have had the cooperation of many countries, including those in the European Union where its human rights charter clearly prohibits those forms of covert action (Smith and Mekhennet 2006).

A critical understanding of human rights abuses in the war on terror benefits from acknowledging the structural aspects of impunity, most notably a reconfigured form of power since 9/11 (chapter 2, 3) and its extensions to the political economy embodied in colonization (chapter 6, 7) as well as outsourcing and privatization (chapter 8). Nonetheless, it is important to delve further into a sociology of denial for additional insights into crimes of power.

Denial theory claims to understand not the structural causes of the behaviour (the reasons), but the accounts typically given by deviants themselves (their reasons). It is concerned less with the literal denial than with
interpretations or implications—especially attempted evasions of judgement
('It's not as bad as you say'). (Cohen 2001, 58)

Long before the term discourse entered the American lexicon of social
thought, sociologists have had a keen interest in deciphering how people talk
about their personal motives that determine how they act. In the 1940s,
C. Wright Mills turned attention to the "vocabulary of motives" to reveal how
ordinary persons explain their actions even when their conduct contradicts
the prevailing norm. Cohen similarly notes that perpetrators and bystanders
resort to unique "motivational accounts" or "speech acts" which serve to justify their actions (see Scott and Lyman 1968). Unlike the classic Freudian
rationalization aimed at repressing shameful deeds, vocabulary of motives provide initial authorization for one's behavior which is indeed deliberated in
advance. By doing so, the account is made to make the decision to do something seem more rational and justifiable than it usually is. The internal solilo-
quy might sound like, "If I do this, what will I then be able to say to myself
and others?" (Cohen 2001, 59). Such personal dialogue is intended not to
keep one's actions secret; rather, it anticipates others finding out what one
does and tries—at times strenuously—to make one's behavior seem within the
social norm. However, since one's deviant or even criminal behavior is
squarely outside the norm such moral accounting constitutes denial, delivered
prior to action. Nevertheless, such justifications are offered with the expectation that they will be accepted by others; moreover, vocabulary of motives
often is tailored to match a particular audience. Consider, for example, White
House memos assembled in *The Torture Papers* (Greenberg and Dratel 2005), in
which government lawyers attempted to lay out in advance a legal argument
that would override the conventional definition of torture. As mentioned previously, Joshua Dratel observes, "Rarely, if ever, has such a guilty governmental conscience been so starkly illuminated in advance" (2005, xxi). In denying
charges that his administration was condoning torture, Bush not only engaged
in act adjustment ("It's not what it looks like") but also actor adjustment
("I am not the sort of person who does things like this"). Similarly, he repeatedly told the world "torture is never acceptable, nor do we hand people to
countries that do torture" (Mayer 2005, EV1 see Cohen 2001, 62).

Denial theory distinguishes between justifications and excuses. The former
refers to accounts in which a person accepts responsibility for certain acts but
denies that there is anything wrong with their conduct. In the latter, one concedes that the act was wrong but denies full responsibility for it, thereby claiming impunity (Cohen 2001; Scott and Lyman 1960). The infamous "just

following orders" defense is aimed at averting not only responsibility but more importantly accountability as described in Kelman and Hamilton's *Crimes of Obedience* (1989), which examines the My Lai massacre in Vietnam where some 500 unarmed old men, women, and children were slaughtered by U.S. soldiers. Moreover, the "just following orders" excuse transcends mere organizational objectives; rather, it is embedded into a more convoluted discourse over patriotism, nationalism, and service to one's country, all of which echoes the "defense of the eternal good" (Katz 1988). The work of Sykes and Matza (1957) contributes enormously to a sociology of denial, particularly since their study involving the techniques of neutralization are intended to undo the moral bind of law in pursuit of impunity. Perhaps anticipating accusations of war crimes for the invasion of Iraq, members of the Bush administration resorted to the following forms of denial so as to justify their actions. As Kramer and Michalowski (2005, 463) put it, "They denied responsibility (the war was Saddam's fault), denied the victims (most were terrorists), denied injury (there was only limited 'collateral damage'), condemned the condemners (protestors were unpatriotic and the French were ungrateful and cowardly) and appealed to higher loyalties (God directed Bush to liberate the Iraqi people)."

Apart from the obvious significance of neutralization theory there are some limitations, as Cohen (2001) reminds us. In the realm of moral indifference, the five techniques of neutralization do not address "consistent repudiations" of conventional moral codes. Consider, for instance, American exceptionalism contained in the U.S. campaign to undermine the International Criminal Court (Ignatieff 2005; Rothe and Mullins 2006). A sociology of denial, however, reaches further into the nature of ideology and its influence over denial. Contained in consistent repudiations is a denial of the moral legitimacy of widely accepted principles aimed at protecting human rights, including absolute prohibitions against torture and the right to a fair trial: both of which have failed to be recognized at Guantanamo Bay and various secret prisons operated by the CIA. Consistent repudiations of such human right protections are not necessarily opportunistic; rather, there is an inherent justification existing before and after the act. "Pure ideological crimes do not require neutralization, because there is no morally legitimate universe outside the ideology. There is no need to be innocent of 'troubling recognition'—because the recognition is not troubling" (Cohen 2001, 98). As pure ideological narratives become embedded in the political process, their stridence serves to ward off external reality checks. Even in the face of evidence that a particular action was politically unwise, morally wrong, and damaging to a particular population, perpetrators—and many bystanders—stick to their narrative of ideological indifference: "I still think what I did was right" (Cohen 2001, 99). Several years into the war in Iraq which clearly has produced more harm than good, Bush and a vast majority of his fellow Republicans consistently claim that the decision to invade was the right thing to do. Moreover, a large segment of the general population also concurs.[5] Here it is important not to characterize political support for the war in Iraq as mindless social conformity. The ideological frame of denial keeps ordinary people from fully realizing the harm and immorality of the many controversial features of America's war on terror (e.g., torture, the unlawful enemy combatant designation). Moreover, such psychological insulation allows them to find comfort in adopting a form of "pseudo-stupidity, not grasping what the fuss was about" (Cohen 2001, 100; see Arendt 1994[1965]).

Fortunately for the sake of the human rights not all Americans stand firmly behind the government and its harmful—and self-defeating—tactics in the war on terror. Moreover, today's multimediated political forum makes dissent possible in numerous ways, especially via the Internet with websites, emails, and the growing popularity of blogs where ordinary people can post their thoughts on issues for the entire world to read. Against that backdrop of resistance, however, governments go on the offensive to shore up support for its policies. Among its tactics are preemptive attacks to "shoot the messenger" and depict allegations of human rights abuses as politically motivated lies, radical propaganda, or simply naïve criticism of a very complicated problem (Cohen 2001). Internal critics are expected to be hit sharply by political whips. Consider the case of Valerie Plame, the CIA agent whose secret identity was revealed by White House operatives when her husband, Ambassador Joe Wilson, published a *New York Times* op-ed challenging the U.S. government's claim that Hussein had attained bomb-making ingredients (i.e., enriched uranium) from Niger.[6] To be sure, denial and discourse contribute further to a cultural frame that serves to threaten human rights; still, as the next passage describes, there are other harmful sources.

THREATS TO HUMAN RIGHTS

Whereas an emerging field of human rights studies offers optimistic outlooks for improved social relations, there remain voices of caution and skepticism, especially in light of the crimes of power contained in the war on terror. In *Can Human Rights Survive?* Conor Gearty gives us reason to pause. Looking at recent developments in the way governments—namely, the United Kingdom and United States—proceed with antiterrorism policy and practice, Gearty is left wondering whether human rights can withstand such repressive and belligerent strategies. Consider the following scenario. In central London, a terrorist attack kills six people and injures more than forty. The prime minister moves to repeal habeas corpus, having recently banned all political demonstrations in the city. The London metropolitan police chief announces to the media his assessment that there are 10,000 armed terrorists in the city poised to strike more innocent people. To shore up security, the chief deputizes an additional

50,000 special constables. Teams of special police units search the sewer systems for explosives. The queen weighs into the emergency, suggesting that terrorists be lynched on the spot. Whereas those events seem as if they occurred over the past few years, they actually took place in 1867 (Bennett 2005). The terrorists were the Irish Fenians, considered the Al-Qaeda of their day. "Their totemic status as the bogeyman of British society was enjoyed for far longer than Osama Bin Laden and his cohorts are likely to be able to manage, though the state's reaction to both is hauntingly similar" (Gearty 2006, 100).

Plots by Irish nationals would continue to preoccupy British politicians, police, and citizens for more than a century. During one week in 1939, the home secretary rushed through antiterrorism legislation after the government claimed that it had discovered the "S Plan" in which it was believed that the Irish Republican Army was scheming to attack London's water supply, drainage system, transport lines, and electrical grid before moving to blow up Parliament. It was later determined that the government possessed knowledge of the plan for seven months but decided not to publicize it since intelligence revealed that the Irish Republican Army was being stimulated by foreign organizations. When the home secretary finally made public his investigation, he asked the media "not to press me for details," leaving the nation to assume that the IRA had the backing of the German Nazis or Italian fascists. It later turned out that the foreigner supporters were neither of those groups; rather, it was the Irish-Americans (Ewing and Gearty 2000). Despite decades of renewed antiterrorism legislation and police tactics, the IRA campaign persisted, even as recently as the Omagh bombing in 1998. Paradoxically, the Terrorism Act of 2000 was passed as the Irish-based political violence was coming to an end, but the story of Britain's war on terror is not purely one of ethical police work; on the contrary, in the face of a well-armed and highly motivated IRA, the government resorted to lengthy detentions, kangaroo courts, prisoner abuse, and torture, even against innocent people. Human rights had indeed taken a back seat to aggressive—and illegal—security measures (Campbell and Connolly 2006; *Ireland v. United Kingdom* 1978; McEvoy 2003).

Nowadays both the American and Britain versions of the war on terror have fixed their sights on the "new" terrorism, most notably political violence committed by so-called Islamic fundamentalists. As a result, the new discourse on terror emphasizing danger and fear are in direct competition with a human rights movement committed to dignity and hope. At the political level, the war on terror undermines two major ethical ideas of the contemporary age: democracy and the rule of law (Gearty 2006; see Crelinsten 2003; Hoffman 2000). As noted previously, recent antiterrorism strategies have created an enhanced executive which rides roughshod over the separation of governmental powers at the domestic level and the rule of law at the international one (Agamben 2005; Butler 2004). Still, the suspension of law in the wake of a national emergencies echoes broader anxieties in late modern society (Ericson 2007). Anxieties over insecurity are reflected in the new terror discourse, prompting Gearty to ask, Why is terrorism so different from other forms of violent crime? Why does it warrant such extreme state actions that would otherwise not be considered legitimate even by the mainstream public? Alluding to the notion of governing through terror, Gearty goes on to wonder how terrorism become so central to political discourse, paving the way for greater state control which subverts the entire human rights project.

In trying to answer such far reaching questions, critical attention is turned to how terrorism is currently framed. Gearty's analyis parallels Garland's (2001) critique of the criminology of the other as well as Feeley and Simon's (1992) new penology, which concentrates on aggregates of perceived lawbreakers: concluding that terrorism is not so much viewed as a method of violence but as a category of people and the sort of thing a person is rather than the kind of thing a person does. That way of thinking about terrorism suggests a form of criminal anthropology whereby it is presumed that persons who engage in political violence are inherently different from the rest of society (see Foucault 1977 on criminal anthropology). Although those labels do resonate in the public imagination, it is the state that determines who or which (ethnic) group is defined as a terrorist, and in doing so, rarely do the authorities have to provide evidence to back up their claims. And, indeed, once the label is assigned it sticks, demonstrating the sheer power of state-sponsored definitions (Welch, Fenwick, and Roberts 1997). Discourse on the "new" terrorism also depicts perpetrators as particularly dangerous, thereby inviting more extreme tactics to be used by the state, including lengthy detentions without trial, kidnapping (i.e., extraordinary renditions), prisoner abuse, and torture. Such state crime is remarkable similar to crimes committed by terrorists; however, because the governments actions are defined as legitimate and necessary to ensure national security, the public usually accepts the alibi, making it complicit in crimes of power.

Threats to human rights also are located in a key paradigm shift in the war on terror. The ideal of human rights has traditionally been upheld by the criminal justice model in which defendants have rights to due process, a lawyer of their choice, a fair trial, and so forth. Moreover, the state has the burden to prove its case before a jury and is obliged to obey rules concerning evidence, discovery, et cetera. The criminal justice model offers a durable process regardless of the nature of the offense, however heinous. Furthermore, it provides a framework and orientation that keeps the state from deviating off course into unethical or even illegal domains of governance. The criminal justice model rests on longstanding principles of the rule of law, thereby precluding the need for a different discourse such as the language of "new" terrorism. By contrast, the terror model, in the words of Gearty, "blows a hole in this system. It disregards the criminal in favour of a language rooted in generalities which has little time for individual dignity or the rule of law" (2006, 125). Similar to the notion of counter-law or the undoing of law, the terror paradigm abandons safeguards against overzealous policing and prosecutions. The emphasis on security rather than criminal justice has indeed compromised human rights. In the United Kingdom, for instance, human rights law has largely accommodated security-oriented changes such as ethnic profiling in the form of stop and searches of South Asian males. Without clearly defining what terrorism actually is, the state permits executive judgment on who is involved in terror-related activities without the safeguards that would be required had the criminal justice model be followed (Gearty 2006, 2005b, 2003).

Similarly, in the United States, the criminal justice model also continues to be compromised by the terror paradigm, as the 2007 conviction of Jose Padilla illustrates. Padilla, initially accused of planning to detonate a "dirty" radioactive bomb, was transferred from military custody (after three and a half years) to stand trial in federal criminal court, where he was convicted on con-spiracy charges (Goodnough and Shane 2007). Apart from the securing the conviction, legal experts note that the real innovation was the justice depart-ment's use of a seldom-tested conspiracy law that requires relatively thin evi-dence, thereby cementing a new prosecutorial model in terrorism cases. The central charge against Padilla was conspiracy to murder, maim, and kidnap people in a foreign country: punishable by life in prison. However, as Robert M. Chesney, a law professor at Wake Forest University, adds, "There is no need to show any particular violent crime. You don't have to specify the particular means used to carry out the crime" (Liptak 2007, EV2). In the prosecution of Padilla, the strongest piece of evidence was what the government claimed to be an application form that Padilla filled out to attend a training camp run by Al-Qaeda in Afghanistan in 2000. "It is a pretty big leap between a mere indi-cation of desire to attend a camp and a crystallized desire to kill, maim and kidnap," said attorney Peter S. Margulies (Liptak 2007, EV2).

Also in the United States, similar shifts to the terror model have not only allowed the executive to carry out policies without much resistance from other branches of government but in doing so has produced an open rejection of the rule of law: including presidential claims that the Geneva Conventions to do not extend to certain combatants and that the Convention against Torture did not apply to the non-Americans outside the United States. Expressing hostility toward the criminal justice model, Bush proclaimed in his 2004 state of the union address, "It is not enough to serve our enemies with legal papers." Likewise, Rumsfeld declared in the 2005 National Defense Strategy: "Our strength as a nation state will continue to be challenged by those who employ a strategy of the weak using international fora, judicial processes, and terrorism" (Greenberg 2005). Of course, the terror model is empowered by its very language, particularly with respect to how it depicts the post–9/11 world, becoming a battleground between good and evil. Days following September 11, Bush delivered the memorable words that would continue to shape America's response to terror: "Our responsibility to history is already clear: to answer these attacks and rid the world of evil" (Lifton 2003, 12).[7] Certainly talking about terror in mystical terms presents a formidable challenge to human rights since it serves to excuse extraordinary renditions, abuse of prisoners, torture, and other forms of state crime all in the name of national security. That "ends justify the means" approach to the antiterrorism has support from some otherwise liberal commentators and professors, some of whom even claim to be advocates of human rights (Dershowitz 2002; see *Nation* 2005). In Ignatieff's *The Lesser Evil: Political Ethics in Age of Terror*, he argues that "Western" society either fights evil with evil or it will succumb to terrorist movements. In riposte, Gearty observes that those

> manifestations of state power are not any longer simple wrongs to be avoided and severely punished when they occur; rather they have become a set of proposed solutions to supposed ethical dilemmas that need now to be considered and debated, as you might consider any other policy proposal. The unspeakable is no longer unspoken. Even the greatest of our human rights taboos—the prohibition on torture and inhuman and degrading treatment—has become just another point of view—and to some an eccentrically absolutist one at that. (2006, 131–132; see Welch 2008b)

Adopting mystical language embodied in the security model leads to other threats to human rights in the form of militant humanitarianism which played a role in the invasion of Afghanistan, Iraq, and perhaps future imperial adventures disguised as "spreading freedom" (see chapter 6). So as to preserve human rights conceived as a set of principles aimed at protecting individual dignity while holding the state in check with democratic governance, traditional criminal justice ought not be replaced with paradigms that encourage official wrongdoing so as to rid the world of evil. Gearty (2006) reminds us that one of the great achievements of international law has been the removal of mystical rhetoric from the relationship between states (see Oberleitner 2004). As the next and penultimate section suggests, there are other ways to reinstate a genuine commitment to human rights.

REINSTATING HUMAN RIGHTS

Of course, another way to reinstate human rights is to hold nations and their actors accountable for their transgressions, especially in the realm of extraordinary renditions, torture, and other serious abuses of power. In 2007, an Italian judge ordered the first trial involving the U.S. program of kidnapping terror suspects on foreign soil, indicting twenty-six Americans most of whom are CIA agents. The case also includes Italy's former top spy. The controversy stems from the abduction of a radical Egyptian cleric, Hassan Mustafa Osama Nasr (known as Abu Omar) who disappeared near his mosque in Milan in 2003 and transported to an Egyptian jail where he was held for nearly four years and tortured. Despite the potent legal language contained in the indictment, it is unlikely that any of the Americans will ever stand trial in Italy. The case nevertheless presents an opportunity for observers to see how such proceedings may contribute efforts to protect human rights. In Europe, the indictment marks a turning point where public anger is growing over extraordinary rendition. Those U.S. operations not only violate European Union human rights law but also breach national sovereignty.

Also in 2007, the Swiss government approved an investigation into the flight that allegedly carried Nasr from Italy to Germany across Swiss airspace; the plane is believed to have departed from an American air base in Germany to Egypt. With similar concerns, a European parliamentary committee issued an extensive report claiming that since September 11, 2001, there have been as many as 1,245 secret CIA flights in Europe. The investigation is troubling for many EU member states since it infers that they had knowledge of those operations or even cooperated with the United States. Baroness Sarah Ludford of Britain, member of the European Parliament, replied, "We believe there has been either active collusion by several European Union governments or turning a blind eye" (Fisher 2007, EV2). The politics surrounding the Italian case are particularly sensitive since it implies possible complicity of the government of then-Prime Minister Silvio Berlusconi. Among the Italians indicted was Nicolo Pollari, who until early 2007 was the chief of military intelligence, along with Marco Mancini, his former deputy. Pollari denies responsibility, adding that he cannot adequately defend himself because he would need to use evidence that is classified as state secrets: his defense suggests that officials outranking him approved the kidnapping (Associated Press 2007c; Grey and Povoledo 2006).

While similar investigations into extraordinary renditions are unfolding in Portugal and Spain, it is the case the German courts that is attracting much interest since it is regarded as the most serious legal challenge yet to the CIA's secret transfers of terrorism suspects. The court issued an arrest warrant for thirteen people in connection with the mistaken kidnapping and jailing of Khaled el-Masri, a German citizen of Lebanese descent who was seized in Macedonia in 2003 and flown to Afghanistan. There he was imprisoned there for five months and reports being shackled, beaten, and interrogated about his alleged ties to Al-Qaeda, before being released without charges. The case is considered the most documented episode involving extraordinary renditions. August Stern, the deputy prosecutor in Munich, explained, "This is a very consequential step. It is a necessary step before bringing a criminal case against these people" (Landler 2007, EV2). Investigators are seeking the identities of the thirteen people, including the four-member crew of the Boeing 737 that picked up Masri, a mechanic, and several other CIA operatives in Macedonia. Compared to the Italian case, the arrest warrant in Germany appears to carry greater weight, according to legal experts, because of the reputation of its courts for painstaking deliberation; moreover, strong diplomatic ties between Germany and the United States are expected to figure prominently. Since the Frankfurt airport has been used for many of the flights (along with the American air base at Ramstein), Germans are searching to determine whether its government has been tolerating or facilitating the renditions. There remain complications, because German courts do not permit trials in absentia, unlike in Italy; furthermore, it is unlikely that the Bush administration would cooperate in the extradition of the thirteen people covered by the arrest warrant. Still, the indictment could hinder the defendants' ability to move around Europe, and the German news media has published and broadcasted the names of those believed to be involved.

Masri petitioned—albeit unsuccessfully—the U.S. Supreme Court to reinstate a lawsuit he filed against the CIA after a federal appeals court threw out the suit. In both courts, the judiciary accepted the government's argument that it would be impossible to try the case without revealing state secrets (Stout 2007c). The U.S. justice department also declined to help German prosecutors in their investigation, citing pending legal cases. Those roadblocks have prompted the Germans to depend on information from other sources, including journalists. The German prosecutor concedes a major break in the case emanates from a Spanish reporter who assembled a list of the names of people who participated in the abduction from sources in the Civil Guard, a Spanish paramilitary unit. The Spanish island of Majorca has been used by the CIA as a logistics point for its flights, and investigators located the names of members of the rendition team on local hotel log. In addition, prosecutors received supportive information from government lawyers in Italy as well as from Dick Marty, a Swiss senator who conducted an inquiry into the rendition program on behalf of the Council of Europe (Smith and Mekhennet 2006).[8] The role of Germany in the abduction is being questioned since Masri claims that while imprisoned in Kabul, he was interrogated by a German who went by the name of Sam. Also, German Foreign Minister Frank-Walter Steinmeier is under scrutiny since he served as chief of staff to the former chancellor, Gerhard Schroder. During that period he had oversaw all German intelligence services. Steinmeier has been asked to explain his activity in another case involving Murat Kurnaz, a German-born Turkish man who was imprisoned for more than four years at Guantanamo Bay. Kurnaz, was released by the United States in 2006 following lengthy negotiations between Berlin and Washington; however, internal German intelligence documents indicate that the Germans declined an offer by the Americans to send Mr. Kurnaz home as early as 2002 (Landler 2007).

While human rights advocates await further developments in the Italian and German cases against CIA agents, another recent episode suggests that some victims of extraordinary renditions may find recourse in the judiciary. In a widely publicized rendition case, Maher Arar, a Canadian citizen born in Syria, was arrested in 2003 while connecting flights at New York's Kennedy Airport after returning from vacation with his family in Tunisia. American officials said that Arar's name appeared on a watch list of suspected terrorists and detained and questioned him for thirteen days but never formally charged of any violation. Then, bound in handcuffs and leg irons, he was loaded onto an executive jet to Damascus, where he was placed in the custody of Syrian interrogators. For a year, Arar was beaten and tortured. It was not until the Canadian government eventually took up his cause, that he was released, without charges (Mayer 2005). Eventually Arar took his case to federal court in Brooklyn where the suit was dismissed; in a controversial ruling, the judge reiterated the government's concerns over national security. Undeterred, Arar took his complaint to the Canadian courts were he was awarded than $10.5 million Canadian ($8.9 million U.S.). The judicial inquiry found that the expulsion to Syria stemmed from false assertions made by Canadian police to U.S. officials, saying that Arar was linked to Al-Qaeda. The inquiry cleared Arar of any terrorism connections and concluded that Canadian officials had also orchestrated a smear campaign against him following his return from Syria. Arar has renewed calls for the United States to remove his name from its terrorist watch list. However, Attorney General Gonzales and Michael Chertoff, the homeland security secretary, had told Canadian officials that Arar remains on the watch list based on information about him that U.S. law enforcement agencies have obtained (Austen 2007).

Other developments in the campaign to hold accountable those responsible for extraordinary renditions and torture are also being tracked. In 2007, a former British resident being held at Guantánamo has filed suit against Jeppesen Dataplan, a subsidiary of the Boeing corporation, which he alleges was a participant scheme that transported him to secret American prisons scattered around the world. While in detention, Benyam Mohammed says he was tortured. His lawyers argue Jeppesen Dataplan has been providing logistical support for the CIA's extraordinary rendition program (Cobain 2007). It is revealing that in response to an emerging prospects for litigation, that CIA counterterrorism officers in growing numbers have signed up for a government-reimbursed, private insurance plan that would pay their civil judgments and legal expenses if they are sued or charged with criminal wrongdoing, particularly in cases involving abuse, harsh interrogation tactics, and torture carried out as part of the war on terror. Whereas the Bush team contends the methods were legal, some CIA officers are worried that they may have violated international law or domestic criminal statutes; furthermore, they express concern that they will not have justice department representation in court or congressional inquiries. Indeed, incriminating details of rough interrogations could come to light if trials take place for detainees currently held at Guantanamo Bay. As evidence of human rights abuses become more frequently aired, "People are worried about a pendulum swing" that could lead to accusations of wrongdoing, said another former CIA officer (Smith 2006, A1). The insurance package can be purchased from Arlington, Virginia–based Wright and Company, a subsidiary of the private Special Agents Mutual Benefit Association created by former FBI officials. Still, as part of the administration's plan to protect intelligence officers from liability, Bush called for Congress to pass legislation drafted by the White House that would exempt CIA officers and other federal civilian officials from prosecution for humiliating and degrading terrorism suspects in U.S. custody. The measure is carefully worded so as to prevent prosecutors or courts from considering a wider definition of actions that constitute torture. Bush further requested that Congress keep federal courts from considering lawsuits by detainees who were in CIA or military custody that allege violations of international treaties and laws governing treatment of detainees (Shane 2008; Shane and Mazzetti 2007b; Smith 2006).[9]

Concluding Comment

It is clear that further legal activities are necessary to hold accountable those responsible for serious human rights abuses. In dismantling states of denial, however, it is crucial to confront broader social and cultural forces that encourage turning a blind eye to state crime, even as so much evidence stares us in the face. Still, when a full realization of atrocities does register, it is then important to channel public outrage into action, thereby confronting official denial while reversing bystander passivity (S. Cohen 2001). At the core of the human rights movement, spearheaded by such organizations as Amnesty International and Human Rights Watch, rests the goal of consciousness raising: not only to "wake people up" and "get the message across" but also to "get people to do something." Becoming aware of unlawful and unethical government conduct is the first step in challenging its policies and practices. For the short and long term, it is vital to democracy that the public not tolerate misguided tactics in the war on terror, such as the abuse and torturing detainees who are often held for years without a fair trial, as well as the invasion and occupation of Iraq. A sound platform for national security is integral to the modern state; nevertheless, political leaders ought to be shunned for stoking fear and anxiety in efforts to garner support for antiterrorism operations that violate domestic and international law. Should Americans be committed to countering states of impunity, they must keep from slipping into a collective amnesia that allows crimes of power to be "airbrushed" out of history (see S. Cohen 2001, 243).

APPENDIX:
VIOLATIONS OF INTERNATIONAL AND U.S. LAWS

Note: The list is not intended to be exhaustive; rather, it serves as a general overview of major violations of international and U.S. laws discussed throughout this work.

I. Unlawful Invasion of Iraq
United Nations Charter, Article 2(4), Article 51
Nuremberg Charter
Hague Convention (1907)
Geneva Conventions (1949)

II. Illegal Transformation of Iraqi Economy
Hague Convention (1907: Article 55)
Geneva Conventions (1949)
International Humanitarian Law (IHL, law of armed conflict)
U.N. Security Council, Resolution 1483
Federal Acquisition Regulation (FAR)

III. Failure to Provide Security and Protect Civilians, Indiscriminate Attacks, and Deliberate Acts of Violence against Noncombatants
Hague Convention (1907)
Geneva Conventions (1949)
International Humanitarian Law (IHL, law of armed conflict)
International Covenant on Civil and Political Rights (ICCPR)
U.N. Security Council, Resolution 1483
War Crimes Act (WCA)
Uniform Code of Military Justice
U.S. Army Field Manual

IV. Torture and Cruel, Inhuman, or Degrading Treatment of Prisoners
Hague Convention (1907)
Geneva Conventions (1949, Common Article 3)
International Humanitarian Law (IHL, law of armed conflict)

International Covenant on Civil and Political Rights (ICCPR)
U.N. Conventions against Torture (CAT)
U.N. Universal Declaration of Human Rights
The Torture Act
War Crimes Act (WCA)
Uniform Code of Military Justice
U.S. Army Field Manual
Fifth, Eight, and Fourteenth Amendments to the Constitution of the United States of America
Torture Victims Protection Act of 1991 (TVPA)

V. Arbitrary Arrest, Indefinite Detention, and Deprivation of the Right to Access to Independent Courts and to a Fair Trial
Geneva Conventions (1949)
International Covenant on Civil and Political Rights (ICCPR)
Inter-American Convention on the Forced Disappearance of Persons
U.N. Convention against Torture (CAT)
Habeas Corpus Act of 1867
Fifth, Eight, and Fourteenth Amendments to the Constitution of the United States of America

Notes

Chapter 1   A Post–9/11 World

1. The body of literature on elite criminality features numerous influential books. The list provided here is not intended to be exhaustive: Barak (1991), Chambliss (1988), Ermann and Lundman (1987), Friedrichs (2004), Green and Ward (2004), Haveman and Smeulers (2008), Kauzlarich and Kramer (1998), Michalowski and Kramer (2006a), Passas and Goodwin (2005), Ross (2000a, 2000b), Ruggiero (2001), Schafer (1974), Sutherland (1985), Tillman and Indergaard (2005), Tombs and Whyte (2003), Tunnell (1993), Welch (2006a).

2. Michalowski and Kramer examined three top journals: *Criminology* (the official journal of the American Criminological Society), *Justice Quarterly* (the official journal of the Academy of Criminal Justice Sciences), and the *British Journal of Criminology*. Between 2000 and 2005, those journals together published 575 articles, of which 18 fell into the category of state, corporate, white collar, or political crimes.

3. Green and Ward do not argue that all deprivations of human freedom and well-being constitute crimes: "That would be to equate 'crime' with the much broader concept of 'social harm,' and would call for a kind of analysis that goes beyond criminology (2004, 8; see Hillyard, Pantazis, Gordon, and Tombs 2004). Moreover, it is important to be wary of how the language of human rights is being used to justify war, or what Chomsky (1999) refers to the "new military humanism," whereby political leaders of powerful nations claim that bombings and other military adventures are important tools to protect human rights (see Gearty 2006).

Chapter 2   A New Configuration of Power

1. Ericson (2007) distinguishes between two fundamental forms of counter-law. First is counter-law I—known as laws against law—and second is counter-law II—or surveillant assemblages. Throughout this work, the term *counter-law* refers to the first form, laws against law.

2. "Military order on detention, treatment and the trial of certain noncitizens in the war on terrorism," 66 *Federal Register* 57831, 2001.

3. "Procedures for trials by military commissions of certain non–United States citizens in the war on terror against terror," Department of Defense Military Commission Order No. 1, March 21, 2002.

4. P.L. 107–40 Sec.2(a), September 18, 2001.

5. Efforts by the White House to sidestep its obligations under the Convention against Torture, in addition to the International Covenant on Civil and Political Rights ICCPR ratified in 1992 and key federal statutes that prohibit torture, worry the human rights community. Compounding matters, several government officials have publicly revealed that they endorse interrogation tactics that reside in the ambit of

torture. While being questioned by the Senate, Porter J. Goss, director of the CIA, was confronted by Senator John McCain (R–AZ), who spent five years as a prisoner of war in Vietnam. When McCain asked Goss about the CIA's reported use of "waterboarding," in which a prisoner is made to believe that he will drown, Goss replied only that the approach fell into "an area of what I will call professional interrogation techniques" (Jehl 2005, A11).

6. With an expansionist ambition, known as manifest destiny, the United States participated in the slave industry, expropriated land from indigenous Americans, and devised the Monroe Doctrine by declaring North and South America as an exclusive American region of the globe. Wars with Mexico and later Spain furthered American borders and established several colonies in the Philippines, Hawaii, and Puerto Rico. Given the relative youthfulness of the United States as a nation, there is considerable evidence that it has had—and continues to have—a unique imperial streak (Ferguson 2005, see Aronowitz and Gautney 2003)

7. While maintaining its status as a superpower since World War II, the United States became truly hegemonic at the end of the Cold War, when the Soviet Union collapsed along with its own brand of imperialism. That historical moment gave rise to the United States as an unrivaled hyperpower, producing an era in which American military would operate with relative impunity as evidenced by the quick invasions of Panama and Grenada. Both of those military interventions served as virtual tuneups for the first Gulf War. Still, there emerged a political contest over how to capitalize on the opportunities delivered by the decline of the Soviet Union. On one side of the debate are the global friendly internationalists typified in the presidencies of George H.W. Bush and Bill Clinton; on the other are the neoconservatives known for their fiercely nationalist, unilateralist, and militarist versions of American open-door imperialism. "It was this latter group that would, surprisingly, find itself in a position to shape America's imperial project for the 21st century" (Kramer and Michalowski 2005, 456).

CHAPTER 3   UNLAWFUL ENEMY COMBATANTS

1. "Military order on detention, treatment and the trial of certain noncitizens in the war on terrorism," 66 *Federal Register* 57831, 2001.

2. "Procedures for trials by military commissions of certain non-United States citizens in the war on terror against terror," Department of Defense Military Commission Order No. 1, March 21, 2002.

3. P.L. 107–40 Sec. 2 (a), September 18, 2001.

4. Foucault (1977, 296–287) does suggest that perhaps Mettray reformatory in France might serve as a good example of the historical birth of prison; however, he still emphasizes its emerging technologies rather than its institutional origin.

5. Under the Detainee Treatment Act, passed in December 2005, defendants could only appeal convictions that resulted in a sentence of death or more than ten years imprisonment.

6. International Covenant on Civil and Political Rights (ICCPR), adopted December 16, 1966, G.A. Res. 2200A (XXI), 21 U.N. GAOR Supp. (No. 16) at 52, U.N. Doc. A/6316 (1966), 999 U.N.T.S. 171, entered into force March 23, 1976, art. 9, para. 4.; Convention against Torture and Other Cruel, Inhuman or Degrading Treatment or Punishment (Convention against Torture), adopted December 10, 1984, G.A. res. 39/46, annex, 39 U.N. GAOR Supp. (No. 51) at 197, U.N. Doc. A/39/51 (1984), entered into force June 26, 1987, art. 13, art. 14, para. 1.

7. The Bush administration claims to have the authority to suspend habeas corpus as constitutional during times of invasion and rebellion, citing President Lincoln's order to suspend of habeas corpus during the Civil War (*Ex Parte Merryman* 17 Fed. Cas. 144 [C.C.D. M.D. [1861]).

CHAPTER 4　GUANTÁNAMO BAY

1. Elaborating on two key features of the panopticon, Foucault writes, "Visible: the inmate will constantly have before his eyes the tall outline of the central tower from which he is spied upon. Unverifiable: the inmate must never know whether he is being looked at any one moment; but he must be sure that he may always do so" (1977, 201).
2. "Guard" rather than "correctional officer" is used as it exists in the literature on GITMO and helps to avoid confusing the term with the military officers stationed there.
3. Foucault states, "The military camp—the short lived, artificial city, built and reshaped almost at will; the seat of power that must be all the stronger, but also all the more discreet, all the more effective and on the alert in that it is exercised over armed men. In the perfect camp, all power would be exercised solely through exact observation; each gaze would form a part of the overall functioning of power. The geometry of the paths, the number and distribution of the tents, the orientation of their entrances, the disposition of files and ranks were exactly defined; the network of gazes that supervised on another was laid down" (1979, 171).
4. Lieutenant-Colonel Jerald Phifer requested authorization of category 2 techniques, including prolonged solitary confinement (for a period of thirty days), painful "stress and duress" positions (compounded by chaining), continuous interrogations (up to twenty hours straight), and psychological techniques such as tapping into detainees phobias (e.g., fear of dogs). Each of those techniques is prohibited by the Geneva Conventions; however, the Bush team argues that unlawful enemy combatants are not afforded such protections. The request for additional measures also included the use of category 3 methods such as death threats, exposure to extreme heat and cold, and "waterboarding" (Rose 2004). Soon thereafter, military officials began exploring tactics that would clearly constitute torture; as a result, they were poised to consider the White House's revised definition of torture as a way of sidestepping international law (Greenberg and Dratel 2005).
5. Garland offers a full critique of Foucault's interpretation of the failure of the prison, noting, "The prison may thus be retained for all sorts of reasons—punitiveness, economy, or plain lack of any functional alternatives—which have little do with any latent success as effective control or political strategy" (1990, 164–166). Indeed, this analysis of Guantánamo Bay also takes into account those instrumental and expressive dimensions of penality, as the next passage suggests.
6. Of course, the entire literature on interrogation techniques aimed at prisoners invites the Foucauldian perspective on criminology as a science of "individual differences" (see McCoy 2006). Moreover, Foucault viewed scientific criminology as a discipline that is not only coopted by the state but also an indispensable, functional part of the modern penal complex (1977, 1991).
7. Later Miller was transferred to Abu Ghraib, where he imported his harsh tactics from GITMO; published photographs furnished the world with visual evidence of brutal and humiliating treatment of detainees (Harbury 2005; Hersh 2004; Rose 2004).

CHAPTER 5　TORTURE

1. Again, for in-depth analyses of a newly configured power emerging since 9/11, see chapter 2.
2. It should be noted that similar techniques were used by the British interrogators against suspected IRA operatives. Moreover, British scientists also replicated CIA research conducted at McGill University, Canada (Smith and Lewty 1959). In addition, French torture methods used in Algeria until the 1960s (Alleg 1959) and those

practiced by Israel offer other evidence of the use of state-sponsored brutality (Cohen 2001, 1995, 1996).

3. For example, Congress revealed the following items drawn from a host of graduation theses:

> We have 4 sorts of torture: use of force such as; threats; physical suffering, imposed indirectly; and mental or psychological torture. (Luu Van Huu, of the South Vietnamese police)
>
> Despite the fact that brutal interrogation is strongly criticized by moralists, its importance must not be denied if we want to have order and security in daily life. (Le Van An, of the South Vietnamese police; Senate 1974).

4. A history of modern torture also includes the ways in which the CIA trained police and soldiers in Iran during the 1950s and the Philippines in the 1970s and 1980s (McCoy 1999; Rejali 1994).

5. At the international level, the widely accepted definition of torture clearly laid out in Article 1 of the Convention against Torture and Other Cruel, Inhuman or Degrading Treatment or Punishment (1984):

> [T]he term "torture" means any act by which severe pain or suffering, whether physical or mental, is intentionally inflicted on a person for such purposes of obtaining from him or a third person information or a confession, punishing him for an act he or a third person has committed or is suspected of having committed, or intimidating or coercing him or a third person, or for any reason based on discrimination of any kind, when such pain or suffering is inflicted by or at the instigation of or with the consent or acquiescence of a public official or other person acting in an official capacity. It does not include pain or suffering arising only from, inherent in or incidental to lawful sanctions.

6. Another key component of interrogation in the war on terror that serves to diminish accountability is the use of private military firms and intelligence contractors. One military law analyst noted, "Legally speaking [military contractors] fall into the same gray zone as the unlawful combatants detained at Guantánamo Bay" (Singer 2005, 121, 2003; see Newburn, 2007).

7. Mistreatment of detainees is forbidden by three sources of law: the Geneva Conventions, the United Nations Convention against Torture, and the Uniform Code of Military Justice which makes cruelty, oppression or maltreatment of prisoners a crime. Even armed services lawyers worried that some tactics might violate the Uniform Code and federal criminal statutes, exposing interrogators to prosecution. A Pentagon memorandum obtained by ABC News said a meeting of top military lawyers on March 8, 2003, concluded that "we need a presidential letter" approving controversial methods, to give interrogators immunity (A. Lewis 2005b, EV1). Reports of abuse are consistent with those prepared by the International Red Cross and Physicians for Human Rights that says "since at least 2002, the United States has been engaged in systematic psychological torture" at Guantánamo Bay (Lewis and Schmitt 2005, 35).

8. The "few bad apples" explanation of Abu Ghraib has retained steady currency even as the scandal makes its way through a series of commissions, none of which are independent from the Defense Department. For example, the Church report based on an investigation by Vice Admiral Albert Church III concludes that only the lowest-ranking soldiers are to be held accountable, not their commanders or civilian overseers. Critics, however, note that it selectively ignores Bush's declaration that terrorist are not covered by the Geneva Conventions and that Iraq is part of the war against terror. The Church commission also ignored Rumsfeld's approval of interrogation techniques for Guantánamo Bay that violate Geneva Conventions and it glossed over the way military attorneys were ordered to ignore their own legal

opinions and instead adhere to Justice Department memos on how to make torture appear legal (Greenberg and Dratel, 2005; Danner, 2004). The Church report said "none of the pictured abuses at Abu Ghraib bear any resemblance to approved policies at any level, in any theatre. Admiral Church and his investigators must have missed the pictures of prisoners in hoods, forced into stress positions and threatened by dogs. All of those techniques were approved at one time or another by military officials, including Mr. Rumsfeld" (*New York Times* 2005, A22).

CHAPTER 6 ORDERING IRAQ

1. To be clear, any act of warfare that cannot be justified as a form of self-defense is prohibited under international law. The United Nations' Charter, as the legal foundation governing the laws of war, declares, "All members shall refrain from the threat or use of force against the territorial integrity or political independence of any state or enforcement action (United Nations 2006, Article 2, chapter 1, 4; see Kauzlarich 2007; appendix).
2. In the House of Representatives, eighty-nine Democrats contacted the White House to determine whether the memo accurately reported the administration's thinking at the time, eight months before the invasion of Iraq. John Conyers Jr. (D–MI), top Democrat on the House Judiciary Committee said the British memo "raises troubling new questions regarding the legal justification for the war as well as the integrity of your own administration" (Jehl 2005a, A10).
3. Enthusiasts of Foucauldian thought should refer to his theory of the verb in which he proposes that "the verb is the indispensable condition for all discourse" (Foucault 1970, 103).
4. The term *ordering* has been used in the previous colonial projects, in particular America where the colonial elite enacted legislation aimed to guarantee an endless supply of slaves as well as to establish a unique code of punishments to discipline them. The "Act for a Better Ordering and Governing of Negroes and Slaves, South Carolina 1712" became a model for other American colonies as they expanded their reliance on slavery for economic gains (Chowdhry and Beeman 2007; Rothenberg 2001; see also Banks 2007).
5. Early on, many Iraqis viewed the occupation as the "the Palestinisation of Iraq," even throwing rocks at U.S. troops as forms of symbolic resistance common in the West Bank and Gaza (Abunimah and Ibish 2003; Reeves 2003). Similarly, Campbell and Connelly (2006) offer global lessons from Northern Ireland.
6. Britain's Attorney General warned the Blair government in March 2003 that a U.N. Security Council resolution would be required to authorize the reconstruction (Dyer 2003; Innes 2003). In May 2003, U.N. Security Council passed Resolution 1483, thereby regularizing the reconstruction. But in doing so, the United Nations not only recognized the United States and United Kingdom as occupying powers but also constituted them as a "unified command" or "the Authority" (Gregory 2004, 229).
7. Tariq Ali (2003a, 2003b) adds that a privatization of the Iraqi oil wells—the second largest reserves in the world—would strengthen U.S. control over the industry while weakening OPEC. Former speechwriter David Frum writes in his book *The Right Man*, that an American-led overthrow of Saddam Hussein followed by a form of government closely aligned with Washington would put the United States in charge of the region more than any power since the Ottomans or even the Romans.
8. Other evidence of Iraqi dependency upon external capital is found in the controversy over how the Defense Fund for Iraq (DFI, an account located at the Federal Reserve Bank in New York) is managed with respect to oil revenue confiscated by the U.N. oil-for-food program, because it is blamed for deepening the Iraqi debt (Catan 2004; Whyte 2007).

9. As Tariq Ali puts it, "The peoples of the Arab world view Operation Iraqi Freedom as a grisly charade, a cover for an old-fashioned European-style colonial occupation, constructed like its predecessor on the most rickety of foundations—innumerable falsehoods, cupidity, and imperial fantasies" (2003a, 9).

10. It was reported in July 2004 that 150 U.S. firms had collectively landed reconstruction contracts in Iraq and Afghanistan worth $48.7 billion. One analysis of Iraqi reconstruction contracts concludes that U.S. and U.K. companies received 85 percent of the value of contracts worth more than $5 million tendered by the CPA whilst Iraqi firms received just 2 percent of the value of those contracts (Iraq Revenue Watch 2004a, 2004b). Most went to U.S. firms. In one period examined between 2003 and 2004, more than 80 percent of prime contracts were given to U.S. companies, with the remainder of the revenue split between U.K., Australian, Italian, Israeli, Jordanian and Iraqi companies (Herring and Ragwala, 2005; see Giraldi 2005).

11. A roster of business ties between U.S. corporations engaged in the Middle East (and the Iraqi reconstruction) and Bush administration officials along with high-ranking Republicans is a lengthy one, but a short list is as follows: Condoleeza Rice, formerly served on the board of directors of Chevron oil; Former President George Herbert Walker Bush worked as senior advisor to the Carlyle Group, an influential firm with close ties to the defense industry; James A. Baker, III, is a key player with Washington Group, a powerful political lobby; former Secretary of State George Schulz has been a leading force at Bechtel Group, which is also involved in the Iraqi reconstruction (see Keen 2006; Hogan, Long, Stretesky, and Lynch 2006; Long, Hogan, Stretesky, and Lynch 2007).

12. "In addition to about 140,000 U.S. troops, Iraq is now filled with a hodgepodge of contractors. DynCorp International has about 1,500 employees in Iraq, including about 700 helping train the police force. Blackwater USA has more than 1,000 employees in the country, most of them providing private security. Kellogg, Brown and Root, one of the largest contractors in Iraq, said it does not delineate its workforce by country but that it has more than 50,000 employees and subcontractors working in Iraq, Afghanistan and Kuwait. MPRI, a unit of L-3 Communications, has about 500 employees working on 12 contracts, including providing mentors to the Iraqi Defense Ministry for strategic planning, budgeting and establishing its public affairs office. Titan, another L-3 division, has 6,500 linguists in the country" (Merle 2006, D1).

13. In addition to the three largest U.S. defense contractors (i.e., Lockheed Martin, Boeing, and Raytheon) which earned more than $30 billion per year in Pentagon contracts (Keen 2006), there are other major players in the private military industry currently doing business in Iraq. Most notable are the following firms:

Aegis Defence Services (United Kingdom): the biggest British winner in Iraq, it increased its turnover from £554,000 in 2003 to £62 million in 2005. The company, run by Lieutenant-Colonel Tim Spicer, was awarded a contract worth $293 million (£154 million) by the CPA in Iraq.

ARMORGROUP (United Kingdom): The company's turnover has increased from $71 million in 2001 to $233 million in 2005. The Foreign Office and Department for International Development have awarded it contracts in Kabul, Baghdad, and Basra.

Control Risk Group (United Kingdom): Turnover rose from £47m in 2003 to £80m in 2004. In Iraq it has been employed by the Pentagon, the CPA, the Office of Reconstruction and Development and US AID. It also provides guards for British government staff in Iraq.

Erinys International (United Kingdom/South Africa): Formed in 2003 with a contract of $100 million from the CPA to guard oil sites and pipelines in Iraq. Led by a former political adviser to ex-Angolan opposition leader Jonas Savimbi.

Blackwater (United States): Provided security guards and helicopters for the former CPA head, Paul Bremer, and the former U.S. ambassador, John Negroponte (Sengupta 2006, EV2–3; also see Pincus 2007).

14. Documents filed with the Securities and Exchange Commission reveal a host of investigations into KBR's work in Iraq, raising the possibilities that investors and the parent company (i.e., Halliburton) could foot the bill for settlements against KBR. The justice department is investigating overcharges in its work in the Balkans from 1996 to 2000 as well as payments in Nigeria that may have violated the Foreign Corrupt Practices Act, which bars the bribing of foreign officials (Glanz and Norris 2006, EV3).

Chapter 7   Collateral Damage

1. An improvised explosive device (or I.E.D.) buried in the road about two miles from their base exploded under the fourth vehicle, killing instantly Lance Corporal Miguel Terrazas, and wounding two other marines, Lance Corporal James Crossan and Lance Corporal Salvador Guzman (Broder 2006).

2. Some witnesses described the men as college students on their way to a technical school college in Baghdad, and said they had been shot while waiting in the car. Others said they had been dragged out the car, forced to lie on the ground and then executed (Broder 2006).

3. Military prosecutors also charged four officers, including a lieutenant colonel in charge of the First Marine Regiment's 3rd Battalion, with dereliction of duty and failing to ensure that accurate information about the killings was delivered up the Marine Corps chain of command (Broder 2006).

4. The last soldier to be executed was John A. Bennett, hanged in 1961; he was convicted of the rape and attempted murder of an eleven-year-old Austrian girl. Incidentally, in Vietnam ninety-five American soldiers and twenty-seven marines were convicted of killing noncombatants (Worth 2006a).

5. Corporal Dustin M. Berg of the Indiana National Guard was sentenced to eighteen months in prison for killing his Iraqi police partner, saying he acted because he feared his partner was going to shoot him. Staff Sergeant Johnny Horne claimed he killed a wounded sixteen-year-old Iraqi boy to put him out of his misery; he pleaded guilty to unpremeditated murder and was sentenced to three years in prison, later reduced to one year (Worth 2006a).

6. By early 2007, the American detention camps in Iraq held 15,500 detainees and by the end of the summer, the number jumped 50 percent, to 24,500, during the "surge" of more troops ordered by Bush (Shanker 2007). The camps are filled with detainees who are being held without charge and without access to tribunals where their cases are reviewed (Moss and Mekhennet 2007).

7. For additional coverage on the abuse and torture of detainees held in Iraq as well as Afghanistan, see McCoy (2006) and (Welch 2006a).

8. Ani slept in a wooden barracks-like structure, with a mattress on the ground and a nail on the wall for hanging clothes. When the guards found an improvised needle that he said was used to repair clothes, guards forced him into an isolated cell, where he was kept for twenty-four days: "You cannot see the difference between day and night," he said. "There was no opening, not even in the door" (Moss and Mekhennet 2007, EV6).

9. A former detainee from Samarra said such a stun gun had been used on him for speaking out of turn. Ahmed Majid al-Ghanem, fifty, a former Baath Party official who was also freed from Camp Bucca and is now living in Syria, said in a separate interview that he witnessed the electric prods being used as punishment on other detainees (Moss and Mekhennet 2007, EV3).

10. General Formica's inquiry concentrated on the Combined Joint Special Operations Task Force-Arabian Peninsula, which included soldiers from the Army's 5th and 10th Special Forces Groups. It did not examine the actions in Iraq of more highly classified special operations units, including Delta Force and some navy Seal groups, or other specialized units including Task Force 6–26, a subject of extensive allegations of misconduct that were reported by the *New York Times* in March 2006 (Schmitt 2007, EV3).

11. Sergeant Girouard has been charged with premeditated murder, a capital offense, as have three other soldiers: Specialist William B. Hunsaker, Private First Class Corey R. Clagett, and Specialist Juston R. Graber. Private Clagett and Specialist Hunsaker are accused of actually shooting the prisoners. The colonel who allegedly gave the order to "kill all military-age men," is Michael Steele the brigade commander; he led the 1993 mission in Somalia made famous by the book and movie *Black Hawk Down* (Worth 2006b, 28; see Shanker and Tavernise 2006, EV1–3).

CHAPTER 8 GOVERNING THROUGH TERROR

1. "Since its formation in 1973, the National Intelligence Council (NIC) has served as a bridge between the intelligence and policy communities, a source of deep substantive expertise on critical national security issues, and as a focal point for Intelligence Community collaboration. The NIC's key goal is to provide policymakers with the best, unvarnished, and unbiased information" (National Intelligence Council 2007, 2).

2. According to Foucault's view on the emergence of governmentality, he explains:
   This schematic presentation of the notion and theory of the art of government did not remain a purely abstract question in the sixteenth century, and it was not a concern only to political theoreticians. I think we can identify its connections with political reality. The theory of the art of government was linked, from the sixteenth century, to the whole development of the administrative apparatus of the territorial monarchies, the emergence of governmental apparatuses; it was also connected to a set of analyses and forms of knowledge which began to develop in the late sixteenth century and grew in importance during the seventeenth, and which were essentially to do with knowledge of the state, in all its different elements, dimensions, and factors of power, questions which were termed precisely 'statistics,' meaning the science of the state; finally, as a third vector of connections. I do not think one can fail to relate this search for an art of government to mercantilism and the Cameralists' science of police. (1991, 96)
   In Foucault's writings, it has been noted that the word "policy" is a better equivalent for the word "police" because it is a term that refers to a whole set of techniques and strategies by which a government in the framework of the state is able to govern people as individuals deemed as being useful (Foucault 1988 [1982]: 155; see Dupont and Pearce 2001, 129; Gordon 1991, 10). Also "statistics" refers to "political arithmetic" meaning knowledge of the states' respective forces (Foucault 1988 [1982], 151; see Dupont and Pearce 2001, 129). See Foucault (1991, 102–103) where he expands on his notion of power as it pertains to "security, territory, and population" and the "history of governmentality."

3. Writing from a Foucauldian perspective, Rose explores government and control: "Of course, programmes of crime control have always had less to do with the control of crime than they have to do with the government of the moral order" (2000, 321).

4. Dupont and Pearce (2001) offer the following description of governmentality:
   "Governmentality," for Foucault, referred to a historically specific economy of power—in which societies are ordered in a decentered way and wherein society's members play a particularly active role in their own self-governance.

In such societies there is a concern with both individuals and aggregates of populations. Governmentality gives consideration to the organization of the social into distinctive domains, and having various immanent logics. Governmentality considers the construal of individuals in relation to different sites—for example, the family, schools, business establishments—and in relation to different regularities—including a biopolitics of birth, longevity, health, death, etc. In each of these domains and sites one finds the deployment of distinctive modes of governance—all of which generate knowledge of subject populations in order to govern the "conduct of conduct" and to intensify and perfect the inherent nature of their object. This creates the possibilities that those human subjects who are so governed are well equipped to govern themselves. Governmental practices are not restricted to the state and the state moreover has learnt or should have learnt the limits of what it can know and do, a realization, incidentally, which emerged first in the context of the economy. (125–126)

Also see Foucault's 1982 essay "The Subject and Power," where power is described as "actions on others actions" which differs from mere physical force and violence insofar as the individuals are free to act in one way or another (see Gordon 1991, 5).

5. The term *problematization* refers to the process by which putative problem is seen as requiring special attention particularly by the government (Castel 1994; Rose and Valverde 1998).

6. Foucault (1991) views liberalism not simply as a set of a set of doctrines stemming from political and economic theory, but as "a style of thinking quintessentially concerned with the art of governing" (Gordon 1991, 14).

7. Since the 1990s, every multilateral peace operation conducted by the United Nations has included private security companies (see Avant 2005).

8. Details about that incident not clear. The Blackwater guards said the driver moved too close to their convoy when they opened fire on his vehicle. Fearful about a possible car bomb or other threat, the guards said they shouted instructions to back away from the convoy, then fired a warning shot into the radiator followed by a shot into the windshield. Those steps are recommended under the rules for the use of force by contractors in Iraq specified in Memorandum 17, a set of guidelines adopted in 2004 by the CPA and still in effect. Some witnesses, however, said the shooting was unprovoked. The driver is reported to have wounds in his shoulder, chest, and head (Fainaru and al-Izzi 2007, A2).

9. One witness, Mohammed Mahdi, said the skirmish lasted about an hour, adding that he saw "at least four or five" people "who were certainly dead" but that he did not know how the people were killed, who killed them or whether they were civilians or combatants (Fainaru and al-Izzi 2007, A4).

10. Immunity aims to protect the Fifth Amendment right against self-incrimination while allowing investigators to still gather evidence. In general, individuals suspected of crimes are not given immunity and such grants are not made until after the probable defendants are identified. Prosecutors often face significant barriers in bringing a prosecution in cases in which defendants have been immunized (Johnston 2007).

11. Fleisher's general remark was further aimed at Bill Maher, a political humorist and host of ABC's show *Politically Incorrect*. In the wake of 9/11, Maher stunned the political and military establishment by saying, "We have the cowards, lobbing cruise missiles from two thousand miles away. . . . Staying in the airplane, when it hits the building—say what you want about that, it's not cowardly (Silverglate 2002, A21).

12. Bush also employs empty language to induce others to surrender to his will. Empty language refers to statements that carry little meaning. In fact, they are tremendously broad and vague, making it virtually impossible to oppose. Such language is not benign; rather it is manipulative precisely because it intends to distract listeners

from examining the content of the message. It is through empty language that dominators conceal faulty generalizations; ridicule viable alternatives; attribute negative motivations to others. By doing so, critics and skeptics are portrayed as contemptible (Brooks 2003a, 2003b).

13. The Patriot Act's surveillance powers are enhanced by Section 215 that lowers the requirements and extends the reach of the Foreign Intelligence Surveillance Act of 1978 (FISA: 50 U.S.C. 1978). Under that section, the FBI director (or a designee as low in rank as an assistant special agent) may apply for a court order demanding the production of "any tangible things (including books, records, papers, documents, and other items)" to accompany an investigation "to protect against international terrorism or clandestine intelligence activities." Civil liberties attorneys complain that the Section 215 removes a key FISA restriction that obligates the government to specify in its application for a court order that "there are specific and articulable facts giving reason to believe that the person to whom the records pertain is a foreign power or an agent of a foreign power." The FBI need not suspect of any wrongdoing, the person whose records are being sought (see Chang 2002).

14. Chang (2002) points out that confrontational protests are by their very nature acts that "appear to be intended . . . to influence the policy of a government by intimidation or coercion" (Chang 2002). Even instances of civil disobedience—including those that do not result in injuries or are entirely nonviolent—could be interpreted as "dangerous to human life" and "in violation of the criminal laws." Protestors that engage in direct action, such as environmentalists, antiabortionists, and antiglobalization activists risk being arrested as "domestic terrorists," should prosecutors find their dissent particularly disruptive. For an overall critique of the Patriot Act see Welch (2006a, chapter 9).

CHAPTER 9 STATES OF IMPUNITY

1. Despite the 2007 executive order authorizing the interrogation program, human rights organizations insist that those who participate in enhanced techniques could face criminal sanctions (see Mazzetti, 2007b EV2). In its recent report *Leave No Marks: Enhanced Interrogation Techniques and the Risk of Criminality*, Physicians for Human Rights and Human Rights First (PHR and HRF 2007; see also PHR 2005) state that U.S. policymakers and interrogation personnel should understand if "enhanced" techniques are practiced, it would be reasonable for courts to conclude that the resulting harm was inflicted intentionally, leading to felony criminal prosecutions, for instance, under the Torture Act or the War Crimes Act (see Appendix).

2. Ignatieff (2005) examines closely the ambivalent pattern in the United States with respect to human rights. In describing American exceptionalism, he identifies three elements: exemptionalism, double standards, and a commitment to a self-contained authority in the form of legal isolation.

3. By 2002, the U.S. had successfully enticed thirteen states to sign on the U.S. Article 98(2) impunity agreements: Afghanistan, Dominican Republic, East Timor, Gambia, Honduras, Israel, Marshall Islands, Mauritania, Micronesia, Palau, Romania, Tajikistan, and Uzbekistan (Amnesty International 2002).

4. Addressing the political economy of antitreaty discourse, Koh draws on the work of Cuellar (2003) by concluding that American opposition to the ICC has "arisen less from broadly entrenched American cultural beliefs than from the skill and maneuvering of particular well-positioned individuals, who, by serving as key institutional choke points, have successfully promoted well-publicized acts of American exceptionalism" (2005, 130).

5. In 2007, a *New York Times*/CBS poll, 35 percent of those surveyed said that taking military action against Iraq was the right thing to do. Sixty-one percent of Americans

said the United States should have stayed out of Iraq. In capturing the public's view of how the war is proceeding, two percent said things are going "very well," and 21 percent said "somewhat well." Seventy-six percent said things are "going badly," including 47 percent who said things are going "very badly." Still, the majority of Americans support continuing to finance the war as long as the Iraqi government meets specific goals (Sussman 2007, EV1). In a related endorsement of public support for state crimes, a CNN poll revealed that 45 percent of those surveyed would not object to having someone tortured if it would produce information about terrorism (Williams 2001).

6. In that case, I. Lewis Libby Jr., former chief of staff to Vice President Cheney and one of the principal architects of Bush's foreign policy, was sentenced today to thirty months in prison for lying during a the leak investigation (Lewis 2007). Soon thereafter, Bush used his power of clemency to commute Libby's sentence; however, he is required to pay a $250,000 fine (Stolberg 2007; for a discussion on " hardball" political culture as within the Bush administration see Dean 2004).

7. The cultural significance of mystical language in the war on terror is examined in detail in Welch (2006a; chapters 1 and 4). Still, it should be briefly mentioned here that Bush—even by his own admission—assumes a messianic force committed to ridding the world of evil (Woodward 2004). The mystical character of the war on terror also has drawn support from Bush's religious constituency, and in extreme instances transposes historical references to the Crusades into the present. Lieutenant-General William Boykin drew considerable attention when it became known that his speeches to church groups not only mischaracterized Islam as an inferior religion but also advocated conversion to Christianity as a tactic in the war on terror (Reuters 2003).

8. The investigation reports that rendition missions departed from airports in Azerbaijan, Germany, Spain and Turkey, and airports in the Czech Republic, Greece, Ireland, and Italy were used for refueling. Detainees were picked up for "unlawful transfer" in Bosnia and Herzegovina, Italy, Macedonia and Sweden. Detainees who passed through those places were dropped off for interrogation or transfer onward in Poland, Romania, Egypt, Jordan, Morocco, Afghanistan, Pakistan and Uzbekistan, among other countries. The inquiry relied on seven independent sets of data from Eurocontrol, the European air traffic–control agency, together with specific information from about twenty national aviation authorities (Smith and Mekhennet 2006).

9. As previously discussed, there is considerable debate over role of the international law and the International Criminal Court in controlling state criminality. From the perspective of criminologists studying war, genocide, and crimes against humanity the following works offer considerable range and depth on the subject: Hagan and Greer (2002); Hagan, Rymond-Richmond, and Parker (2005); Hoffman (2000); McEvoy (2003); Morrison (2006); Mullins, Kauzlarich, Rothe (2004); Rothe and Mullins (2006).

Cases

Berrera-Echararria v. Rison, 21 F. 3d 314, 318 (1994)
Chahal v. United Kingdom, Eur. Ct. H.R. (1996)
Ex Parte Merryman, 17 Fed. Cas. 144 [C.C.D. M.D.] (1861)
Hamdan v. Rumsfeld, 415 F. 3d 33 (2005)
Hamdi v. Rumsfeld, 542 U.S. 507 (2004)
Ireland v. United Kingdom, 2 EHRR 25 (1978)
Rasul v. Bush and United States, 542 U.S. 466 (2004)
Wilson v. Arkansas, 514 U.S. 927, 929 (1995)

References

Note: EV refers to electronic version of the publication.

Abunimah, A. and H. Ibish. 2003. War in Iraq and Israeli occupation: A devastating resonance. *Chicago Tribune*, March 28, 34.

Adler, M. and B. Longhurst. 1994. *Discourse, power and justice: Towards a new sociology of prisons*. London: Routledge.

Agamben, G. 1998. *Homo sacer: Sovereign power and bare life*. Translated by Daniel Heller-Roaxen. Stanford: Stanford University Press.

———. 2005. *State of exception*. Translated by Kevin Attell. Chicago: University of Chicago Press.

Ali, T. 2003a. Re-colonizing Iraq. *New Left Review* 21: 5–19.

———. 2003b. *Bush in Babylon: The re-colonizing of Iraq*. London: Verso.

Alleg, H. 1958. *The question*. New York: Braziller.

Allen, J. 2004. The campaign comes to Rome. *New York Times*, June 3, A27.

Amann, D. 2004. Guantánamo Bay. *Columbia Journal of Transnational Law* 42: 263–348.

Amnesty International. 2001. *The International Criminal Court: The need for the European Union to take more effective steps to prevent members from signing US impunity agreements*. New York: Amnesty International.

———. 2003. *Amnesty International condemns Ashcroft's ruling to indefinitely detain non-U.S. citizens, including asylum seekers*. Press release, April 28.

———. 2004. *Iraq: One year on the human rights situation remains dire*. March 18 [www.amnesty.org].

———. 2005. *Guantánamo and beyond: The continuing pursuit of unchecked executive power*. New York: Amnesty International.

Amoore, L. and M. De Goede. 2005. Governance, risk and dataveillance in the war on terror. *Crime, Law and Social Change*, 43:149–173.

Anderson, J. 2004. *The fall of Bagdhad*. New York: Penguin.

Armstrong, D. 2002. Dick Cheney's song for America: Drafting a plan for global dominance. *Harper's Magazine*, October: 76–83.

Arendt, H. (1994 [1965]) *Eichmann in Jerusalem: A report on the banality of evil*. New York: Penguin.

Aronowitz, S. and H. Gautney. 2003. *Implicating empire: Globalization and resistance in the 21st century world order*. New York Basic Books.

Ashworth, A. 2000. Is the criminal law a lost cause? *Law Quarterly Review*, 116: 225–256.

———.2003. *Principles of criminal law*. Oxford: Oxford University Press.

———. 2004. Social control and "anti-social behaviour": The subversion of human rights? *Law Quarterly Review*, 120: 263–291.

Associated Press. 2007a. U.S. psychologists scrap interrogation ban. August 20, EV1–2.

———. 2007b. Puppy from Iraq ties family to slain soldier. May 26, 1.

———. 2007c. Trial opens involving C.I.A. rendition. June 7, EV1–2.

Austen, I. 2007. Canada reaches settlement with torture victim. *New York Times*, January 25, EV1–3.

Avant, D. 2004. Mercenaries. *Foreign Policy*, August, 20–28.

———. 2005.) *The market for force: The consequences of privatizing security*. New York: Cambridge University Press.

Banks, C. 2007. Ordering the other: Reading Alaskan native culture past and present. In *Race, gender, and punishment: From colonialism to the war on terror*, edited by M. Bosworth and J. Flavin. New Brunswick, NJ: Rutgers University Press.

Barak, G. 1991. *Crimes by the capitalist state: An introduction to state criminality*. Albany: SUNY Press.

Barnes, J.E. 2007. America's own unlawful combatants? Using private guards in Iraq could expose the U.S. to accusations of treaty violations, some experts think. *Los Angeles Times*, October 15: EV1–5.

Bauman, Z. 2000. *Liquid modernity*. Oxford: Blackwell Publishing.

Beccaria, C. (1764 [1856]). *On crimes and punishment*. London.

Beck, U. 1992. *Risk society: Towards a new modernity*. London: Sage.

———. 2002a. The terrorist threat: world risk society revisited. *Theory, Culture and Society*, 19: 39–55.

———. 2002b. The silence of words and political dynamics in the world risk society, *Logos*, 1: 1–18.

Beck, U., A. Giddens, and S. Lash. 1994. *Reflexive modernity: Politics, tradition, and aesthetics in the modern social order*. Cambridge: Polity Press.

Bennett, W. J. and J. DiIulio.1996. *Body count: Moral poverty and how to win America's war against crime and drugs*. New York: Simon and Schuster.

Bentham, J. 1970 [1789]. *An introduction to the principles of morals and legislation*. Edited by H.L.A. Hart and J.H. Burns. London.

Beyani, C. 2003. International law and the "war on terror." In *Humanitarian action and the "global war on terror,"* edited by J. Macrae and A. Harmer. HPC Report 14: London: Overseas Development Institute.

Biderman, A. D. and H. Zimmer. 1961. *The manipulation of human behavior*. New York: Wiley.

Blass, T. 2004. *The man who shocked the world: The life and legacy of Stanley Milgram*. New York: Basic Books.

Bolton, J. 2002. United States Under Secretary of State for Arms Control and International Security, "Letter to Secretary-General Kofi Annan," May 6 [http://www.state.gov/r/pa/prs/ps/2002/9968.htm]

Bonger, W. 1916. *Criminality and economic conditions*. Boston: Little, Brown.

———. 1936. *An introduction to criminology*. London: Methuen.

Bonn, S. 2007. Whoppers of mass deception (WMD): Presidential rhetoric, moral panic, and the war in Iraq. Ph.D. dissertation, University of Miami.

Borradori, G. 2003. *Philosophy in a time of terror: Dialogues with Jurgen Habermas and Jacques Derrida*. Chicago: University of Chicago Press.

Bosworth, M.1999. *Engendering resistance: Agency and power in women's prisons*. Dartmouth: Ashgate.

Bosworth, M. and E. Carrabine. 2001. Reassessing resistance: Race, gender, and sexuality in prison. *Punishment and Society* 3(4): 501–515.

Bosworth, M. and J. Flavin. 2007. Introduction: Race, control, and punishment. In *Race, gender, and punishment: From colonialism to the war on terror*, edited by M. Bosworth and J. Flavin. New Brunswick, NJ: Rutgers University Press.

Bottoms, A. E. 1995. The philosophy and politics of punishment and sentencing. In *The politics of sentencing reform*, edited by C. Clarkson and R. Morgan. Oxford: Clarendon.

Bowart, W. 1978. *Operation mind control*. New York: Dell.

Bowden, M. 2003. The dark art of interrogation: A survey of the landscape of persuasion. *The Atlantic Monthly*, October, 51–76.

Bradley, C. A. and J. Goldsmith. 2005. Congressional authorization and the war on terrorism. *Harvard Law Review* 118: 2047–2130.

Brighenti, A. 2006. On territory as relationship and law as territory. *Canadian Journal of Law and Society* 21(2): 65–86.

———. 2007. Visibility: A category for the social sciences. *Current Sociology* 55(3): 323–342.

Bremer, L. P. 2003. Operation Iraqi prosperity. *Wall Street Journal*, June 20, 33.

———. 2006. *My year in Iraq: The struggle to build a future of hope*. New York: Simon and Schuster.

Broder, J. 2006. Contradictions cloud inquiry into 24 Iraqi deaths. *New York Times*, June 17, EV1–10.

Broder, J. and D. Johnston. 2007. U.S. military to supervise Iraq security convoys. *New York Times*, October 31, EV1–4.

Broder, J. and J. Risen. 2007a. Armed guards in Iraq occupy a legal limbo. *New York Times*, September 20, EV1–5.

———. 2007b. Blackwater tops firms in Iraq in shooting rate. *New York Times*, September 27, EV1–6.

Broder, J. and D. Rohde. 2007. State Department use of contractors leaps in 4 years. *New York Times*, October 24, EV1–6.

Brooks, R. 2003a. The character myth: To counter Bush, the Democrats must present a different vision of a safe world. *Nation*, December 29, 25–28.

———. 2003b. A nation of victims: Bush uses well-known linguistic techniques to make citizens feel dependent. *Nation*, June 30, 20–22.

Brown, W. 2005. The governmentality of tolerance. In *Regulating aversion: A critique of tolerance in the age of identity*, edited by W. Brown. Princeton: Princeton University Press.

Brzezinski, Z. 2004. *The choice: Global domination or global leadership*. New York: Basic Books.

Burchell, G., C. Gordon, and P. Miller. 1990. *The Foucault effect: Studies of governmentality*. Chicago: University of Chicago Press.

Butler, J. 2004. *Precarious life: The powers of mourning and violence*. London: Verso.

Calhoun, C., P. Price, and A. Timmer. 2002. *Understanding September 11th*. New York: Free Press.

Callon, M. and B. Latour. 1981. Unscrewing the big Leviathan: How actors macrostructure reality and sociologists help them to do so. In *Advances in social theory and methodology: Toward an integration of micro-and macro-sociologies*, edited by K. Knorr-Cetina and A. Cicourel. London: Routledge & Kegan Paul.

Cambanis, T. 2003. Strike at Hussein left neighborhood shattered, angry. *Boston Globe*, April 13: 1.

Campbell, C. and I. Connolly. 2006. Making war on terror? Global lessons from Northern Ireland. *Modern Law Review* 69(6): 935–957.

Cameron, D. E. 1956. Psychic driving. *The American Journal of Psychiatry* 112 (7): 502–509.

Carrabine, E. 2000. Discourse, governmentality and translation: Towards a social theory of imprisonment. *Theoretical Criminology* 4(3): 309–331.

————. 2004. *Power, discourse and resistance: A genealogy of the Strangeways prison riot.* Dartmouth: Ashgate.

Castells, M. 1997. *The information age: Economy, society, and culture. Vol. II: The power of identity.* Oxford: Basil Blackwell.

Castle, R. 1991. From dangerousness to risk. In *The Foucault Effect: Studies in Governmentality*, edited by G. Burchell, C. Gordon, and P. Miller. Chicago: University of Chicago Press.

Castle, R. 1994. Problematization as a mode of reading history. In *Foucault and the writing of history*, edited by J. Goldstein. Oxford: Blackwell.

Catan, T. 2004. Big spender: What happened to $20bn of Iraqi funds? *Financial Times*, December 9: 25.

CBS News. 2003. Cheney's Halliburton ties remain. September 26: [cbsnews.com]

Central Intelligence Agency. 1963. *KUBARK Counterintelligence Interrogation* [http://www.kimsoft.com/2000/kubark.Htm].

Chambliss, W. 1988. *On the take: From petty crooks to presidents.* Bloomington: Indiana: Indiana University Press.

————. 1989. State-organized crime. *Criminology* 27(2): 183–208.

Chandrasekaran, R. 2006. *Imperial life in the emerald city: Inside Iraq's green zone.* New York: Alfred A. Knopf.

Chang, N. 2002. *Silencing political dissent: How post-September 11 anti-terrorism measures threaten our civil liberties.* New York: Seven Stories Press.

Chatterjee, P. 2004. *Iraq inc.: A profitable occupation.* New York: Seven Stories Press.

Chemerinsky, E. 2005. Enemy combatants and separation of powers. *Journal of National Security Law and Policy* 1: 73–125.

Cheney, R. 2005. The sleeper scenario: Terrorism-support laws and the demands of prevention. *Harvard Review of Legislation* 42, 1–90.

Chivers, C. J. 2006. Black-market weapon prices surge in Iraq chaos. *New York Times*, December 10, EV1–8.

Chowdhry, G. and M. Beeman. 2007. Situating colonialism, race, and punishment. In *Race, gender, and punishment: From colonialism to the war on terror*, edited by M. Bosworth and J. Flavin. New Brunswick, NJ: Rutgers University Press.

Chomsky, N. 1999. *The new military humanism: Lessons from Kosovo.* London: Pluto.

————. 2002a. The world after September 11 (2001). In *Pirates and emperors, old and new*, edited by N. Chomsky. London: Pluto.

————. 2002b. *Pirates and emperors, old and new.* London: Pluto.

————. 2003. *Hegemony or survival: America's quest for global dominance.* New York: Henry Holt.

Christadoulou, L. 2006. *Corporate carve-up: The role of UK companies in Iraq since 2003.* Oxford: Corporate Watch.

Christian Aid. 2003. *Iraq: The missing billions: Transition and transparency in post-war Iraq.* Briefing Paper for the Madrid Conference on Iraq, 23–24 October 2003. London: Christian Aid.

Clarke, R. 2004. *Against all enemies: Inside America's war on terror.* New York: Simon and Schuster.

Clegg, S. 1989. *Frameworks of power.* London: Sage.

Clemmer, D. 1958. *The prison community.* New York: Rhinehart and Co.

Cloud, D. 2006. Ex-G.I. in rape killing case left army under mental illness rule. *New York Times*, July 6, EV1–3.

Cloud, D. and M. Gordon. 2006. Violence in Iraq reaches new high, report says. *New York Times*, December 18, EV1–3.

Cobain, I. 2007. Firm to be sued over "torture flights." *Guardian*, June 4, 1–3.

Cockburn, A. and J. St. Clair. 1988. *Whiteout: The CIA, drugs and the press.* New York: Verso.

Cockburn, P. 2003. Real looting. *Independent*, April 28, 28.

Cohen, R. 2006. Iraq's biggest failing: There is no Iraq. *New York Times*, December 10, EV1–6.

Cohen, S. 1979. The punitive city: Notes on the dispersal of social control. *Contemporary Crisis* 3, 339–363.

———. 1985. *Visions of social control.* Cambridge: Polity Press.

———. 1995a. *The impact of information about human rights violations: Denial and acknowledgement.* Jerusalem: Center of Human Rights, Hebrew University.

———. 1995b. State crimes of previous regimes: Knowledge, accountability, and the policing of the past. *Law and Social Inquiry* 20: 7–50.

———. 1996. Government responses to human rights reports: Claims, denials, and counterclaims. *Human Rights Quarterly* 18, 3: 517–543.

———. 2001. *States of denial: Knowing about atrocities and suffering.* Cambridge, UK: Polity.

———. 2005. Post-democratic torture. *Index on Censorship* 34,1.

———. 2006. Neither honesty nor hypocrisy: The legal reconstruction of torture. In *Politics of crime control: Essays in honour of David Downes*, edited by T. Newburn and P. Rock. Oxford: Oxford University Press.

Cohen, S. and L. Taylor. 1981. *Psychological survival: The experience of long-term imprisonment*, 2nd ed. London: Penguin.

———. 1992. *Escape attempts: The theory and practice of resistance to everyday life* (2nd edition). London: Routledge.

Cole, D. 2003. *Enemy aliens: Double standards and constitutional freedoms in the war on terror.* New York: New Press.

Cole, S. 2001. *Suspect identities: A history of fingerprinting and criminal identification.* Cambridge, MA: Harvard University Press.

Colliers, R. 2003. Imports inundate Iraq under new U.S. policy. *San Francisco Chronicle*, July 10, 4.

Conover, T. 2003. Land of Guantánamo. *New York Times*, June 29, A1, A17.

Conrad, J. 1926. Geography and some explorers. In *Last essays*, edited by R. Curle. Oxford: Blackwell.

Cook, R. 2003. The financial scandals of occupation are worse than the errors of judgement. *Independent*, November 7, 29.

Cooper, H. and D. Sanger. 2006. Rice's counselor gives advice others may not want to hear. *New York Times*, October 28, EV1–4.

Cotter, L. H. 1967. Operant conditioning in a Vietnamese mental hospital. *American Journal of Psychiatry* 124(1): 23–28.

Corporate Pirates. 2005a. Economic occupation of Iraq back on trial. Press statement, August 16.

———. 2005b. R v. Quinton and Jasiewicz. Legal briefing attached to Economic Occupation of Iraq Back on Trial. Press statement, August 16.

Cousins, M. and A. Hussain. 1984. *Michel Foucault.* New York: St. Martin's Press.

Cowell, A. 2006. Briton wants Guantánamo closed. *New York Times*, May 11, EV1–2.

Crawford, A. 2002. *Crime and insecurity: The governance of safety in Europe.* Devon, UK: Willan Publishing.

———. 2003. "Contractual governance" of deviant behavior. *Journal of Law and Society* 30: 479–505.

————. 2006. Networked governance and the post-regulatory state? Steering, rowing, and anchoring the provision of policing and security. *Theoretical Criminology* 10(4): 449–479.

Crelinsten, R. 2003. The world of torture: A constructed reality. *Theoretical Criminology* 7(3): 293–318.

Croft, S. 2006. *Culture, crisis and America's war on terror.* Cambridge: Cambridge University Press.

Cuellar, M.F. 2003. The International Criminal Court and the political economy of antitreaty discourse. *Stanford Law Review* 55: 1597–1614.

Danner, M. 2004. *Torture and truth: America, Abu Ghraib, and the war on terror.* London: Granta Books.

Danzelot, J. 1979. *The policing of families.* London: Hutchinson.

Dean, J. 2004. *Worse than Watergate: The secret presidency of George W. Bush.* New York: Little, Brown.

Deflem, M. 2004. Social control and the policing of terrorism: Foundations for a sociology of counter-terrorism. *American Sociologist* 35(2): 75–92.

Deflem, M. 2008. *Sociology of law: Visions of a scholarly tradition.* New York: Cambridge University Press.

De Lint, W. and S. Virta. 2004. Security in ambiguity: Toward a radical security politics. *Theoretical Criminology* 8(4): 465–489.

Department of Defense. 1991. Memorandum for the record, subject: USSOUTHCOM CI Training—Supplemental Information (U). Office of the Assistant Secretary of Defense Command, Control, Communications and Intelligence, July 31.

Dershowitz, A. 2002. *Why terrorism works.* New Haven, Conn.: Yale University Press.

Didion, J. 2003. *Fixed ideas: America since 9/11.* New York: New York Review Books.

Dodge, T. 2003. *Inventing Iraq: The failure of nation building and a history denied.* New York: Columbia University Press.

Doerr-Zegers, O., L. Hartman, E. Lira, and E. Weinstein. 1992. Torture: Psychiatric sequelae and phenomenology. *Psychiatry* 55(2): 177–184.

Downes, D., P. Rock, C. Chinkin and C. Gearty. 2007. *Crime, social control and human rights—Essays in honour of Stanley Cohen.* Cullumpton, Devon (UK): Willan Publishing.

Dratel, J. 2005. The legal narrative. In *The torture papers: The road to Abu Ghraib,* edited by K. Greenberg and J. Dratel. New York: Cambridge University Press.

Dreyfus, H.L., and P. Rabinow. 1983. *Michel Foucault: Beyond structuralism and hermeneutics.* Chicago: University of Chicago Press.

Dunlap, J.W. 1955. Psychologists and the Cold War. *The American Psychologist* 10(3): 107–109.

Dupont, D. and F. Pearce, 2001. Foucault contra Foucault: Rereading the "governmentality" papers. *Theoretical Criminology* 5(2): 123–158.

Durkheim, E. 1933/1883. *The division of labor in society.* English version, George Simpson, trans. New York: Free Press.

————. 1966/1897. *Suicide: A study in sociology.* New York: Free Press.

Dussel, E. 1995. *The invention of the Americas: Eclipse of "the other" and the myth of modernity.* New York: Continuum.

Dwyer, J. and R. Worth. 2006. Accused GI was troubled long before Iraq. *New York Times,* July 14, EV1–6.

Dyer, C. 2003. Occupation of Iraq illegal, Blair told. *Guardian,* May 22, 29.

Edkins, J. 2000. Sovereign power, zones of indistinction and the camp. *Alternatives* 25: 3–25.

Ekman, I. 2007. Far from war, a town with a well-used welcome mat. *New York Times*, June 13, EV1.

Ericson, R.V. 2007. *Crime in an insecure world*. Cambridge: Polity.

Ericson, R.V. and K. Haggerty. 1997. *Policing the risk society*. Toronto: University of Toronto Press.

Ermann, M.D. and R.J. Lundman. 1987. *Corporate and governmental deviance: Problems of organizational behavior in contemporary society*. New York: Oxford University Press.

Eviatar, D. 2003. Free-market Iraq? Not so fast. *New York Times*, January 10, A37.

Ewald, F. 1991. Insurance and risk. In *The Foucault effect: Studies in governmentality*, edited by G. Burchell, C. Gordon, and P. Miller. Chicago: University of Chicago Press.

Ewing, K.D. and C. Gearty. 2000. *The struggle for civil liberties*. Oxford: Oxford University Press.

Fagen, P.W. and M.A. Garreton. 1992. *Fear at the edge: State terror and resistance in Latin America*. Berkeley: University of California Press.

Fainaru, S. and S. al-Izzi. 2007. U.S. security contractors open fire in Baghdad: Blackwater employees were involved in two shooting incidents in past week. *Washington Post*, May 27, A1–5.

Fallows, J. 2004. Blind in Baghdad. *Atlantic Monthly*, 293(1): 52–74.

Farge, A. and M. Foucault. 1982. *Le desorde des familles: Lettre de cachet des archives de la Bastille au XVIIIe siecle*. Paris: Gallimard.

Farley, M. and R. Wright. 2003. US solicits help in Iraq—to a point. *Los Angeles Times*, August 22, 36.

Feeley, M. and J. Simon. 1992. The new penology: Notes on the emerging strategy of corrections and their implications. *Criminology* 30(2): 449–474.

Feitlowitz, M. 1998. *A lexicon of terror: Argentina and the legacies of torture*. New York: Oxford University Press.

Ferguson, N. 2001. Welcome to the new imperialism. *Guardian*, October 31, 35.

———. 2005. *Colossus: The rise and fall of the American empire*. New York: Penguin Books.

Fisher, I. 2007. Italy indicts 26 Americans in C.I.A. abduction case. *New York Times*, February 16, EV1–3.

Fisher, L. 2005. *Military tribunals and presidential power*. Lawrence: University of Kansas Press.

Fisher, S. 1977. *The use of hypnosis in intelligence and related military situations*. Washington: Study SR 177-D, Contract AF18 [600].

Fisk, R. 2003a. Who is to blame for the collapse in morality that followed "liberation?" *Independent*, April 12, 22.

———. 2003b. The dogs were yelping. They knew bombs were on the way. *Independent*, April 9, 21.

Fitzpatrick, P. 2001. Bare sovereignty: *Homo sacer* and the insistence of law. *Theory and Event* 5(2): 1–24.

Foucault, M. 1970. *The order of things: An archaeology of the human sciences*. London: Routledge.

———. 1972/1969. *The archaeology of knowledge*. London: Tavistock.

———. 1977. *Discipline and punish: The birth of the prison*. Translated by Alan Sheridan. New York: Vintage.

———. 1978. *The history of sexuality, Vol. 1: The will to knowledge*. Translated by Robert Hurley. London: Penguin.

————. 1980. Prison talk. In *Power/Knowledge: Selected interviews and other writings 1972–1977*, edited by C. Gordon. New York: Pantheon.

————. 1982. The subject and power. In *Michel Foucault: Beyond structuralism and hermeneutics*, edited by H.L. Dreyfus and P. Rabinow. Chicago: University of Chicago Press.

————. 1988a. The dangerous individual. In *Michel Foucault: Politics, philosophy, culture: Interviews and other writings, 1977–1984*, edited by L.D. Kritzman. London: Routledge.

————. 1988b. *Power/Knowledge: Selected interviews and other writings, 1972–1977*, edited by C. Gordon. . Brighton, England: Harvester.

————. 1988c/1982. The political technology of individuals. In *Technologies of the self: A seminar with Michel Foucault*, edited by L. Martin, H. Gutman, and P. Hutton. Amherst: The University of Massachusetts Press.

————. 1989. What calls for punishment. In *Foucault live: Collected interviews, 1966–84*, edited by S. Lotringer. New York: Semiotext(e).

————. 1991a. Questions of method. In *The Foucault effect: Studies of governmentality*, edited by G. Burchell, C. Gordon, and P. Miller. Chicago: University of Chicago Press.

————. 1991b. Governmentality. In *The Foucault effect: Studies of governmentality*, edited by G. Burchell, C. Gordon, and P. Miller. Chicago: University of Chicago Press.

————. 1996. What is critique? What is enlightenment? *Eighteenth-century answers and twentieth-century questions*, edited by J. Schmidt. Translated by Kevin Paul Geiman. Berkeley: University of California Press.

————. 2003. *"Society must be defended": Lectures at the College de France, 1975–1976.* New York: Picador.

Fowler, J. 2003. US bridles as Annan calls it "occupying power." *Toronto Star*, April 24, 1.

Friedrichs, D. 1996. Governmental crime, Hitler and white collar crime: A problematic relationship. *Caribbean Journal of Criminology and Social Psychology* 1: 44–63.

————. 1998. *State crime: Volumes I and II.* Aldershot, UK: Aldershot/Dartmouth.

————. 2004. *Trusted criminals: White collar crime in contemporary society.* Belmont, CA: Wadsworth.

Frosch, D. 2007. Fighting the terror of battles that rage in soldiers' heads. *New York Times*, May 13, EV1–6.

Frum, D. 2005. *The right man: An inside account of the Bush White House.* New York: Random House.

Fukuyama, F. 2006. *After the Neo-Cons: America at the crossroads.* London: Profile.

Gallant, T. 1999. Brigandage, piracy, capitalism and state-formation: Transnational crime from a historical world systems perspective. In *States and illegal practices*, edited by J. Heyman. Oxford: Berg.

Garland, D. 1990. *Punishment and modern society: A study in social theory.* Chicago: University of Chicago Press.

————. 1992. Criminological knowledge and its relation to power: Foucault's genealogy and criminology today. *British Journal of Criminology* 32(4): 403–421.

————. 1996a. The limits of the sovereign state: Strategies of crime control in contemporary society. *British Journal of Criminology* 36(4): 445–471.

————. 1997a. "Governmentality" and the problem of crime. *Theoretical Criminology* 1(2): 173–214.

————. 1997b. The punitive society: penology, criminology and the history of the present. *Edinburgh Law Review* 1: 180–199.

————. 2006. Concepts of culture in the sociology of punishment. *Theoretical Criminology* 10(4): 419–448.

Garrison, J. 2004. *America as empire: Global leader or rogue power?* San Francisco: Berrett: Koehler.

Gatrell, V.A.C. 1994. *The hanging tree: Execution and the English people, 1770–1886.* Oxford: Oxford University Press.

Gearty, C. 1997. *The future of terrorism.* London: Phoenix.

———. 2003. Terrorism and morality. *European Human Rights Law Review* 4: 377–383.

———. 2005a. With a little help from our friends. *Index on Censorship* 34,1: 46–51.

———. 2005b. 11 September 2001, counter-terrorism and the Human Rights Act. *Journal of Legal Studies* 32: 18–32.

———. 2006. *Can human rights survive?* Cambridge: Cambridge University Press.

Giddens, A. 1984. *The constitution of society.* Cambridge: Polity.

———. 1990. *The consequences of modernity.* Cambridge: Polity.

Gilroy, P. 2002. Raise your eyes. [http://www.opendemocracy.net]. September 11.

———. 2003. "Where ignorant armies clash by night": Homogeneous community and the planetary aspect. *International Journal of Cultural Studies* 6: 261–276.

Giraldi, P. 2005. Money for nothing: Billions of dollars have disappeared, Gone to bribe Iraqis and line contractors' pockets. *The American Conservative*, October 24: 12–18.

Glanz, J. 2006. Congress tells auditor in Iraq to close office. *New York Times*, November 3, EV1–4.

———. 2007a. Billions in oil missing in Iraq, U.S. study says. *New York Times*, May 12, EV1–6.

———. 2007b. Inspector of projects in Iraq under investigation. *New York Times,* May 4, EV1–3.

———. 2007c. Inspectors find rebuilt projects crumbling in Iraq. *New York Times*, April 29, EV1–3.

Glanz, J., D. Johnston, and T. Shanker. 2006. Democrats aim to save inquiry on work in Iraq. *New York Times*, November 12, EV1–5.

Glanz, J. and F. Norris. 2006. Report says Iraq contractor is hiding data from US. *New York Times*, October 28, EV1–4.

Glanz, J. and S. Tavernise. 2007. Blackwater shooting scene was chaotic. *New York Times*, September 28, EV1–5.

Goffman, E. 1961. *Asylums.* Hammondsworth: Penguin.

Golden, T. 2006a. The battle for Guantánamo. *New York Times Magazine*, September 17, EV1–17.

———. 2006b. Military taking a tougher line with detainees. *New York Times*, December 16, EV1–6.

Golden, T., and D. Van Natta, Jr. 2005. In U.S. report, brutal details of 2 Afghan inmates' deaths. *New York Times*, May 20, A1, A12.

Goldfarb, M. 2006a. Boys in the bubble. *New York Times Book Review*, December 17, EV1–6.

———. 2006b. *Ahmad's war, Ahmad's peace: Surviving under Saddam, dying in the new Iraq.* New York: Avalon.

Gordon, Colin (1991) Government rationality: An introduction. In *The Foucault effect: Studies of governmentality,* edited by G. Burchell, C. Gordon, and P. Miller. Chicago: University of Chicago Press.

Goodnough, A. and S. Shane. 2007. Padilla is guilty on all charges in terror trial. *New York Times*, August 17, EV1–6.

Gourevitch, A. 2003. Detention disorder: Ashcroft's clumsy round-up of foreigners lurches forward. *American Prospect*, January: EV1–7.

Graham, B. and D. Morgan. 2003. US has no plans to count civilian casualties. *Washington Post*, April 15: 1.

Green, P. and T. Ward. 2000. State crime, human rights, and the limits of criminology. *Social Justice* 27(1): 101–115.

———. 2004. *State crime: Governments, violence and corruption*. London: Pluto.

———. 2005. Special issue: State crime. *British Journal of Criminology*, 45(4).

Greenberg, K. 2005. From fear to torture. In *The torture papers: The road to Abu Ghraib* edited by K. Greenberg and J. Dratel. New York: Cambridge University Press.

Greenhouse, L. 2004. Justices affirm legal rights of "enemy combatants." *New York Times*, June 29, A1, A14.

Gregory, D. 1995. Imaginative geographies. *Progress in Human Geography* 19: 447–485.

———. 2004. *The colonial present: Afghanistan, Palestine, Iraq*. Oxford: Blackwell.

Greider, W. 2003. Occupiers and the law. *Nation*, November 17, 5–6.

Grey, S. 2006. *Ghost plane: The true story of the CIA torture program*. New York: St. Martin's Press.

Grey, S. and P. Elisabetta. 2006. Italy arrests 2 in kidnapping of Imam in '03. *New York Times*, July 6, EV1–5.

Hacking, I. 1986. Making people up. In *Reconstructing individualism*, edited by T.C. Heller, et al. Stanford: Stanford University Press.

———. 1990. *The taming of chance*. Cambridge: Cambridge University Press.

Hagan, J. and S. Greer. 2002. Making war criminal. *Criminology* 40(2): 231–264.

Hagan, J., W. Rymond-Richmond, and P. Parker, 2005. The criminology of genocide: The death and rape of Darfur. *Criminology* 43(3): 525–561.

Haggbloom, S.J. 2002. The 100 most eminent psychologists of the 20th century. *Review of General Psychology* 6(2): 139–152.

Hall, S. 1988. *The hard road to renewal: Thatcherism and the crisis of the left*. London: Verso.

Harbury, J. 2005. *Truth, torture, and the American way: The history and consequences of U.S. involvement in torture*. Boston: Beacon Press.

Harcourt, B. E. 2007. *Against Prediction*. Chicago: University of Chicago Press.

Hardt, M. and A. Negri. 2000. *Empire*. Cambridge, MA: Harvard University Press.

———. 2003. Globalization and democracy. In *Implicating empire: Globalization and resistance in the 21st century world order* edited by S. Aronowitz and H. Gautney. New York Basic Books.

———. 2004. *Multitude: War and democracy in the age of empire*. New York: Penguin Putnam.

Harriman, E. 2005. So, Mr. Bremer, Where did all the money go? *Guardian*, 7 July 7, 32.

———. 2006. Cronyism and kickbacks. *The London Review of Books*, January 26, 4–9.

Hartung, W. 2004. *How much are you making on the war Daddy? A quick and dirty guide to war profiteering in the Bush administration*. New York: Nation Books.

Haveman, R. and A. Smeulers 2008. *Towards a criminology of international crimes*. Antwerp, Belgium: Intersentia.

Held, D. 1995. *Democracy and the global order: From the modern state to cosmopolitan governance*. Cambridge: Polity.

Herbert, B. 2004. A war without reason. *New York Times*, October 18, A17.

———. 2005. Torture, American style. *New York Times*, February 11, A25.

Hiro, D. 2004. One Iraqi, one vote. *New York Times*, January 27, A1.

Herring, E. and G. Ragwalla. 2005. Iraq, imperialism and global governance. *Third World Quarterly* 26: 18–31.

Hersh, S. M. 2004. *Chain of command: The road from 9/11 to Abu Ghraib*. New York: HarperCollins Publishers.

Hillyard, P., C. Pantazis, S. Tombs, D. Gordon. 2004. *Beyond criminology: Taking harm seriously*. London: Pluto.

Hinton, M. 2006. *The state on the streets: Police and politics in Argentina and Brazil*. London: Lynne Rienner Publishers.

Hirst, P. and G. Thompson. 1996. *Globalization in question*. Cambridge: Polity.

Hirst, P. and P. Woolley. 1982. *Social relations and human attributes*. London: Tavistock.

Hoffman, M. H. (2000) Emerging combatants, war crimes, and the future of international law. *Crime, Law & Social Change* 34: 99–110.

Hoffman, S. (2005) American exceptionalism: The new version. In *American exceptionalism and human rights*, edited by M. Ignatieff. Princeton, NJ: Princeton University Press.

Hogan, M., M. Long, P. Stretesky, and M. Lynch. 2006. Campaign contributions, post-war reconstruction contracts, and state crime. *Deviant Behavior* 27: 269–297.

House of Representatives. 1971. 92nd Congress, 1st Session, Subcommittee of the Committee on Government Operations, Hearings on August 2, page 349: Washington: Government Printing Office.

Hudson, B. 2003. *Justice in the risk society*. London: Sage.

Huff, R. 2001. White house sees red over Maher's remarks. *Daily News* (New York): 112.

Huggins, M., M. Haritos-Fatouros, and P.G. Zimbardo. 2002. *Violence workers: Police torturers and murderers reconstruct Brazilian atrocities*. Berkeley: University of California Press.

Human Rights Watch. 1997. *Cold storage: Supermaximum confinement in Indiana*. New York: Human Rights Watch.

———. 2000. *Out of sight: Supermaximum security confinement in the United States*. New York: Human Rights Watch.

———. 2002. *Presumption of guilt: Human rights abuses of post- September 11th detainees*. New York: Human Rights Watch.

———. 2004. *Guantánamo: Detainee accounts*. New York: Human Rights Watch.

———. 2005. *Guantánamo: Three years of lawlessness*. New York: Human Rights Watch.

———. 2006a. *Q and A: Military Commissions Act of 2006*. New York: Human Rights Watch.

———. 2006b. *Human Rights Watch world report 2006: U.S. policy of abuse undermines rights worldwide*. New York: Human Rights Watch.

———. 2007. *US mark five years of Guantánamo by closing it: Congress should restore detainees' access to courts*. New York: Human Rights Watch.

Ignatieff, M. 1978. *A just measure of pain: The penitentiary in the industrial revolution*. London: Penguin.

———. 2004. *The lesser evil: Political ethics in an age of terror*. Princeton, NJ: Princeton University Press.

———. 2005. *American exceptionalism and human rights*. Princeton, New Jersey: Princeton University Press.

Ikenberry, G. J. 2002. America's imperial ambition. *Foreign Affairs* 81 (5): 52–61.

Innes, J. 2003. US and UK action in post-war Iraq may be illegal. *Scotsman,* May 22, 24.

International Advisory and Monitoring Board (IMAB) (2005a) Statement by the International Advisory and Monitoring Board on the Development Fund for Iraq. May 23.

———. 2005b. Statement by the International Advisory and Monitoring Board on the Development Fund for Iraq. November 4.

International Crisis Group. 2003. *Baghdad: A race against the clock*. International Crisis Group, June 11.

Iraqi Revenue Watch. 2003. Iraq keeping secrets: America and Iraq's public finances. *Iraq Revenue Watch, Report No. 3*. New York: Open Society Institute.

———. 2004a. Iraq fire sale: CPA rushes to give away billions in Iraqi oil revenues. *Iraq Revenue Watch, Briefing No. 7*. New York: Open Society Institute.

———. 2004b. Disorder, negligence and mismanagement: How the CPA handled Iraq reconstruction funds. *Iraq Revenue Watch, Report No. 7*. New York: Open Society Institute.

———. 2004c. Auditors find poor practices in management of Iraqi oil revenues. *Iraq Revenue Watch, Briefing No. 8*. New York: Open Society Institute.

———. 2004d. Audit finds more irregularities and mismanagement of Iraq's revenues. *Iraq Revenue Watch, Briefing No. 9*. New York: Open Society Institute.

Ivanovich, D. 2004. Houston Halliburton's refunds $27 million after auditors check war food bills. *Houston Chronicle*, February 3, A1.

Jackson, D. 2003. US stays blind to Iraqi casualties. *Boston Globe*, November 14, 1.

Jackson, R. 2005. *Writing on the war on terrorism*. Manchester: Manchester University Press.

Jacobs, J.B. 1977. *Stateville: The penitentiary in mass society*. Chicago: University of Chicago Press.

Jacques, M. 2006. America faces a future of managing imperial decline: Bush's failure to grasp the limits of US global power has led to an adventurism for which his successors will pay a heavy price. *Guardian*, November 16, EV1–16.

Jamieson, R. 1998. Towards a criminology of war in Europe. In *The new European criminology* edited by V. Ruggiero, N. South, and I. Taylor. London: Routledge.

Jameson, F. 2003. The end of temporality. *Critical Inquiry* 29: 695–718.

Janis, I. 1949. *Are the cominform countries using hypnotic techniques to elicit confessions in public trials?* Santa Monica: Rand Corporation, Air Force Project Rand Research Memorandum, RM-161, April 25.

———. 1982. *Groupthink*. Boston: Houghton Mifflin.

Janofsky, M. 2004. Rights experts see possibility of a war crime. *New York Times*, November 13, A8.

Jehl, D. 2003. US-backed exiles return to reinvent nation. *New York Times*, May 4, A16.

———. 2005a. Questions left by C.I.A. chief on torture use: Goss vouches only for current practices. *New York Times*, March 18, A1, A11.

———. 2005b. British memo on U.S. plans for Iraq war fuels critics. *New York Times*, May 20, A10.

Jehl, D. and D. Johnson. 2005. Renditions and case-by-case approval. *New York Times*, December 22, A14.

Jenkins, P. 2003. *Images of terror: Fanaticism and the arms of mass destruction*. New York: Oxford University Press.

Jinks, D. and D. Sloss. 2004. Is the president bound by the Geneva Conventions? *Cornell Law Review* 90: 97–202.

Jones, T. and T. Newburn. 1998. *Private security and public policing*. Oxford: Oxford University Press.

Johnston, D. 2007. Immunity deals offered to Blackwater guards. *New York Times*, October 30, EV1–4.

Juhasz, A. 2004. Ambitions of empire: The Bush administration economic plan for Iraq (and beyond). *LeftTurn Magazine*, January 20.

Kacprowski, N. 2004. "Stacking the deck" against suspected terrorists. *Seattle University Law Review* 26: 651–697.

Kagan, R. 2004. *Of paradise and power: America and Europe in the new world order.* New York. Alfred A. Knopf.

———. 2006. *Dangerous nation.* New York. Alfred A. Knopf.

Kahn, R. 1996. *Other people's blood: U.S. immigration policies in the Reagan decade.* Boulder: CO: Westview.

Kafka, F. 1999. *The trial.* New York: Random House.

Kaplan, E. 2004a. Follow the money: Bush has revived the Christian right through direct federal largesse. *Nation,* November 1, 20–23.

———. 2004b. *With God on their side: How Christian fundamentalism trampled science, policy, and democracy in George W. Bush's White House.* New York. New Press.

Katyal, N. and L.H. Tribe. 2002. Waging war, deciding guilt: Trying the military tribunals. *Yale Law Journal* 111: 1259–1310.

Katz, J. 1985. *Seductions of crime: Moral and sensual attraction to doing evil.* New York: Basic Books.

Kauzlarich, D. 2007. Seeing war as criminal: Peace activist views and critical criminology. *Contemporary Justice Review* 10(1): 67–85.

Kauzlarich, D. and R. Kramer. 1998. *Crimes of the American nuclear state: At home and abroad.* Boston: Northeastern University Press.

Kauzlarich, D. and R. Matthews. 2006. Taking stock of theory and research. In *State-corporate crime: Wrongdoing at the intersection of business and government,* edited by R. Michalowski and R. Kramer. New Brunswick, NJ: Rutgers University Press.

Kauzlarich, D., R. Matthews, and W. J. Miller. 2001. Toward a victimology of state crime. *Critical Criminology* 10: 173–194.

Kauzlarich, D., C. Mullins, and R. Matthews 2003. A complicity continuum of state crime. *Contemporary Justice Review* 6(3): 241–254.

Keen, D. 2006. *Endless war? Hidden functions of the "war on terror."* London: Pluto Press.

Kelley, M. 2003. The next step for CSR: Economic democracy. *Business Ethics,* August.

Kelling, G. and J.Q. Wilson. 1982. Broken windows. *Atlantic Monthly* 249: 29–38.

Kelly, C. 2004. The war on jurisdiction: Troubling questions about Executive Order 13303. *Arizona Law Review* 46: 221–246.

Kelman, H. and L. Hamilton 1989. *Crimes of obedience: Toward a social psychology of authority and responsibility.* New Haven: Yale University Press.

Kennedy, R. (director, producer) (2007) *Ghosts of Abu Ghraib.* HBO (Home Box Office): aired February 22.

Kerr, D. 1999. Beheading the king and enthroning the market. A critique of Foucauldian governmentality. *Science and Society* 63(2):173–202.

King, R. 1999. The rise and rise of super-max: An American solution in search of a problem? *Punishment and Society* 1: 163–186.

Klare, M. 1972. *War without end: American planning for the next Vietnams.* New York: Knopf.

Klein, N. 2003a, Bring Halliburton home. *Nation,* November 24, 10.

———. 2003b. Bomb before you buy. *Guardian,* April 14, 32.

———. 2004a. Baghdad year zero. In *No war: America's real business in Iraq,* edited by N. Klein et al. London: Gibson Square.

———. 2004b. Why is war-torn Iraq giving $190,000 to Toys R Us?. *Guardian,* October 16, 22.

———. 2007. *Shock doctrine: The rise of disaster capitalism.* New York: Henry Holt.

Knowlton, B. 2005. Poll shows modest changes in levels of anti-U.S. mood *International Herald Tribune,* June 24, EV1–3.

Koh, H.H. 2005. America's Jekyll-and-Hyde exceptionalism. In *American exeptionalism and human rights*, edited by M. Ignatieff. Princeton, NJ: Princeton University Press.

KPMG Bahrain. 2004. Development Fund for Iraq: Report of Factual Findings in Connection with Disbursements for the Period from January 1 2004 to June 28 2004. Baghdad: International Advisory and Monitoring Board of the Development Fund for Iraq and the Project and Contracting Office.

Krahmann, E. 2003. Conceptualizing security governance. *Cooperation and Conflict*, 38, 1, 5–26

Kramer, R., and R. Michalowski 2005. War, aggression and state crime: A criminological analysis of the invasion and occupation of Iraq. *British Journal of Criminology* 45: 446–469.

Kramer, R. and Michalowski, R. 2006. The original formulation. In *State-corporate crime: Wrongdoing at the intersection of business and government,* edited by R. Michalowski and R. Kramer. New Brunswick, NJ: Rutgers University Press.

Kramer, R., R. Michalowski, and D. Kauzlarich. 2002. The origins and development of the concept and theory of state-corporate crime. *Crime & Delinquency*, 48, 2: 263–282.

Kramer, R., R. Michalowski, and D. Rothe. 2005. "The supreme international crime": How the U.S. war in Iraq threatens the rule of law. *Social Justice* 32, 2: 52–81.

Krugman, P. 2004. Ignorance isn't strength. *New York Times,* October 6, A27.

Kurtz, S. 2003. Democratic imperialism. *Policy Review* 118: 26–39.

Labaton, S. 2007. Court endorses law's curbs on detainees. *New York Times*, February 21, EV1–2.

Lakoff, G. and M. Johnson. 1999. *Philosophy in the flesh: The embodied mind and its challenge to western thought.* New York: Basic Books.

Landler, M. 2007. German court seeks arrest of 13 C.I.A. agents. *New York Times*, January 31, EV1–5.

Langbein, J.H. 1977. *Torture and the law of proof: Europe and England in the Ancien Regime.* Chicago: University of Chicago Press.

Larner, W. and W. Walters. 2004. Introduction: Global governmentality: governing international spaces. In *Global governmentality: Governing international spaces*, edited by W. Larner and W. Walters. London: Routledge.

Lautenberg, F. 2003. Constituting a financial interest in Halliburton. Press release: September 25.

Lawson, A. and S. Halford. 2004. *Fuelling suspicion: The coalition and Iraq's oil billions.* London: Christian Aid.

Levi, M. and D.S Wall. 2004. Technologies, security, and privacy in the post-9/11 European information society. *Journal of Law and Society* 31(2): 194–220.

Lewis, A. 2004. Making torture legal. *New York Book Review of Books*, July 15.

———. 2005a. Introduction. In *The torture papers: The road to Abu Ghraib,* edited by K. Greenberg and J. Dratel. New York: Cambridge University Press.

Lewis, A. 2005. Guantánamo's long shadow. *New York Times*, June 21, EV1.

Lewis, N.A. 2004. Fate of Guantánamo Bay detainees is debated in federal court. *New York Times*, December 2, A36.

———. 2007. Libby receives 30 months in prison in C.I.A. leak case. *New York Times*, June 5, EV1–6.

Lewis, N.A. and E. Schmitt. 2005. Inquiry finds abuses at Guantánamo Bay: Pentagon's Report follows F.B.I. complaints about practices. *New York Times*, May 1, 35

Lifton, R.J. 1961. *Thought reform and the psychology of totalism: A study of brainwashing in China*. London: Victor Gollancz.

————. 2003. American apocalypse. *Nation*, December 22, 11–17.

Liptak, A. 2007. Padilla case offers a new model of terrorism trial. *New York Times*, August 18, EV1–4.

Lipton, E. 2006. Former antiterror officials find industry pays better. *New York Times*, June 18, EV1–10.

Lind, E. et al. 1989. The changing face of war: Into the fourth generation. *Marine Corps Gazette,* October, 22–26.

Loader, I. and N. Walker. 2001. Policing as a public good: Reconstituting the connections between policing and the state. *Theoretical Criminology*, 5, 1: 9–35.

Lockwood, D. 1992. *Solidarity and schism: The problem of disorder in Durkheimian and Marxist sociology.* Oxford: Clarendon Press.

Long, M., M. Hogan, P. Stretesky, and M. Lynch. 2007. The relationship between postwar reconstruction contracts and political donations: The case in Afghanistan and Iraq. *Sociological Spectrum* 27: 453–472.

Lumpkin, J. and D. Linzer. 2003. US officials were reluctant to call troops occupiers. *Associated Press,* November 27, 1.

Lupton, D. 1999. *Risk.* London: Routledge.

Lyon, D. 2006. *Theorizing surveillance: The panopticon and beyond.* Collompton, Devon, UK: Willan Publishing.

MacKinnon, M. 2003. How to make friends and occupy people. *Globe and Mail*, July 26, 24.

Mann, M. 1986. *The sources of social power.* Cambridge: Cambridge University Press.

Mannheim, K. 1991. *Ideology and utopia: An introduction to the sociology of knowledge.* London: Routledge.

Marchetti, V. and J. Marks. 1974. *The CIA and the cult of intelligence.* New York: Knopf.

Margulies, P. 2004. Judging terror in the "zone of twilight." *Boston University Law Review* 84: 383–443.

Marks, J. 1979. The *search for the "Manchurian candidate": The CIA and mind control.* New York: Times Books.

Mathiesen, T. 1997. The viewer society: Michel Foucault's "panopticon" revisted. *Theoretical Criminology* 1(2): 215–234.

Matza, D. 1964. *Delinquency and drift.* New York: Wiley.

Mayer, J. 2005. Outsourcing torture. *New Yorker,* February 21, EV1–14.

Mazzetti, M. 2007a. Rules lay out C.I.A.'s tactics in questioning. *New York Times*, July 21, EV1–4.

————. 2007b. C.I.A. destroyed tapes of interrogations. *New York Times*, December 6, EV1–5.

McCoy, A. W. 1999. *Closer than brothers: Manhood at the Philippine military academy.* New Haven, CT: Yale University Press.

————. 2006. *A question of torture: CIA interrogation, from the Cold War to the war on terror.* New York: Metropolitan Books.

McEvoy, K. 2003. Beyond the metaphor: Political violence, human rights and "new" peacemaking criminology. *Theoretical Criminology* 7(3): 319–346.

McGrory, D. 2003. UN and army at odds as troops encourage looting. *London Times*, April 5, 38.

McLaughlin, E., J. Muncie, and G. Hughes. 2001. The permanent revolution: New labour, new public management and the modernization of criminal justice. *Criminal Justice* 1(3): 301–318.

Mekay, E. 2004. "Staggering amount" of cash missing in Iraq. *Inter Press Service*, August 21.

Melossi, D. 2001. The cultural embeddedness of social control: Reflections on the comparison of Italian and North-American cultures concerning punishment. *Theoretical Criminology* 5(4): 403–424.

Melossi, D. and M. Pavarini. 1981. *The prison and the factory: Origins of the penitentiary system.* London: Macmillan.

Merkin, D. 2004. Terror-filled: Preparing for the worst by never ceasing to think about it. *New York Times Magazine,* August 15, 13–14.

Merle, R. 2006. Census counts 100,000 contractors in Iraq. *Washington Post,* December 5, D1.

Michalowski, R. and R. Kramer. 2006a. *State-corporate crime: Wrongdoing at the intersection of business and government.* New Brunswick, NJ & London: Rutgers University Press.

Michalowski, R. and R. Kramer. 2006b. The critique of power. In *State-corporate crime: Wrongdoing at the intersection of business and government,* edited by R. Michalowski and R. Kramer. New Brunswick, NJ & London: Rutgers University Press.

Milgram, S. 1964. Group pressure and action against a person. *Journal of Abnormal and Social Psychology* 9(2):137–143.

———. 1974. *Obedience to authority: An experimental view.* New York: Harper & Row.

Miller, V. 2007. Tough men, tough prisons, tough times: The globalization of supermaximum security prisons. In *Race, gender, and punishment: From colonialism to the war on terror,* edited by M. Bosworth and J. Flavin. New Brunswick: Rutgers University Press.

Mills, C. W. 1940. Situated actions and vocabulary of motives. *American Sociological Review* 15: 904–913.

———. 1956. *The power elite.* New York: Oxford University Press.

Moran, J. 2006. State power in the war on terror: A comparative analysis of the UK and USA. *Crime, Law & Social Change* 44: 335–359.

Morgan, M. 2004. The origins of new terrorism. *Parameters* Spring Edition: 29–43.

Morgan, R. and T. Newburn. 1997. *The future of policing.* Oxford: Oxford University Press.

Morrison, W. 2006. *Criminology, civilization and the new world order.* London: Routledge.

Moss, M. and S. Mekhennet. 2007. Jailed 2 years, Iraqi tells of abuse by Americans, *New York Times,* February 17, EV1–7.

Mroue, B. 2007. Iraqis revoke license of U.S. security firm involved in killings. *Associated Press,* September 17, EV1–3.

Mullins, C., D. Kauzlarich, and D. Rothe. 2004. The international criminal court and the control of state crime: Prospects and problems. *Critical Criminology* 12: 285–308.

Mythen, G. 2004. *Ulrich Beck: A critical introduction to the risk society.* London: Pluto Press.

Mythen, G. and S. Walklate. 2006. Criminology and terrorism: Which thesis? risk society or governmentality. *British Journal of Criminology* 46: 379–389.

Nation 2005. The torture tree. December 26, 28–29.

National Intelligence Council. 2007. *National intelligence estimate: The terrorist threat to the US homeland.* (July) Washington, D.C.: National Intelligence Council.

NBC "Meet the Press." 2003. Pentagon report news coverage. September 14.

New York Times 2004a. Abu Ghraib, whitewashed. July 24, A12.

———. 2004b. Politics and the Patriot Act. April 21, A22.

———. 2004c. In defense of civil liberties. September 24, A24.

———. 2005a. Mr. Cheneyís imperial presidency. December 23, A26.

———. 2005b. Abu Ghraib, whitewashed again. March 11, A22.

———. 2006. Money down the drain in Iraq. October 26, EV1–2.

———. 2007. Under fire, State Dept. watchdog quits. December 8, EV1–2.

————. 2008. The FISA follies, redux. January 26, EV1–2.

Newburn, T. 2007. Governing security. In *Crime, social control and human rights—Essays in honour of Stanley Cohen*, edited by David Downes, Paul Rock, Christine Chinkin, and Conor Gearty (Editors). Cullumpton, Devon (UK): Willan Publishing.

Nietzsche, F. 1996 [1887. *The genealogy of morals (in Birth of tragedy and genealogy of morals)*. Translation by Douglas Smith. New York: Anchor Books.

Normand, R. 2004. Presentation on the crimes committed during the ongoing occupation. World Tribunal on Iraq. New York, May 8. [http://worldtribunal-nyc.org/document/index.htm]

Norris, A. 2003. The exemplary exception—Philosophical and political decisions in Giorgio Agamben's *homo sacer*. *Radical Philosophy*, 119: 6–16.

Oberleitner, G. 2004. A just war against terror. *Peace Review* 16: 263–276.

O'Connell, M.E. 2005. Enhancing the status of non-state actors through a global war on terror. *Columbia Journal of Transnational Law* 43: 435–458.

O'Malley, P. 1996. Risk and responsibility. In *Foucault and political reason*, edited by A. Barry, T. Osborne, and N. Rose. Chicago: University of Chicago Press.

————. 1999. Volatile and contradictory punishment. *Theoretical Criminology* 3(2): 175–196.

————. 2004. *Risk, uncertainty and government*. London: Glasshouse.

O'Reilly, C. 2005. State /corporate symbiosis: The role of security consultants in Iraq. British Society of Criminology, Leeds, England, July 14.

O'Reilly, C. and G. Ellison. 2006. Eye spy private high: Re-conceptualizing high policing theory. *British Journal of Criminology* 46: 641–660.

Osborne, D. and T. Gaebler. 1992. *Rethinking government*. Harmondsworth: Penguin.

Parenti, C. 2004. *The freedom: Shadows and hallucinations in occupied Iraq*. New York: The Free Press.

Parry, R. 1997. *Lost history: Contras, cocaine, and other crimes*. Arlington, VA: Media Consortium.

Passas, N. and N. Goodwin. 2005. *It's legal but it ain't right : Harmful social consequences of legal industries*. Ann Arbor: University of Michigan Press.

Paust, J. 2003. The US as occupying power over portions of Iraq and relevant responsibilities under the law of war. *ASIL Insights* (American Society of International Law. [www.asil.org]) April 15.

Paust, J. 2005. Executive plans and authorizations to violate international law concerning the treatment and interrogation of detainees. *Columbia Journal of Transnational Law* 43: 811–863.

Physicians for Human Rights. 2005. *Break them down: The systematic usse of psychological torture by U.S. forces*. Washington, DC: Physicians for Human Rights.

Physicians for Human Rights and Human Rights First. 2007. *Leave no marks: Enhanced interrogation techniques and the risk of criminality*. Washington: Physicians for Human Rights and Human Rights First.

Pincus, W. 2007. Security contracts to continue in Iraq: New top commander counts hired guards among his assets. *Washington Post*, February 4, A19.

Pious, R.M. 2006. *The war on terrorism and the rule of law*. Los Angeles: Roxbury.

Pratt, J. 2007. *Penal populism*. London: Routledge.

Pratt, J., D. Brown, S. Hallsworth, M. Brown, and W. Morrison. 2005. *The new punitiveness: Theories, trends, and perspectives*. Cullompton, UK: Willan Publishing.

Priest, D., and B. Gellman. 2002. U.S. decries abuse but defends interrogations "stress and duress" tactics used on terrorism suspects held in secret overseas facilities. *Washington Post*, December 26: A1.

Quinney, R. 1977. *Class, state and crime: On the theory and practice of criminal justice.* New York: Longman.

Rabinow, P. 1986. Representations are social facts: Modernity and post-modernity in anthropology. In *Writing culture: The poetics and politics of ethnography,* edited by J. Clifford and G. Marcus. Berkeley: California University Press.

Rawlinson, P. 2002. Capitalists, criminals and oligarchs: Sutherland and the new "robber barons." *Crime Law and Social Change* 37: 293–307.

Reeves, P. 2003. Iraqis emulate Palestinians by stoning troops. *Independent,* April 27, 39.

Rejali, D.M. 1994. *Torture and modernity: Self, society, and state of modern Iran.* Boulder, CO: Westview Press.

Reuters. 2003. Rumsfeld praises general who ridicules Islam as "Satan." October 17, EV1.

———. 2007. Not all troops would report abuse, study says. May 5, EV1–2.

Rhodes, L. 2004. *Total confinement: Madness and reason in the maximum security prison.* Berkeley: University of California Press.

Rhodes, R. 1997. *Understanding governance: Policy networks, governance, reflexivity and accountability.* Buckingham: Open University Press.

Risen, J. 2006. *State of war: The secret history of the CIA and the Bush administration.* New York: Free Press.

———. 2008. 2005 Use of gas by Blackwater leaves questions. *New York Times,* January 10, EV1–6.

Risen, J. and T. Golden. 2006. 3 prisoners commit suicide at Guantánamo. *New York Times,* June 11: EV1–5.

Rodriguez, J. 2006. *Civilizing Argentina: Science, medicine, and the modern state.* Chapel Hill: University of North Carolina Press.

Rose, D. 2004. *Guantánamo: America's war on human rights.* London: Faber and Faber.

———. 2006. Now they tell us. *Vanity Fair,* November 3, EV1–12.

Rose, N. 1990. *Governing the soul: The shaping of the private self.* London: Routledge.

———. 1996. The death of the social: refiguring the territory of government. *Economy and Society* 25: 327–356.

———. 2000. Government and control. *British Journal of Criminology* 40: 321–339.

Rose, N. and P. Miller. 1992. Political power beyond the state: Problematics of government. *British Journal of Sociology,* 43(2): 173–204.

Rose, N. and M. Valerde. 1998. Governed by law? *Social and Legal Studies* 7(4): 541–551.

Rosen, N. 2007. The flight from Iraq. *New York Times Magazine,* May 13, EV1–20.

Ross, J.I. 2000a. *Controlling state crime: An introduction (2nd edition).* New Brunswick, NJ: Transaction.

———. 2000b. *Varieties of state crime and its control.* Monsey, NY: Criminal Justice Press.

Ross, L. 1998. *Inventing the savage: The social construction of Native American criminality.* Austin: Texas University Press.

Rothe, D. 2006. Iraq and Halliburton. In *State-corporate crime: Wrongdoing at the intersection of business and government,* edited by R. Michalowski and R. Kramer. New Brunswick, NJ & London: Rutgers University Press

Rothe, D. and C. Mullins. 2006a. The international criminal court and the United States opposition. *Crime, Law & Social Change,* 45: 201–226.

———. 2006b. *Symbolic gestures and the generation of global social control: The International Criminal Court.* Landham, MD: Lexington.

Rothenberg, P. 2001. *Race, class, and gender in the United States.* New York: Wirth Publishers.

Rothman, D. 1971. *The discovery of the asylum in the new republic.* Boston: Little Brown.

————. 1980. *Conscience and convenience: The asylum and its alternatives in progressive America.* Boston: Little Brown.

Roy, A. 2001. *Power politics.* Cambridge, MA: South End Press.

Rubin, A. 2007. After Iraqi troops do dirty work 3 detainees talk. *New York Times,* April 21, EV1–7.

Ruggiero, V. 2001. *Crime and markets: Essays in anti-criminology.* Oxford: Oxford University Press.

Ruggiero, V. 2007. War, crime, empire and cosmopolitanism. *Critical Criminology* 15(3): 211–221.

Ruggiero, V. and M. Welch. 2009. Special issue on Power Crime. *Crime, Law & Social Change: An International Journal.* In press.

Said, E. 1978. *Orientalism.* New York: Pantheon.

————. 1993. *Culture and imperialism.* New York: Vintage.

Sands, P. 2006. *Lawless world: Making and breaking global rules.* Harmondsworth (UK): Penguin.

Sanger, D. and D. Cloud. 2006. Bush faces a battery of ugly choices on war. *New York Times,* October 20, EV1–4.

Sante, L. 2004. The Abu Ghraib photos: Here's-me-at-war.jpeg. *International Herald Tribune,* May 12, 6.

Savelsberg, J. 2002. Cultures of control in modern societies. *Law and Social Inquiry* 27(3): 685–710.

Scahill, J. 2007. *Blackwater: The rise of the world's most powerful mercenary army.* New York: Avalon.

Schabas, W. 2004. *An introduction to the International Criminal Court* (2nd edition). Cambridge: Cambridge University Press.

Schafer, S. 1974. *The political criminal: The problems of morality and crime.* New York: Free Press.

Schama, S. 2003. America's Iraq. *Middle East Report* 227, 14–28.

Scheer, R. 2004. Give Iraqis the election they want. *Los Angeles Times,* January 20, 39.

Scheer, C., R. Scheer, and L. Chaudhry. 2003. *The five biggest lies Bush told us about Iraq.* New York: Seven Stories Press.

Scheffer, D.J. 1999. The United States and the International Criminal Court. *American Journal of International Law* 93: 12–22.

Scheuer, M. 2004. *Imperial hubris: Why the west is losing the war on terror.* Washington, D.C.: Brassey's.

Schmitt, C. 1985. *Political theology: Four chapters on the concept of sovereignty.* Cambridge, MA: MIT Press.

Schmitt, E. 2005. 3 in 82nd Airborne say beating Iraqi prisoners was routine. *New York Times,* September 24, A1, A6.

————. 2007. Pentagon study describes abuse by units in Iraq. *New York Times,* June 17, EV1–4.

Schmitt, M. 2003. The law of belligerent occupation. *Crimes of War Project* [www.crime-sofwarproject], April 15.

Schuman, M. 2004. Fullajaís health damage. *Nation,* December 13, 5–6.

Sciolino, E. 2006. Spanish judge calls for closing U.S. prison at Guantánamo. *New York Times,* June 4, EV1–4.

Scott, M.B. and S. M. Lyman. 1968. Accounts. *American Sociological Review* 33: 46–62.

Seelye, K. 2005. Pentagon says acquittals may not free detainees. *New York Times,* March 22, A13.

Semple, K. 2007. U.S. sweeps Iraq seeking 3 soldiers missing in attack. *New York Times,* May 13: EV1–6.

Senate. 1974. 93rd Congress, 2nd Session, Congressional Record. Vol.120, pt. 25, October 2, pages 33474–5. Washington: Government Printing Office.

Senate. 1977. 95th Congress, 1st session. Project MKUltra: The CIAís Program of Research in Behavioral Modification. Joint Hearing before the Select Committee on Intelligence and the Subcommittee on Health and Scientific Research of the Committee on Human Resources. Washington: Government Printing Office.

Sengupta, K. 2006. UK Blair accused of trying to privatize war in Iraq. *Independent,* October 30, EV1–3.

Sewall, S. and C. Kaysen. 2000. *The United States and the International Criminal Court: Security and international law.* Lanham, MD: Rowman and Littlefield.

Sewell, W.H. 1999. The concept(s) of culture. In *Beyond the cultural turn,* edited by V.E. Bonnell and L. Hunt. Berkeley: University of California Press.

———. 2005. *Logics of history: Social theory and social transformation.* Chicago: University of Chicago Press.

Shane, S. 2008. CIA officers turn to legal insurer. *New York Times,* January 19, EV1–4.

Shane, S. and M. Mazzetti. 2007a. Interrogation methods are criticized. *New York Times,* May 30, EV1–6.

———. 2007b. Tapes by CIA lived and died to save image. *New York Times,* December 30, EV1–4.

Shane, S., S. Grey, and M. Williams. 2005. C.I.A. expanding terror battle under guise of charter flights. *New York Times,* May 31, A1, A14.

Shanker, T. 2007a. Army career behind him, General speaks out on Iraq. *New York Times,* May 13, EV1–3.

Shanker, T. 2007b. With troop rise, Iraqi detainees soar in number. *New York Times,* August 25, EV1–5.

Shanker, T. and S.L. Myers. 2008. US asking Iraq for wide rights on war. *New York Times,* January 25, EV1–5.

Shanker, T., E. Schmitt, and R.A. Oppel, Jr. 2006. Military to report marines killed Iraqi civilians. *New York Times* May 26: EV1–8.

Shanker, T. and S. Tavernise. 2006. Murder charges for 3 GIs in Iraq. *New York Times,* June 20: EV1–3.

Shearing, C. 2005. Policing our future. In *Police and people,* edited by D. Smith, D. and A. Henry. Aldershot: Ashgate.

Shearing, C. and J. Wood. 2000. Reflections on the governance of security: A normative inquiry. *Police Research and Practice* 1, 4: 457–476.

Shenon, P. 2007. House panel questions monitoring of cash shipped to Iraq. *New York Times,* February 7, EV1–3.

Shiner, P. 2007. A coverup of torture, racism and complicity in war crimes. *Guardian,* April 23, 32.

Silverglate, H. 2002. First casualty of war. *National Law Journal* December 3, A21.

Simon, J. 1988. The ideological effects of actuarial practices. *Law and Society Review,* 22: 772–800.

———. 1997. Governing through crime: In *The crime conundrum: Essays on criminal justice,* edited by L. Friedman and G. Fisher. Boulder, Colorado: Westview Press.

———. 1998. Refugees in a carceral age: The rebirth of immigration prisons in the United States. *Public Culture* 10(3): 577–607.

————. 2007. *Governing through crime: How the war on crime transformed American democracy and created a culture of fear.* New York: Oxford University Press.

Simpson, C. 1994. *Science of coercion: Communication research and psychological warfare, 1945–1960.* Oxford: Oxford University Press.

Singer, P.W. 2003. *Corporate warriors: The rise of the privatized military industry.* Ithaca: Cornell University Press.

————. 2005. Outsoucing war. *Foreign Affairs* March/April: 119–133.

Slim, H. 2003. Why protect civilians? Innocence, immunity, and enmity in war. *International Affairs* 79: 481–501.

Sloboda, J. and H. Dardagan. 2003. The holes in the map: Mapping civilian casualties in the conflict in Iraq. [www.iraqbodycount.net] April 28.

Smith, C.S. and S. Mekhennet. 2006. European nations aided C.I.A. renditions, report says. *New York Times* June 6, EV1–3.

Smith, D. 1996. Introduction. *The genealogy of morals (in Birth of tragedy and genealogy of morals)* by F. Nietzsche. Translation by Douglas Smith. New York: Anchor Books.

Smith, P. 2003. Narrating the guillotine: Punishment, technology as myth and symbol. *Theory, Culture and Society* 20(5): 27–51.

Smith, R.J. 2006. Worried C.I.A. officers buy legal insurance: Plans fund defense in anti-terror cases. *Washington Post* September 11, A1.

Smith, S. and W. Lewty. 1959. Perceptual isolation in a silent room. *Lancet* 2 (September 12): 342–345.

Sontag, S. 2004. The photographs are us. *New York Times Magazine*, May 23, 24–29, 42.

Soros, G. 2004. *The bubble of American supremacy: Correcting the misuse of American power.* New York: Public Affairs.

Southern Studies. 2003/2004. *Winter report 2003/2004.* [http://www.southernstudies.org]

Special Inspector General for Iraq Reconstruction (SIGIR). 2005a. Report to Congress, January 30.

————. 2005b. Report to Congress, October 30.

————. 2006. Report to Congress, April 30.

Spierenburg, P. 1984. *The spectacle of the suffering: Executions and the evolution of repression.* Cambridge: Cambridge University of Press.

Squitieri, T. 2003. US troops, journalists investigated for looting. *USA Today*, April 23, 34.

Stanley, A. 2007. Abu Ghraib and its multiple failures. *New York Times*, February 22, EV1–5.

Steel, M. 2003. Knock it down, then build it up again. *Independent*, April 10, 30.

Steel, R. 2004. Fight fire with fire: In the war on terror, Michael Ignatieff argues, draconian methods may well be justified. *New York Times Book Review*, July 25, 13.

Steinert, H. 2003. The indispensable metaphor of war: On populist politics and the contradictions of the state's monopoly of force. *Theoretical Criminology* 7(3): 265–291.

Stenson, K. 1993. Community policing as government technology. In *Economy and society special issue on liberalism and governmentality*, edited by A. Barry, T. Osborne, and N. Rose. London: Routledge.

————. 2003. The new politics of crime control. In *Crime, risk and justice*, edited by K. Stenson and R. Sullivan. Devon: Willan.

Stolberg, S.G. 2006a. Bush signs new rules to prosecute terror suspects. *New York Times*, October 18, E1–2.

————. 2006b. Bush signs bill setting detainee rules. *New York Times*, October 17, E1–2.

————. 2007. Bush pays tribute to fallen U.S. troops. *New York Times*, May 28, EV1–2.

Stout, D. 2007a. Fissures grow on eve of Bush speech on Iraq. *New York Times*, January 9, EV1–3.

———. 2007b. Report cites continued Qaeda threat. *New York Times*, July 17, EV1–5.

———. 2007c. Supreme Court won't hear torture appeal. *New York Times*, October 9, EV1–4.

———. 2008. Mukasey demurs on waterboarding. *New York Times*, January 30: EV1–3.

Stover, E., H. Megally, and H. Mufti. 2005. Bremer's "gordian knot": Transitional justice and the US occupation of Iraq. *Human Rights Quarterly* 27: 830–857.

Suskind, R. 2004. *The price of loyalty: George W. Bush, the White House, and the education of Paul O'Neill*. New York: Simon and Schuster.

———. 2006. *The one percent doctrine: Deep inside America's pursuit of its enemies since 9/11.* New York: Simon & Schuster.

Sussman, D. 2007. Poll shows view of Iraq war is most negative since start. *New York Times*, May 25, EV1–4.

Sutherland, E. 1985. *White collar crime: The uncut version*. New Haven, CT: Yale University Press.

Swanson, S. 2004. Enemy combatants and the writ of habeas corpus. *Arizona State Law Journal* 35: 939–1022.

Sykes, G. 1958 *The society of captives*. Princeton: Princeton University Press.

Sykes, G., and D. Matza. 1967. Techniques of neutralization: A theory of delinquency. *American Sociological Review* 22: 664–670.

Tavernise, S. 2006. U.N. reports deadliest month in Iraq. *New York Times*, November 22, EV1–4.

———. 2007. Bomb's lasting toll: Lost laughter and broken lives. *New York Times*, January 6, EV1–5.

Taylor, C. 2004. *Modern social imaginaries*. Durham: Duke University Press.

Tenet, G. 2007. *At the center of the storm*. New York: HarperCollins.

Thomas, G. 1988. *Journey into madness: Medical torture and the mind controllers*. London: Bantam Press.

Thomas, N. 1989. *Out of time: History and evolution in anthropological discourse*. Cambridge: Cambridge University Press.

———. 1994. *Colonialism's culture: Anthropology, travel and government*. Cambridge: Polity.

Tillman, R. and M. Indergaard. 2005. *Pump and dump: The rancid rules of the new economy*. New Brunswick, NJ & London: Rutgers University Press.

Tilly C. 1985. War making and state making as organised crime. In *Bringing the state back in*, edited by P. Evans, D. Rueschmeyer and T. Skocpol. Cambridge: Cambridge University Press.

Tombs, S. 2001. Thinking about "white collar" crime. In *White collar crime research: Old view and future potentials*, edited by S.A. Lingren. Stockholm: National Council for Crime Prevention, Sweden.

Tombs, S. and D. Whyte. 2003a. *Unmasking the crimes of the powerful*. New York: Peter Lang.

———. 2003b. Unmasking the crimes of the powerful. *Critical Criminology* 11(3): 217–236.

Tunnell, K. 1993. *Political crime in contemporary America*. New York: Garland.

Turner, B. 1997. From governmentality to risk. In *Foucault, health and medicine*, edited by A. Petersen and R. Bunton. London: Routledge.

Tyler, P.E. 2004a. Ex-Guantánamo detainee charges beating. *New York Times*, March 12, A10.

Tyler, P. 2004b. U.N. chief ignites firestorm by calling Iraq "illegal." *New York Times*, September 17, A11.

Tyler, P. and R. Bonner. 2003. Questions are raised on awarding of contracts in Iraq. *New York Times*, October 4, A10.

Tyler, T., P. Callahan, and J. Frost. 2007. Armed and dangerous (?): Motivating rule adherence among agents of social control. *Law & Society Review* 41(2): 457–492.

Unger, C. 2004. *House of Bush, House of Saud: The secret relationship between the world's two most powerful dynasties*. New York: Simon and Schuster.

United Nations. 2006. *The United Nations charter*. [www.un.org/aboutun/charter/]

Urbina, I. 2007. Even as loved ones fight on, war doubts arise. *New York Times*, July 15, EV1–8.

Usborne, D., R. Cornwall, and P. Reeves. 2003. Iraq, inc.: A joint venture built on broken promises. *Independent*, May 10, 27.

Valentine, D. 1990. *The Phoenix program*. New York: Morrow.

Venn, C. 2002. World dis/order. *Theory, Culture and Society* 19: 121–136.

Verlio, P. 1994. *The vision machine*. Bloomington: Indiana University Press.

Von Zielbauer, P. 2006. 4 GIs tell of how Iraqi raid went wrong. *New York Times*, August 7, EV1–8.

———. 2007a. Military cites negligence in aftermath of Iraq killings. *New York Times*, April 22, EV1–4.

———. 2007b. Propaganda fear cited in account of Iraqi killings. *New York Times*, May 6: EV1–5.

———. 2007c. Marine says his staff misled him on killings. *New York Times*, May 11, EV1–4.

Von Zielbauer, P. and C. Marshall. 2006. 8 marines charged in killings of Iraqi civilians. *New York Times*, December 21: EV1–3.

Waldman, A. 2004. Guantánamo and jailers: Mixed review by detainees. *New York Times*, March 17, A6.

Walker, N. 1999. Decoupling police and state. In *The boundaries of understanding: Essays in honour of Malcolm Anderson*, edited by E. Bort and R. Keat. Edinburgh: International Social Science Institute.

Ward, D. and T. Werlich. 2003. Alcatraz and Marion: Evaluating supermaximum custody. *Punishment and Society* 5(1) 53–75.

Watson, P. 1978. *War on the mind: The military uses and abuses of psychology*. New York: Basic Books.

Waxman, H. 2004. Iraq on the record: The Bush administration's public statements on Iraq. Committee on Government Reform, Minority Staff, Special Investigation Division. Washington, D.C: U.S. House of Representatives.

Weber, M. 1948. *From Max Weber: Essays in sociology*. Edited and translated by H. Gerth and C.W. Mills). London: RKP.

———. 1978/1920. *Economy and society*. Edited and translated by G. Roth and C. Wittich, 2 volumes. Berkeley: University of California Press.

———. 1985/1905. *The protestant work ethic and the spirit of capitalism*. London: Unwin Paperbacks.

Weiner, T. 2007. *Legacy of ashes: The history of the C.I.A.* New York: Doubleday.

Weinstein, H. 1990. *Psychiatry and the CIA: Victims of mind control*. Washington: American Psychiatric Press.

Weisman, S. 2005. Jail term for soldier in abuse case. *New York Times*, May 23, A10

Welch, M. 2002. *Detained: Immigration laws and the expanding I.N.S. jail complex*. Philadelphia: Temple University Press.

———. 2003. Trampling of human rights in the war on terror: Implications to the sociology of denial. *Critical Criminology: An International Journal* 12(1): 1–20.

————. 2005. Los delitos del estado en la guerra estadounidense contra el terror: Una mirada a la cultura de la impunidad (State crimes in America's war on terror: Examining a culture of impunity). *Capitulo Criminologico: Revista de las Disciplinas del Control Social* (Venezuela), 33(4): 22–43.

————. 2006a. *Scapegoats of September 11th: Hate crimes and state crimes in the war on terror.* New Brunswick, New Jersey & London: Rutgers University Press.

————. 2006b. Seeking a safer society: America's anxiety in the war on terror. *Security Journal* 19(2):93–109.

————. 2006c. Immigration, criminalization, and counter-law: A Foucauldian analysis of laws against law, Merging Immigration and Crime Control: An Interdisciplinary Workshop, Baldy Center for Law and Social Policy, University at Buffalo Law School, Buffalo, New York, April 28–29.

————. 2007a. Control social Foucaultiano en el mundo Post 9/11: Desarrollos recientes a través de fronteras sociales y culturales (Foucauldian social control in a post-9/11 world: Recent developments across social and cultural boundaries), *Revista CENIPEC* (Centro de Investigaciones Penales y Criminologicas Universidad de Los Andes Facultad de Ciencias Juridas y Politicas, Venezuela), 26: 113–136.

————. 2007b. Immigration lockdown before and after 9/11: Ethnic constructions and their consequences." In *Race, gender and punishment: From colonialism to the war on terror*, edited by M. Bosworth and J. Flavin. New Brunswick, NJ & London: Rutgers University Press.

————. 2007c. Moral panic, denial, and human rights: Scanning the spectrum from over-reaction to under-reaction." In *Crime, social control and human rights—Essays in honour of Stanley Cohen*, edited by D. Downes, P. Rock, C. Chinkin and C. Gearty. Cullumpton, Devon (UK): Willan Publishing.

————. 2007d. Fare l'impensabile. Genealogia della tortura moderna (Doing the unthinkable: A genealogy of modern torture). *Studi Sulla Questione Criminale* (Faculty of Law, University of Bologna, Italy), anno 11 n. 3:41–64.

————. 2008a. Militarizing power in the war on terror: Unlawful enemy combatants and the Military Commissions Act. In *Supranational Criminology: Towards a criminology of international crimes*, edited by R. Haveman and A. Smeulers. Antwerp: Intersentia.

————. 2008b. Ordering Iraq: Reflections on power, discourse, and neocolonialism. *Critical Criminology: An International Journal*. In press.

————. 2009. Fragmented power and state-corporate killings: A critique of Blackwater in Iraq. *Crime, Law & Social Change: An International Journal*. In press.

Welch, M., M. Fenwick, and M. Roberts. 1997. Primary definitions of crime and moral panic: A content analysis of experts' quotes in feature newspaper articles on crime. *Journal of Research in Crime and Delinquency* 34(4): 474–494.

Wheatcroft, G. 2006. Manifest destinies. *New York Times Book Review*, December 17, EV1–4.

Whitaker, B. 2003. Free to do bad things. *Guardian*, April 12, 34.

Whyte, D. 2003. Lethal regulation: State-corporate crime and the United Kingdom government's new mercenaries. *Journal of Law and Society* 30, 4: 575–600.

————. 2007. The crimes of neo-liberal rule in occupied Iraq. *British Journal of Criminology* 47(2): 177–195.

Williams, G. (1999) *French discourse analysis: The method of post-structuralism*. London: Routledge.

Williams, P.J. 2001. By any means necessary. *Nation*, November 26, 11.

Williams, W.A. 1969. *The roots of the modern American empire*. New York: Random House

————. 1988. *The tragedy of American diplomacy*. New York: Norton Paperback Edition.

Willis, F. 2005. Evidence to Senate Democratic Policy Committee Hearing: An oversight hearing on waste, fraud and abuse in U.S. Government Contracting in Iraq. February 14.

Wong, E. 2003. Saboteurs, looters, and old equipment work against efforts to restart Iraqi oilfields. *New York Times*, December 14, A1.

Worth, R. 2006a. U.S. military braces for flurry of criminal cases in Iraq. *New York Times*. July 9, EV1–5.

———. 2006b. Sergeant tells of plot to kill Iraqi detainees. *New York Times,* July 28, EV1–7.

Woodward, B. 2004. *Plan of attack*. New York: Simon and Schuster.

Wright, T. 2006. US defends rights record before UN panel in Geneva. *New York Times*, May 6, EV1–2.

Young, J. 2003. In praise of dangerous thoughts. *Punishment and Society* 5: 97–107.

Zedner, L. 2006. Liquid security: Managing the market for crime control. *Criminology and Criminal Justice* 6(3): 267–288.

Zernike, K. 2006. White House asks Congress to define war crimes. *New York Times*, August 3, EV1–4.

Zinn, H. 2003. *A people's history of the United States: 1492-present*. New York: HarperPerennial.

Zoepf, K. 2007. Iraqi refugees turn to the sex trade in Syria. *New York Times*, May 29: EV1–7.

Index

Abu Ghraib, 5, 12, 13, 24, 75, 76, 88, 90–91, 122–123, 165; "bad apples," 184–185; Geoffrey Miller, 89, 183; photos, 126, 166; private military firms, 149–150; prosecution, 161

Agamben, Giorgio, 11, 16, 18, 20, 42, 104, 112, 115, 160; *homo sacer,* 22, 28, 126–129; separation of powers, 72

Al-Qaeda, 3, 23, 26, 33, 52, 140, 170; Geneva Conventions, 122; information deficit, 86; National Intelligence Council, 135; Padilla, 172; special registration program, 142

American Psychological Association, 75, 82

Association of Humanitarian Lawyers, 113

Baker, James A., 118, 186

Beccaria, Cesare, 37

Beck, Ulrich, 29, 140–141. *See also* risk society theory

Bentham, Jeremy, 37, 48, 63. *See also* panopticon

Berrera-Echararria v. Rison, 46

Blackwater, 144–148, 163, 186–187, 189

Bolton, John, 162

Bonger, Willem, 5

Bremer, Paul, 102, 104, 111. *See also* Coalition Provisional Authority (CPA)

Bumgarner, Colonel Mike, 47, 64–67

Bush, George, W., 3, 15, 21–22, 25–27, 33–34, 172; Abu Ghraib, 90; collateral damage, 115–116; Executive Order 13303; GITMO, 73–74; habeas corpus, 182; Halliburton, 106; *Hamdan v. Rumsfeld,* 39; invasion of Iraq, 168; Iraq security plan, 126; Military Commissions Act, 39, 41, 43–44, 46; neoconservatives, 110–111; regime change, 96; renditions, 87; responsibility to history, 173; rhetoric, 152–154, 191;

riot control agents, 148; stonewalling, 109; *Torture Papers,* 24, 86; treatment of prisoners, 177. See also *Rasul v. Bush and United States*

Butler, Judith, 11, 15–16, 18–20, 22, 28, 42, 69, 104, 127, 160; separation of powers, 72

Camp Bucca, 123–124, 187

Camp Cropper, 124

Camp Mercury, 90–91, 123, 166

Canguilhem, Georges, 9

Chahal v. United Kingdom, 46

Chandrasekaran, Rajiv, 95

Cheney, Dick, 15, 22, 25–26, 34, 191; Halliburton, 106; Military Commissions Act, 42; stonewalling, 109; West Point, 115

Coalition Provisional Authority (CPA), 95, 102–108, 111, 145, 186. *See also* Bremer, Paul

Cohen, Stanley, 8, 14, 20, 24, 28, 71, 114; second history of torture, 76; *States of Denial,* 158, 164–169, 177

Convention against Torture, 23–24, 41, 80, 86–87, 172, 181–182, 184

counter-law, 11, 16–18, 24, 29, 36, 38, 159–160, 181; Military Commissions Act, 42–43. *See also* Ericson, Richard V.; Foucault, Michel

Defense Fund for Iraq (DFI), 104, 107, 163, 185

Defense Planning Guidance (DPG), 25–26

Detainee Standards of Conduct, 60

Durkheim, Emile, 67–68, 139

Ericson, Richard V., 11, 15–18, 20, 24, 29, 38, 43, 73, 104, 181; neoliberal political culture, 159–160; new terrorism, 140–141

About the Author

Michael Welch is a professor in the Criminal Justice program at Rutgers University, New Brunswick, New Jersey (USA). He received a Ph.D. in sociology from the University of North Texas and his research interests include punishment, human rights, and social control. His key writings have appeared in *Punishment & Society, Justice Quarterly, Journal of Research in Crime & Delinquency, Crime, Law & Social Change, The Prison Journal, Social Justice,* and *Critical Criminology.* Welch is author of *Scapegoats of September 11th: Hate Crimes and State Crimes in the War on Terror* (2006, Rutgers University Press), *Ironies of Imprisonment* (2005), *Detained: Immigration Laws and the Expanding I.N.S. Jail Complex* (2002), *Flag Burning: Moral Panic and the Criminalization of Protest* (2000), *Punishment in America* (1999), and *Corrections: A Critical Approach* (2nd ed., 2004). He has lectured and delivered papers throughout the United States as well as in Canada, England, Scotland, the Netherlands, France, Germany, Italy, Spain, Poland, Finland, Thailand, Argentina, and Venezuela. Recently, Welch served as a visiting fellow at the Centre for the Study of Human Rights at the London School of Economics. His website is www.professormichaelwelch.com and e-mail address is retrowelch@aol.com.

Printed in the United States
208578BV00002B/127-288/P

9 780813 544359